The NAME GAME

CHRISTOPHER P. ANDERSEN

Simon and Schuster
New York

Designed by Irving Perkins
Manufactured in the United States of America

1 2 3 4 5 6 7 8 9 10

Library of Congress Cataloging in Publication Data
Andersen, Christopher P
    The name game.

    Bibliography: p.
    1. Names, Personal. 2. Names, Personal—
Psychological aspects. I. Title.
CS2367.A52   929.4'01'9   77-8584
ISBN 0-671-22457-3

The author wishes to thank Evil Eye Music, Inc., New York, N.Y.,
for permission to quote lines from the song "A Boy Named Sue," words
and music by Shel Silverstein, © copyright 1969; and Frank Music
Corp., for permission to reprint lines from "How to Succeed in
Business Without Really Trying" by Frank Loesser, © 1961 Frank
Music Corp., 1350 Avenue of the Americas, New York, N.Y. 10019.
International Copyright Secured. All Rights Reserved.

ACKNOWLEDGMENTS

I am grateful to Simon and Schuster Editor-in-Chief Michael Korda for his advice, encouragement and of course his matchless editing skills. I am also indebted to Joan Sanger and Larry Ashmead for their many suggestions, and to Sylvia Porter for her counsel. To Jesse Birnbaum, Dick Stolley, Cran Jones, Otto Fuerbringer and all those who have helped make my work a pleasure, my thanks.

My parents have provided much help and understanding. My sister Valerie, though she may not know it, is always an inspiration. Finally, I thank my wife, my other Valerie, for many things—not the least of which are her invaluable support and patience beyond the call.

DEDICATION
*For Jeanette, Edward
and my two Valeries*

Contents

Who hath not own'd, with rapture-
   smitten frame,
The power or grace, the magic of a
   name?
   —Thomas Campbell

ALICE: *Must* a name mean something?
HUMPTY-DUMPTY: Of course it must. *My* name
   means the shape I am. With a name like
   yours, you might be any shape, almost.
      —Lewis Carroll
      Through the Looking Glass

CHAPTER 1

You Are What You're Named

One classes someone else when that person's name is given to him. Every Christian name has a conscious or subconscious cultural association which parades the images others form of its bearer, and has an influence on shaping the personality in a positive or negative way.
— Claude Lévi-Strauss

Your name is the most important thing you will ever possess. What's in a name? We now know that names are so important that they figure in every human relationship. You must never enter into a business deal, fall in love, get married, have an affair, hire, fire, promote or go to work for someone else without first considering the implications of the other person's name.

What's in a name? Among other things, the difference between success or failure in the business world, or between social acceptability and an emotional, educational, even sexual handicap. Names are far more than mere identity tags. They are charged with hidden meanings and unspoken overtones that profoundly help or hinder you in your relationships and your life.

A rose by any other name may smell as sweet, but many people by another name would undoubtedly be better off. Some names trigger a positive response when we hear them; we tend to associate others with negative qualities. And if after reading this book you discover that you are a victim of your name, there *is* something you can do to make your name work for you.

Onomatology—the study of names—has been confined over the years to examining the etymology (linguistic origins) of names. But a handful of psychologists and other students of human behavior, so few that they scarcely number a dozen, have uncovered a starting new aspect to the science of onomatology. They have discovered that we are all affected in our business, family, social and sexual relationships by the connotations our names carry.

The scientific data are growing steadily. Three separate studies —among Harvard graduates in 1948, among child inmates of a New Jersey psychiatric institute and among mental patients in a Chicago institution—indicated that behavior problems occur much more frequently among those people with "peculiar" names. Not that a name need be bizarre to elicit a strong response from others. John may well inspire trust and confidence, while Benjamin is viewed with suspicion. Whatever the reactions of others, a name is unquestionably a vital part of each individual's psychological profile. For example: People with out-of-the-ordinary names are much more likely to commit crimes or suffer from some psychosis. Girls named Agatha are less popular and generally less attractive than girls named Susan. An Elmer is less likely to get good grades in school than a David. Barbaras tend to be aggressive—and successful. An Allen is generally regarded as serious, sincere and sensitive, and a Nancy as spiteful. Michaels are often perceived as winners, and Oscars as losers. People whose last names begin with the letters A through R generally live longer, healthier lives than do people in the S–Z group. The rich and the super-rich are, as we shall see, much more inclined to have strange names, and use them to intimidate others. Learning about the power and influence of names can help you be a winner at—the Name Game.

In fact, you have been playing the Name Game all your life, whether you are aware of it or not. But even before you could start playing, your parents played, using you as a pawn. "There is no doubt that in many cases given names, short names and nicknames or whatever forename is bestowed or inflicted on the innocent newborn is a clear indicator of where his parents want him to go," contended psychiatrist Eric Berne, author of the bestselling *Games People Play* and originator of Transactional Analysis. "He will have to struggle against such influences, which will be continued in other forms as well, if he is to break away. This is something parents have control over and should be able to foresee." The sorry fact is that parents choose not to recognize the power that they possess. Instead, they show roughly the same degree of care in naming their children as they do in naming their pets, and sometimes less.

Soon enough, it was your turn to play the Game. As a child, you were influenced by your playmates' names, and you picked friends and enemies accordingly. In school, you either benefited or suffered from your name. Teachers viewed you, it has now been scientifically established, in a certain way in large part because of your name. These associations were to be reinforced over the years.

When you enrolled in college, or applied for your first job, you may well have used your full formal name—first, middle and last—to lend weight to your application. Before getting engaged, you almost certainly toyed with your intended's name. Perhaps you scribbled it over and over again next to yours, or tried to imagine what your first name would look like once it was wedded to his surname on a marriage license.

On the job, you have been swayed by the impressive-sounding names of your superiors. But you have also felt superior to some of your co-workers because their names conveyed the unarticulated message that they are losers. If you have ever hired someone, you avoided applications with names that for some reason made you feel uncomfortable. At the same time, you were inclined to give the nod to those whose names, carrying positive connotations, spelled out success. And when your first child arrived, you dipped into your own deep well of prejudices and came up with a name that, as Eric Berne stated, was "a clear indicator of where you want him to go."

Thus the circle closed.

Your Name Is Your Fate

Test your familiarity with the powerful influence names have on our lives by arranging the following men's and women's names according to what you perceive to be their general desirability. Which would *you* choose to name your son, your daughter?

Arlene	Barrett
Maureen	Kevin
Jennifer	Benjamin
Norma	Stephen
Shirley	Michael

Studies indicate that Jennifer should rate at the top of the girls' names, followed by Shirley, then Arlene, Norma and Maureen. Michael is the most positive of the boy's names. Close behind are Stephen and Kevin—two strong, easily accepted names —while Barrett and Benjamin trail at a considerable distance. To you, the differences may have been imperceptible. But they nonetheless would have had an unparalleled impact on your child throughout his life.

The proof that we are either the victims or beneficiaries of our names is all around us. Yet despite the substantial evidence, every year names are inflicted on an estimated 3 million new-born Americans whose parents give little or no thought to the broad implications. More and more parents are consulting astrology charts and numerologists, but the overriding concern in selecting a name (aside from paying homage to a relative) is still the same: How does it sound? Phonetic balance, as name authority Evelyn Wells pointed out as early as 1946, is a legitimate concern. "Science," she wrote, "tells us of the power of sounds and words to influence the mind." But science now tells us that the cadence and the melody of a name are not nearly so significant as the associations it carries.

One who understands all too well is *New York Times* columnist Russell Baker. "At this very moment," he lamented, "it is an almost certain bet that somewhere in America a mother is nam-ing her newborn son Kenneth and thereby freighting him with heavy psychological luggage that he will carry with him to the grave. The difficulty with being a Kenneth is that Kenneths are expected to be lean and fibrous. A Sydney or a Wallace has a perfect right to be shaped like a rail or a balloon, and the Kenneths' knowledge that they are denied this freedom of con-tour must surely fill them with hostility." As for those poor fellows named Irving, Baker continued with tongue firmly planted in cheek, an Irving "knows that he is consigned to the intellectual life, doomed at worst to years with Nietzsche in the library stacks, at best to writing brilliantly denunciatory letters to the editors of elite magazines."

Humorous—and quite plausible. We tend to become what others expect us to become, to conform to society's expectations. That may even extend to one's physical appearance. A person whose name implies obesity—Bertha, for example—may subconsciously try to live up to that preconception. The name Irving *does* have a certain egghead quality; hence the proliferation of Irvings on the faculties of universities. And as Harveys became increasingly incensed over their lackluster image, thousands of them (including one closet Harvey, pianist Van Cliburn) banded together in 1970 to get people to stop thinking of Harveys as bumbling boobs—and thereby lessen every Harvey's chances of becoming one.

There is ample cross-cultural evidence that this phenomenon is by no means restricted to American society. The *British Journal of Psychology* reported that the Ashantis of Ghana name their children after the day of the week on which they were born. According to the old nursery rhyme, "Monday's child is fair of face/ Tuesday's child is full of grace/ Wednesday's child is full of woe/ Thursday's child has far to go/ Friday's child is loving and giving/ Saturday's child works hard for a living/ But the child that is born on the Sabbath Day/ Is bonny, and blithe, and good, and gay."

Monday's child, named Kwadwo, is expected to be quiet and peaceful. The grim forecast for Wednesday's child, named Kwaku, is apparently shared by the Ashanti, who look upon Wednesday's child as aggressive and temperamental—a monumental headache. In accordance with this self-fulfilling prophecy, boys born on Wednesday were found among the Ashanti to have a significantly greater frequency of juvenile court arrests than boys bearing the names of other days of the week.

As author Muriel Beadle says, "For any child a name which interferes substantially with normal interaction is a handicap. The expectations of one's society shape behavior."

The notion is far from new. There is little question that Freud keenly appreciated the value of a socially acceptable name.

Originally called Sigismund, a popular name among Viennese Jews that came to be used by anti-Semites as the nineteenth-century Austrian equivalent of "kike," Freud changed his name to the more Teutonic Sigmund when he was 22.

Like Freud, Werner Erhard, the Gucci-clad guru of EST (which stands both for "it is" and Erhard Seminars Training), changed his name to suit his new persona. Born Jack Rosenberg in Lower Marion, Pennsylvania, Erhard married at 18, fathered four children and worked as a construction company supervisor before becoming a used car salesman under the catchy name of Jack Frost. He dropped out of sight in 1960. Leaving his family behind, Erhard took off for San Francisco with his girlfriend Ellen, now the second Mrs. Erhard and mother of Werner's three youngest children. "I wanted," he explains, "to get as far away from Jack Rosenberg as I could get." Discarding his own identity, he found a new one in the pages of *Esquire* magazine. From one article, he adopted physicist Werner Heisenberg's first name, and from another took the last name of former West German Chancellor Ludwig Erhard for his new alias. "Freudians," Erhard concedes, "would say this was a rejection of Jewishness and a seizure of strength." Accordingly, Erhard's approach to EST—a blend of Zen, Transactional Analysis, Yoga and Transcendental Meditation, with a dash of Dale Carnegie for good measure—has been widely described as sadistic and verging on the Hitlerian. For Jack Rosenberg, the transformation is complete.

Weakness in a name is likely to exact a psychological price. "Many aristocratic English given names," H. L. Mencken observed in his opus *The American Language,* "like Reginald, Algernon, Percy, Wilfred, Cedric, Cyril, Cecil, Aubrey and Claude are commonly looked upon as sissified in the United States, and any boy who bears one of them is likely to have to defend it with his fists." Such names provide some of the clearest examples of how labels and their associations mold our personalities.

One who stuck it out was *Future Shock* author Alvin Toffler. "I hate Alvin," he states flatly. "I have always hated it. Alvin was a sissy name, and I was constantly getting into fistfights over it—even in high school. Thank God, I grew up in the 1940s and not the 1950s. I might have had to live down 'Alvin the Chipmunk' on top of all the rest." A boyhood fraught with this extra degree of stress added to his emotional mettle, but Toffler eventually discovered that Alvin is not considered a "sissy name" the world over. Toffler was once told by then Australian Prime Minister Gough Whitlam, "You are considered a very sexy man in Australia. Really hot stuff." Recalls Toffler: "It turned out that one of the most popular movies in Australia was called *Alvin Purple,* all about the exploits of a particularly lubricious young window-washer. Now, living up to *that* Alvin's reputation might have been a challenge." Still, sighs Toffler, "I would gladly have settled for being a 'Mike Scott.' "

Not everyone is as willing as Toffler to put up with an unpopular name. Maverick nutritionist Carlton Fredericks has long relished a deserved reputation as a hell-raiser and archenemy of the food industry. Fredericks seems perfectly suited for the role of righteous consumer advocate. Compact, impeccably groomed and immaculately attired, the mellifluous-voiced Dr. Fredericks boasts an Adolph Menjou moustache and an unsettlingly sardonic smile. "Your mother must have had a hunch you'd be a celebrity," marveled one interviewer. "Carlton Fredericks is the perfect name for someone in public life." Actually, Fredericks started out as Harold Casper Frederick Caplan, and suffered the misfortune of being known simply as Casper by his doting mother. By the time he was nine, Fredericks recalls, "I knew that Casper was something I just couldn't handle. I was squabbling over my name every week. It got so bad that I cringed whenever a teacher called on me in class. So at my insistence, my mother marched down to City Hall and we had my name legally changed to Carlton Fredericks."

Why Carlton? "The Carltons were cousins, and I always thought that it had such a nice—no, an important—sound. It made a definite change as far as my self-esteem was concerned, and in turn I found that the other kids were finally treating me with some respect."

It's important to remember that the role of a name may change dramatically, given the particular situation and one's status in life. Kingman Brewster is an unfair burden for any lad to bear, but something of an asset in the halls of academe. Conversely, while Bart may look dandy emblazoned across the sweatshirt of a high school halfback, it may turn out to be an embarrassment on a corporate letterhead. From presidents to ax-murderers, many famous people have mastered the art of changing their names to suit their purposes and the different stages of their lives—something from which we can all learn. For example:

> Tommy—never Thomas or even Tom—was freckle-faced, frail and at the age of ten already wearing Ben Franklin spectacles. He would later admit to being a "laughed-at Mamma's boy" whose childhood days in Augusta, Georgia, were generally spent playing with the girls. As he grew to adolescence, Tommy Wilson suddenly found himself isolated from members of both sexes. He was now uneasy in the company of females, and boys were never quite willing to accept the timid youngster as one of their own. On the occasions when they did allow him to join in their games, Tommy still ran home to his mother as soon as the talk or the play showed signs of turning rough. This insecurity—which frequently gave way to outbursts of uncontrolled rage—would continue into adulthood. When he was 24, Wilson suffered such severe indigestion and throbbing headaches that he was forced to drop out of the University of Virginia. Still a virgin, he finally summoned enough courage to propose marriage to his cousin Hattie. She turned him down. Returning home, he decided it was time for a change. Before striking out on his own, Tommy Wilson grew flamboyant sideburns, bought a fashionable new wardrobe and dropped his childish Christian name in favor of the dignified middle name that seemed more fitting for a man of his ambition. From now on, he would be known as Woodrow Wilson.

> From his sprawling 49th-floor Manhattan office, overlooking, ironically enough, Avon's impressive black glass and steel headquarters, Revlon's French-born president and chairman of the board Michel Bergerac recalled his first days in America as a Fulbright student at UCLA.

"It did not take long for me to become a devout Californian, right down to the name. I had not been in this country for more than a few months and I was miraculously transformed from Michel into 'Mike.' " The son of an electric company manager in Biarritz, Bergerac, who had aimed for the French diplomatic corps but discovered that he was curiously adept at business administration, was indeed transformed. He "bummed around" for six months, working as a hired hand on the cattle ranches that are sprinkled along Oregon's Rogue River. He also found time to court and marry a young San Franciscan. Mike Bergerac soon launched his corporate career as a junior executive with the Los Angeles-based Cannon Electric Company. Quickly proving himself a master diversifier, he pyramided Cannon into a 35-company international conglomerate before it was eagerly gobbled up by International Telephone and Telegraph—and he along with it.

At ITT, down-to-earth Mike Bergerac soon rose to become president of the corporation's $5-billion-a-year European subsidiary, where he bought and sold more than 100 companies before Revlon founder Charles Revson sought him out. In the *haut monde* world of Revlon, where he has ruled like a Renaissance prince since Revson's death in 1975, Mike Bergerac is once again the urbane Michel. "I don't think the people around me would be comfortable calling me Mike," he contends. "And in this environment, neither would I." While Bergerac changed his name to suit his surroundings like some corporate chameleon, handsome older brother Jacques never considered changing his. Now president of Revlon's French subsidiary, Jacques, who was married for a time to Ginger Rogers, spent 20 years pursuing screen stardom as a lover.

The year: 1969. Dressed in a blue cotton smock and looking like someone's apple-cheeked grandmother, Marion Lane sat in the visitor's cubicle at the Contra Costa County Jail in northern California and talked, among other things, of her childhood in Illinois. Marion, better known as Winnie Ruth Judd, was awaiting extradition to Arizona, where 38 years before she had been convicted and sentenced to hang for murdering her two best friends, cutting up their bodies, stuffing them in a trunk and shipping the trunks to California for a midnight sea burial. During the sensational murder trial, Mrs. Judd was dubbed the "Tiger Woman" by the nation's tabloids. With good reason. Even during her childhood she had been a schizophrenic's delight. As the flighty Winnie, she shocked local townsfolk by wandering about after dark in a nightgown and fantasizing in a disconcertingly convincing manner that she was searching for her lost baby.

As Ruth, she was given to dark rages. In 1962, after nearly three decades in prisons and mental hospitals, Winnie Ruth Judd escaped. Choosing the angelic-sounding alias Marion Lane—Mary Worth might have been equally appropriate—she embarked on a new life as a nurse for the elderly in Oakland's elegant suburb of Piedmont. After her discovery and capture in 1969, Winnie-Ruth-Marion was (were?) extradited to Arizona and, because she had led an exemplary life on the lam, was pardoned. Marion Lane now lives and works in Danville, California, where she is the housekeeper for a wealthy physician.

Your Name Can Make the Difference

In an NBC studio high up in Rockefeller Center, two of the highest-paid, most forceful and dynamic women in the country chat about their accomplishments. Both are named Barbara. Newswoman and television personality Barbara Walters (who claims she always wanted to be "Babs Elliott" because "it sounds so smart and elegant") has signed a contract to co-anchor the ABC Evening News for a staggering $5 million over five years. Feisty Washington hostess-turned-author Barbara Howar, who has just pocketed $800,000 for the paperback rights to her first novel, says both women earned it.

She may spell her name a bit differently, but Barbra Streisand is much the same type—tough, aggressive, capable, outrageously successful. Then there are other Barbaras—Stanwyck, Hollywood's tough broad of the 1940s; formidable Bain of "Mission Impossible" fame; Hutton, the much-married Woolworth heiress, and Jordan, the implacable black Texas congresswoman. Think of the Barbaras you have known and compare. You will probably find that they share these same qualities of strength and ability. Is this all coincidence?

Seated around a coffee table in midtown Manhattan, three attractive women tried to explain the impressive success each had had in her respective field. The financial analyst, Miss Nelson, said she had had a step-by-step plan, going methodically from one goal to the next. The housewife who had broken through the barriers and begun to establish herself as an author and poet, Mrs. Morgan, attributed her success to sheer will and a belief that anything is possible. The top female broker on Wall Street, Mrs. Hughes, had a very different explanation. "I think," she mused, "that we are all successful because we're all named Paula." The observation is valid; most people describe Paulas as being "determined!" Another coincidence?

The answer, of course, is *no*—people sharing the same name have similar characteristics. Such is the power of a name in determining how others see us, how we see ourselves and how the two combine to influence our personalities and the course of our lives. Take the case of Walter Murphy, the 33-year-old president of a prosperous Manhattan employment agency. "In school I was always supposed to have my homework done on time, so I did," says Walter. "I was expected to get good grades. I did. And there was no doubt that I would be lousy at sports. I was." Now how does he feel about the bookish image that goes with being a Walter? "Since most of my clients are bookkeepers, accountants and bankers, it is absolutely perfect. A Walter is exactly what these people want to see."

Another employment counselor testifies to rampant name prejudice in hiring. One of his clients with a negative name had waited a month without a job offer despite impressive qualifications. Says the counselor: "On a lark, I suggested that he drop the name and just call himself by his initials. He did, and within a week he landed a job."

That our names are tied to the jobs we do is quite evident to those who run the St. Regis Paper Company, fifth-largest producer of paper products in the world. When 6 percent of the grocery bags being produced by St. Regis' Washington and California factories turned out to be defective, concerned company officials tried to solve the problem by hiring more inspectors. That approach failed. So the company tried something new. Instead of putting each machine operator's *number* on the bags he or she produced, the *name* of each operator went onto each bag. "The results," says St. Regis product manager Jack Reed, "are amazing. The 350 employees want to be responsible for their own work. Believe me, they don't want a defective bag with their name on it." End result: the number of flawed bags has dropped dramatically, from 6 percent to less than 1 percent.

Sex and Your Name

Since the vast majority of sexual problems arise out of psychological difficulties, it is not surprising that in a few cases men and women have found their love lives in some way hampered by an unattractive, embarrassing or confusing name. Cleveland-born Claire is a denizen of New York's Upper East Side singles' bars, and he looks the part. Lanky, with a carefully tended moustache, he is equally comfortable wearing his on-the-job three-piece suit (Claire is an assistant buyer for a department store) or his weekend uniform of faded-to-perfection Levi's. When he graduated from high school in 1961, however, Claire was anything but a sexual success. "I would go to a bar with friends, we'd meet a couple of girls, and the minute it came time for the introductions, I could always expect a wisecrack. I had grown up with this problem, but somehow I had convinced myself that once I was out of school it would vanish. Anyway, being laughed at by just about every woman you meet is not the way to begin a relationship." And when he did wind up in bed with a woman, he admitted, "there was always the memory of her first reaction to my name—the raised eyebrows, the giggles." When he was 25, Claire began experimenting with an alias. He picked Bob—"It was the name I always wanted as a kid"—and soon discovered that his relationships with women improved significantly. "Without the stumbling block at the beginning, my confidence and social ability increased."

The emotional tether that connects name and libido is further evidenced by the reluctance of a man to tell a prostitute his first name. With anonymity comes freedom, freedom to perform in ways that one might never dare if he had to take off the mask. Homosexuals often have encounters with one another without ever learning the other person's name—or wanting to. "As long as neither of us knows each other," says one gay New Yorker, "we can do whatever we want and not be inhibited." It is interesting to note that this man and his friends have sexual relations with one another without feeling they've "known" each other until they've divulged their names. For transsexuals, a new name signifies a new life. George Jorgensen became Christine, and tennis personality Dr. Richard Raskin chose a complete overhaul. Changing her surname to Richards, she picked Renee for her first name. Significantly, Renee means "reborn."

Your Name and Your Sanity

Astonishingly, perhaps as many as 50 percent of those who bother to go back and read their birth certificates are surprised to find that the name on the certificate is not what they have been called all their lives. There are often omissions, variations or information that they are not aware of.

There are many reasons behind this. A person may be given a formal name at birth that was never intended for common use. Your parents may have had second thoughts, and simply decided that the original choice of a name would best be forgotten. Or maybe the name, due to the error of some clerk, was never recorded properly in the first place.

In many cases, important clues to the intentions of your parents at the time can be found in your birth certificate. Who chose your name? Whom were you named after and why? A man named Bud by his boyhood friends, for example, might confirm his suspicions that his mother is possessive by reading on his birth certificate that his real name is Valentine—a label perhaps intended to undermine his self-confidence and strengthen her hold. Thus it is wise to find your birth certificate and read it. And if you ever seek professional help from a psychologist or psychiatrist, take your birth certificate along. "If a patient has not seen his birth certificate," advised Dr. Eric Berne, "he should be instructed to do so, or even better, bring it in for the therapist to see."

The Name Game has become enormously complicated because, unlike most other cultures, we have over the decades steadily expanded our pool of standard given names. While a century ago there were a few hundred names from which to choose, there are now thousands upon thousands—a seemingly limitless supply. Nonetheless, traditional favorites like John, Mary, William and Susan have consistently headed the popularity polls.

Until now, that is. A revolution in naming is underway. Archaic names are being rescued from oblivion. New ones are being coined by the score. New sources are being tapped. American blacks, for example, are turning in ever-larger numbers to African and Arabic names for themselves and their children. Will the youngsters who bear the strange names of the 1970s profit or suffer from their parents' imagination? We now have at hand the knowledge to prevent the traumas associated with peculiar names. The question remains: Are you willing to use this knowledge?

Like the rest of us, you had nothing to say about the name your parents bestowed upon you. And like the rest of us, you have probably gone through life without ever consciously using names—yours or others'—to improve your life.

Myron is a case in point. Myron is 29 years old and, for as long as he can remember, has never cared for his name. By the time he reached the University of California at Berkeley, he was the meek, self-effacing mathematics major everyone had expected him to be. After graduating with a far-from-dazzling scholastic record, Myron tried to get a job as an executive trainee with an investment banking firm. But the personnel officers treated him with thinly disguised indifference, and the résumés he sent to personnel agencies inspired only apathy. So Myron went to work for a San Francisco Bank, and there he remains—right where he started, behind a teller's cage.

Not that Myron hasn't tried; whenever there is an opening at the bank, he approaches R. Tompkins Janos, the manager, and requests a tryout as a personal loan officer. But twice the job has gone to somebody else—first to a J. Anthony Marks, then to a Kenneth J. Jenkins. Inevitably, the frustration took its toll at home. Myron's wife, Pamela, who had made it clear from the outset that she would not tolerate failure on the part of her husband, finally left to live with another man. Now Myron is involved with a department store buyer named Sylvia, who is every bit as demanding and difficult as Pamela was.

Had his parents been skilled players of the Name Game, his name would have been different, and so too would his life. Had *he* been a skilled player of the Name Game, there is much Myron could have done to bolster his self-confidence and his esteem in the eyes of others, to improve his scholastic standing, to widen his professional horizons, to get the job he wanted, to move ahead swiftly and to select a more compatible mate. He could have traded in his name, for example, for something that studies show is more positive and effective. Or he could have just used his first and middle initials, which would have drawn a favorable response from professors and personnel officers alike. Once he landed the job he wanted, his memos—signed with initials— would not go unnoticed. He would also be a likelier prospect for promotion. On the private side, he might have been forewarned that Sylvias and Pamelas are generally thought to be aggressive. These are preconceptions that Sylvias and Pamelas are, more likely than not, going to try to live up to. The following pages explain how, and why, once you have mastered the Name Game, you will have learned a newfound freedom to control your own destiny.

As you read the following, you will learn how names have changed the characters, lives and personalities of people. You will learn what *your* name really means to others and, more importantly, to yourself. You will learn how your career, your marriage, your social life, your children and your world are affected by your name and the names of those around you. You will learn how to interpret the psychological meanings of names, and, most importantly, what modifications to make to get the most out of yours.

For the first time, this book gives you alternatives to just putting up with your name. It gives you the freedom not only to tailor your name to your ambitions, but to use your newfound knowledge to comprehend the motivations and the actions of those around you.

CHAPTER 2

What Does Your Name Say About You?

As his name is, so is he.
—I Samuel 25:25

Test Your Name Power: An Exercise

The stakes are high, the odds tough. The beginner needs a little limbering up. How much do you already know about the hidden meanings of names?

Take the following short quiz, then turn the page to see how your impressions of certain names compare with a poll of 1,100 people.

Match the name to the appropriate adjective:

Allan	Mediocre
Andrew	Diffident
Anthony	Aggressive
Benjamin	Manly
Daniel	Very good-looking
Dennis	Spoiled
Donald	Large, soft and cuddly
Edward	Thoughtful
George	Dishonest
Gordon	Serious, sincere, sensitive
Harold	Coarse
Hugh	Cheery, honest and proud
Joseph	Smooth and charming
Keith	Sincere but immature
Mark	Intelligent, earnest but dull
Paul	Red and plodding
Richard	Tall, wiry, elegant

Robert	Introverted and mean
Roger	Hardworking but unsuccessful
Simon	Hard, self-reliant, ambitious
Thomas	Clumsy

Barbara	Plain
Emma	Childish
Florence	Temperamental but likable
Gillian	Spiteful
Louise	Sultry and surly
Maureen	Pretty but silly
Nancy	Masculine
Pamela	Sensual and selfish
Patricia	Hard, ambitious and domineering
Sally	Fat but sexy
Sarah	Pretty

In 1973, psychologist Ralph Winsome polled 1,100 people on their reactions to thirty-two common first names:

Allan	Serious, sincere, sensitive
Andrew	Sincere but immature
Anthony	Tall, wiry, elegant
Benjamin	Dishonest
Daniel	Manly
Dennis	Clumsy
Donald	Smooth and charming
Edward	Thoughtful
George	Aggressive
Gordon	Hardworking but unsuccessful
Harold	Coarse
Hugh	Mediocre
Joseph	Intelligent, earnest but dull
Keith	Hard, self-reliant, ambitious
Mark	Spoiled
Paul	Cheery, honest and proud
Richard	Very good-looking
Robert	Diffident
Roger	Red and plodding
Simon	Introverted and mean
Thomas	Large, soft and cuddly

As for the women:

Barbara	Fat but sexy
Emma	Pretty but silly
Florence	Masculine
Gillian	Pretty
Louise	Temperamental but likable
Maureen	Sultry and surly
Nancy	Spiteful
Pamela	Hard, ambitious and domineering
Patricia	Plain
Sally	Childish
Sarah	Sensual and selfish

Researcher E. D. Lawson asked a group of students to rank 20 men's names—the 10 most common (David, Gary, James, John, Joseph, Michael, Paul, Richard, Robert and Thomas) and 10 selected at random (Andrew, Bernard, Dale, Edmond, Gerd, Ivan, Lawrence, Raymond, Stanley and Matthew). Male and female students felt strongly that people with names like Bernard, Dale, Gerd, Ivan and Stanley were worse than the rest—weaker, less active and generally less desirable.

A rigorously scientific approach was taken by psychologists Barbara Buchanan and James Bruning of Pennsylvania State University in 1967. She selected about 1,350 Ohio University students at random and asked them to rate over 1,000 names according to their personal likes and dislikes. The most popular names turned out to be Michael, James, Linda, Susanne and Kim. Ferde, Isidore, Eugenia and Beulah were the least appreciated names.

The students, who were also asked to rate the names on an active-passive and a masculine-feminine scale, split along sexual lines. Male students, for example, rated Adam, Mac, Samson and Bart as the most masculine-sounding male names, while the women polled thought Dave, Kirk, Michael and James sounded more manly. But everyone agreed that among the male names, Valentine, Claire and Shelly were the most sissified of the lot.

As for women's names, the male students thought Sue, Elizabeth and Linda were most feminine, while the ladies themselves picked Yvette, Sophia and Sheri. Least feminine, according to the men: Sydney, Ronnie and Jerry. Ladies' choices: Lou, Alfreda and Billie.

For most active, the women picked Dierdre, Jody and Tobi, while their male counterparts thought Bobbie, Patty and Bridget sounded least passive. Pansy, Prissy, Agnes, Violet, Rose and Mona were pegged by all as wallflowers.

Showing a certain association between masculinity and activity, four of the eight favorite "masculine" names also showed up on the "active" list. The males agreed that Bart, Johnny and Dave were the most active-sounding fellows, while the women singled out Kirk, Sargeant and James. Again, there was agreement on which names had a certain inert quality: Isidore, Percival, Milton and—also rated as most feminine-sounding—Valentine. It is interesting to note that, in their feelings about names, women tended to be more extreme.

The English prejudices are similar to ours. British psychologist David Sheppard of the University of Reading sampled 146 people from ten widely scattered universities, offices and research stations. More than 93 percent of Sheppard's subjects rated John as trustworthy, William, Jane and Margaret as kind but not aggressive, Tony as sociable, Robin as young and Frederick as pushy. Eleanor was considered average in every category, while Mathilda and Agnes were presumed to be rather homely. Cyril and Miriam, conforming to what Sheppard calls the "sneaky sound" of their names, were deemed totally untrustworthy. Strangely, Ann was regarded as more trustworthy but less beautiful and less sociable than Anne. What a difference an "e" makes.

Fat vs. Thin Names

As Russell Baker has pointed out, many names connote physical characteristics. Of the following, which do you think are "fat" names, and which are "thin"? (Tip: Before answering, close your eyes and visualize the type of person each name conjures up.)

Bertha	Leo
Dominic	Kenneth

Emily	Anthony
Sally	Olga
Ollie	Barbara

ANSWERS: Bertha, Dominic, Ollie, Leo, Olga and Barbara would be expected by most people to carry around a bit of excess poundage. Emily, Sally, Kenneth and Anthony are the likely skinnys.

Attractive vs. Unattractive Names

Pretend you are going on a blind date, and the other person's name leads you to believe that he or she is a certain type. Sometimes, we are pleasantly (or unpleasantly) surprised to find that we were wrong. But more often than not, we find exactly what we had expected to find—solely on the basis of a name. "Funny, you don't look like a Bertha." Or a Sam. Or a Lola. We all have very strong feelings about what people with a certain name are "supposed" to look like because names in fact do have an impact on the way people look. Or, more precisely, on the way people make themselves look in accordance with society's expectations. There are, of course, beautiful Effies and dashing Maynards. But of the following names, which do you think belong to attractive types, and which to markedly less attractive people?

Richard	Carl
Sophia	Norton
Anthony	Nellie
Gertrude	Louise
Sherry	Amanda
Isidore	

ANSWERS: Richard, Sophia, Anthony, Sherry, Carl, Louise and Amanda we would expect to be rather attractive. Gertrude, Isidore, Norton and Nellie are, alas, a different story.

Active vs. Passive Names

People tend to be what we expect them to be. If a person is fortunate enough to have a positive name that is full of strength and life, then those are the qualities we will anticipate—and usually find. While some names we are prone to associate with an active, vibrant, dynamic character, others imply a certain sedentary quality. An active-sounding name gives any person a head start in business and is bound to have the same effect on that individual's self-image. Which of the following do you think fit in the active category, and which are the passive-sounding names that generally serve as a handicap?

Bridget	Boyd
Rose	Sylvia
Johnny	Cliff
Dave	James
Milton	Jody
Mona	Patty
Isidore	

ANSWERS:

The most active-sounding names are Bridget, Johnny, Dave, Sylvia, Cliff, James, Jody and Patty. Rose, Milton, Mona, Isidore and Boyd are, studies show, thought of as fundamentally passive.

Winner vs. Loser Names

A corporate vice-president is told by his secretary that he has an appointment with a young person who wishes to fill that opening as junior account executive. But even before the door opens and the hopeful job hunter walks in, there is a mental strike against that person. To the V.P. and many, many others, the applicant's name spells inadequacy, weakness and a distinct lack of drive. That individual is already stereotyped as a loser, and will have to work that much harder to overcome that overwhelming impression. In the office, on the playing field and even in the bedroom, a name can help transmit the message "I am a winner" or "I am a loser." Which of the following bespeak the positive qualities that mean success to most of us? Which are we likely to view as losers?

Elroy	Claude
Dean	Douglas
Gladys	Durward
Keith	Janet
Beverly	Pamela

ANSWERS:

Dean, Keith, Beverly, Douglas, Janet and Pamela belong in the winner's circle, while Elroy, Gladys, Claude and Durward are names that are associated in most people's minds with anything but great success.

The Name-Makers

Just where do we get preconceived notions about the qualities attached to a name? Personal experience, as Freud maintained, plays an enormous part, of course. But in addition, literature, movies and television have a large role in the formulation of these images. Character actress Beulah Bondi couldn't have been much of an asset to her fellow Beulahs when it came to looks, but what Richard Burton and Elizabeth Taylor have done for their respective namesakes is immeasurable. Every Lucy in the country owes her lighthearted image to some degree to Lucille Ball, and practically every show business Mary from Pickford to Tyler Moore has reinforced the sweetness-and-light image that goes with just being Mary. It will be several years before we know what impact such hit television shows as "Rhoda," "Phyllis" and "Maude" have had on our collective psyche.

Writers, as might be expected, have always been acutely aware of the importance of their characters' names. In the third century B.C., the Roman comedy writer Plautus invented Manducus ("to place in the mouth"), a glutton who became so popular with the audiences of the period that a slang word, *manducare* ("to eat greedily"), was derived from the character's name. Eventually, *manducare* began to replace the original Latin verb meaning "to eat," *edere*. Because of Plautus' insatiable character, the Italians now say *mangiare* and the French, *manger*. The fifteenth-century Italian poet Matteo Boiardo created a boastful character named Rodomonte, literally defined as "I roll away the mountain." The English word rodomontade is the end result.

The great master of tailoring names to characters was Charles Dickens. Consider Ebenezer Scrooge, Mr. Bumble, Mrs. Jellyby, Oliver Twist, Mrs. Sparsit, Tiny Tim, Bob Cratchit, Mrs. Pardiggle, David Copperfield. Although we undoubtedly associate certain characteristics with these names *because* of the Dickens tales, they possess a poetic magic that tells the reader something about each character before that character is actually described. Once we are introduced, for example, to Ebenezer Scrooge, a patently unpleasant-sounding name, we are not at all surprised at the shriveled soul we find. Some have gone so far as to suggest that Dickens followed a formula. The vowel "u" symbolized clumsiness, as in Bugby, Bumble and Nuff. An "i" evoked sympathy—Pip, Fips, Gig and Sniggs. According to this formula, a combination was used to suggest both qualities in one character; hence Nupkins and Spruggins.

Fitzgerald's James Gatz changed his name to Jay Gatsby upon settling on the shores of West Egg. Daisy Buchanan and her cloddish husband Tom seem aptly named. The guileless Good Old Boy narrator, Nick Carraway, spends part of his time courting a society golfer who cheats. Her decidedly snooty, yet intriguing name: Jordan Baker.

James Bond creator Ian Fleming took a more lighthearted approach. Beyond such villains as the infamous Dr. No and Goldfinger, Fleming the unrepentant chauvinist wasted no time putting his women in their place with names like Miss Moneypenny and Pussy Galore. Playwright Tennessee Williams evoked the musky decadence of a fading New Orleans magnolia with Blanche DuBois, and Neil Simon squeezes every last laugh out of his audiences with just the right names. Would *The Odd Couple* have been quite so funny if the main characters were named Steve Johnson and Bob Jones, instead of Felix Unger and Oscar Madison?

In many cases, the artist is fully aware of the process by which he arrives at names for his characters. Often, however, it is a subconscious process by which the writer unknowingly gives us a glimpse at his psychiatric makeup. Biographer Leon Edel, for example, points to a curious conjunction of small facts relating to mystery writer Rex Stout. Edel notes that Stout, whose first name means king in Latin, created a sleuth whose first name is that of a Roman emperor, Nero. Although Stout was anything but, he made his hero grossly overweight. And the man with the two names Nero and Wolfe—words that inspire fear—had as his indispensable assistant a man known as "Goodwin." "Now," sighs Edel, "isn't that curious?"

CHAPTER 3
The Secret History of Your Name

Before you can play to win, you must first understand the rules, the dynamics of names over the centuries and how names have shaped lives in every culture.

The notion that names carry with them some mystical connotations is probably as old as naming itself. The ancient Egyptians regarded one's name as a separate entity with a life of its own, and in Rome the eighth (for girls) or ninth (for boys) day after birth was "Name Day." A sacrifice was offered and a name "purified" so that it would not later be misused as an incantation by practitioners of sorcery. Not wanting to tempt the envy of the gods, the Chinese made a point of giving their children unpleasant-sounding names.

Although English surnames did not appear in large numbers until well after the Crusades, there is no way of pinpointing that historic moment when the first human became the proud possessor of a name. It is safe to assume, however, that as soon as man formed the most elemental social group—the family—he required some verbal method for labeling the group's members. The oldest surviving personal name is believed by some archaeologists to be En-lil-ti, a word that appears on a Sumerian tablet dating from 3300 B.C. that was discovered outside Baghdad in 1936. But some antiquarians insist that En-lil-ti is probably the name of a Sumer deity, Lord of the Air, and that the Sumer gods of silt, Lahma and Lahamu, are older still. If that is true, the first-personal-name honor probably falls to N'armer, the father of Men, Egypt's first pharaoh. N'armer dates back almost 5,000 years, to 3000 B.C.

Among the various linguistic theories that seek to explain the origins of the very first names, the one with the most validity

38

presumes people were named for physical characteristics. To put it simply, a small man might be called "The Short One," a gray-haired woman, "The Gray One," and so on. The belief soon followed that powers and traits—even such physical attributes as size and strength—could be invested in an individual through his name.

As civilization and language advanced, so did the descriptive power of names. The root of the Greek word for thunder shows up in the ancient Greek name Stentor. Thus Stentor's voice was anything but soft, and the adjective *stentorian* evolved to describe anyone with a loud voice. The Slavic word for thunder is *grom,* and the Russian equivalent of Stentor is Gromyko, the family name of the Soviet foreign minister. Oedipus meant "swollen foot." Contrary to popular belief, Moses is probably neither Hebrew nor Aramaic, but perhaps the ancient Egyptian word meaning "child." The Romans came up with, among other names: Agrippa, meaning "born feet-first," Aurelius ("golden"), Dexter ("right-handed"), Sallust ("healthy"), Calvin ("bald"), Seneca ("old"), Cecil ("dim-sighted"), Rufus ("red"), Lucius ("light"), Livy ("bluish"), Crassus ("fat") and Varus ("bow-legged"). The Celtic name Fingal ("fair-complexioned stranger") refers to eighth-century Norwegian invaders. The French Algernon is "bearded" and the German Karl means "a man."

Names describing more than just physical qualities soon flourished. Hebrew was the source for such names as Beulah ("married"), Ephraim ("fruitful"), Solomon ("peaceable"), Isaac ("laughter"), Ann ("gracious"), Job ("afflicted"), David ("beloved") and Abel ("breath"). The Greek name Sophia means "wise," Ambrose, "immortal," and Philander, "lover of men." Names giving some indication of the individual's occupation or location also sprang up. George is Greek for "farmer," Angelos means "messenger" and Philip is "lover of horses." The Hebrew Gideon is a "hewer," while the Welsh Morgan is a "dweller by the sea." The English, however, waited until the Dark Ages to turn to their occupations and locations, primarily for surnames.

Totemic names paying homage to natural phenomena evolved at about the same time. Mata Hari, for example, is Malay for "day's eye" (the sun), and is the unlikely-sounding parallel for

the English "day's eye"—Daisy. The Italian Laura may be derived from "l'aura," the air. Adam is "man of red earth," Eve
is "life," the Latin Stella, "star."

Nowhere was the totemic use of names more evident than
among the American Indians, who invariably took names designed to transfer to the bearer such qualities as the swiftness
of an eagle, the cunning of a fox or the ferocity and strength of
a bear. From Sitting Bull to Crazy Horse to the Aztec Netza-
hualcotyl ("hungry coyote"), the natives of the New World
sought to honor the forces of nature. Even today, Indian tribes
such as the Cherokee and Arapaho permit their members to
change their names several times to suit their personalities at a
given stage of life. Many of those who knew her well might have
said that the temperamental actress daughter of Alabama Congressman William Brockman Bankhead was aptly named. In
Chickasaw the word Tallulah means "terrible."

Realizing what most psychologists are only now beginning to
admit—that character and personality are heavily influenced by
one's given name—the Puritans and their descendants lavished
righteousness on their newborn with the zeal of true believers.
The founder of England's first fire insurance company was Unless-
Christ-had-died-for-thee-thou-shalst-be-damned Barebones. His father, who gave his name to the Barebones Parliament of 1653,
was Praise-God Barebones.

As Arthur Calhoun observed in his *Social History of the American Family from the Colonial Times to the Present,* parents took
the job of naming very seriously, searching for names that might
exercise a favorable influence on the child's life. Not surprisingly,
the Bible was a prime source. In the earlier years, Old Testament
names like Heber, Gershom, Uriah, Zabdiel, Jedidiah, Shem,
Ezra and Zachariah were widely chosen. There were also such
sturdy English standbys as John ("Jehovah has been gracious"
in Hebrew), Christopher ("Christ-bearer"), Michael ("He who
is like God"), Matthew ("Gift of Jehovah"), William ("Determined protector"), Thomas ("The Twin"), Richard ("Wealthy
and powerful"), James ("The Supplanter") and Charles
("Man").

Many of the girls were named for abstractions such as Hope,
Faith, Charity, Patience, Prudence, Honor, Rejoice, True, De-

sire, Unite, Thanks, Experience, Preserved, Wait-still and Submit. Eighteenth-century advances also brought some simplification to girls' names as parents turned to Sally, Ann, Dorothy, Lucy and Elizabeth, or simple biblical names like Abigail, Hannah, Martha, Sarah, Ruth and Deborah.

Still, a baby born after the death of his or her father stood a chance of being named Fathergone or Abiel, Hebrew for "God is my father." One colonial parent, Richard Gridly, named his children Return, Believe and Tremble. Another, Edward Bendall, called his Truegrace, Reform, Hoped-for, More-Mercy and Restore. Heaping piety on their offspring, good Christian parents even saddled them with such "names" as Search-the-Scriptures, Fear-not, Sin-deny, Sorry-for-sin, Faint-not, Stand-fast, Increase, More-trial, Joy-again, From-above, Free-gifts, Be-faithful, More-fruit, Hope-still, Dust, Learn-wisdom, Hate-evil, The Lord-is-near and Fly-fornication.

An eighteenth-century Rhode Island man was named Through-much-tribulation-we-enter-into-the-Kingdom-of-Heaven Clapp. Mr. Clapp was not alone. In 1855, the Editor's Drawer of *Harper's Magazine* noted the passing of a woman called Aunt Tribby by her friends and family. Her extended title: Through-much-tribulation-we-enter-into-the-Kingdom-of-Heaven Crabb. A Texas farmer born in 1883 was baptized Daniel's wisdom may I know, Stephen's faith and spirit choose, John's divine communion seal, Moses' meekness, Joshua's zeal, Win-the-day and Conquer-All Murphy. Such unwieldy titles did not always produce the desired effect. Whom-the-Lord-Preserved Scott, a Midwest farmer, preferred to be known by another name. Whom-the-Lord-Preserved was nicknamed "Canned" Scott.

First Names First

Every person had in the beginning one and only one proper name, among the Iewes, Adam, Joseph, Solomon; among the Egyptians, Anubis, Amasis, Buriris; among the Chaldeans, Ninus, Ninias, Semiramis; among the Medians, Astiages, Bardanes, Arbaces; among the Grecians, Dimodes, Vlisses, Orestes; among the Romans,

Romulus, Remus, Faustulus; *among the Gaules,* Litavi-
cus, Cavarillus; *among the Germans,* Arovistus, Armi-
nius, Nassua; *among the Britains,* Cassibellin, Caratac,
Calgac; *among the ancient English,* Hengest, Aella,
Kenric; *likewise among all other Nations, except the
savages of Mount Atlas of Barbary, which were reported
to be both namelesse and dreamlesse.*
        —William Camden
        Remaines Concerning Britain, 1605

Historically, our lives have always been shaped more by our
given than by our last names. Until relatively recently, the given
or baptismal name was the only one of any real importance in
the English-speaking world. Legal documents were signed with
the given name only, and all court proceedings were conducted
accordingly. From the thirteenth-century records of King Edward I:

> One Matthew came to the market and found in the
> hands of one Robert his horse which had been the
> night before stolen from his house in the town, and
> that he raised the cry on the said Robert and so both
> man and horse were taken.

During the reign of Edward II, a jurist recorded the following
opinion:

> A certain Alice appealed John of rape and breach of
> the peace of our Lord and King. John came forward
> and defended all manner of felony. If Alice, by advice
> of counsel, had not withdrawn her appeal, the judgment
> of the court would have been that Alice should tear out
> John's eyes.

Ironically, the ancient Greeks, Hebrews and even the earliest
Icelandic tribes made use of second or family names, and the ancient Romans came to bestow names in much the same way as
modern Americans. They combined a first name, a clan name and
a patronymic, as in Marcus Claudius Tacitus, Cneius Pompeius
Magnus (Pompey the Great), Marcus Tullius Cicero or Caius

Julius Caesar. But following the fall of the empire, surnames all but disappeared in Europe until the eleventh century, when a burgeoning population, increased travel and improved communications outstripped the supply of available Christian names. Still, as late as the fifteenth century many Englishmen—and nearly all Irishmen—were without surnames. In 1465, King Edward IV decreed that every Irishman should not only dress like an Englishman, but "take to him an English surname, of one town as Sutton, Chester, Trym, Skryne, Cork, Kinsale; or colour as whyte, black, brown; or art of science, as smith or carpenter; or office, as cook, butler and that he and issue shall use this name."

The classic patronymic, which can be found in the Old Testament—"Isaac, son of Abraham"—survives in modern Israel, where the late David Ben-Gurion—"David, son of Gurion—served as the first prime minister. Achilles is introduced in Homer's *Iliad* as Peleiades Achileus—Achilles, son of Peleus; brothers Agamemnon and Menelaus are called the Atreidae—sons of Atreus.

By the time Edward IV issued his decree, scores of patronymics had already been conjured up through a variety of methods. If a man was baptized Michael, for instance, and his father's name was John, he might become known as Michael Johnson. Or David, son of Patrick, might be called David Fitzpatrick, "fitz" being the anglicized form of the Old French word for son brought to England by the Normans.

To be sure, it is not always easy to recognize the original in a patronymic. Ransom, for example, means son of Randolph. The *O'* prefix of O'Hara and O'Dwyer is a regular Irish form meaning "descendant of" and was generally used to describe the grandson of the original. Hence the first O'Malley was often Malley's grandson.

Frequently surnames were formed merely by appending an "s" to the father's name. As a result, we have Abrahams and Abrams, Clements, Collins, Davis (from David), Edmonds, Edwards, Evans, Ewings, Franks, Geoffreys, Gibbs, Griffiths, Hawkins, Hodges, Hughs, Humphreys, Jacks, Jacobs, Jeffreys, Jones (from John), Marks, Martins, Matthews, Parsons, Peters, Phillips, Reynolds, Richards, Roberts, Robins, Rowlands, Solomons, Samuels, Sanders (from Alexander), Simons, Stephens, Stevens, Walters and Williams.

Other cultures and languages have given rise to their own patronymic prefixes and suffixes. In Italian, the predominant form is *de* or *di*, as in di Giovanni, the Italian for Johnson. The Germans and Scandinavians use the standard *son* and *sen* endings, while the Rumanians use the suffix *escu*, meaning "like." The Yugoslavs use *vich* and *ich* as standard endings. Russians and Bulgarians lean toward *ov* or *ev* endings, so that Petrov means "of the Peters," Ivanov, "of the Johns," etc. They even go so far as to have a secondary patronymic ending in *sky* or *ski* that often hitches up with *ov* or *ev* to produce a double patronymic. Ivanovsky, then, means "of the nature of the descendants of John." To make Russian names all the more complicated, a middle patronymic is sometimes used to further describe the individual's forebears. Fyodor Mikhailovich Dostoyevsky's name loses something in the translation. It means "Fyodor, son of Michael of the nature of the descendants of Dostoy."

Less male-chauvinistic is the matronymic, in which the mother supplies the name. Nelson (Nell's son) is a standard matronymic in English, as is Allyson (Alice's son) and Babson (Barbara's son). Piero della Francesca (Peter, son of Frances) was a reknowned Italian artist. In Scandinavia and parts of England settled by the Vikings, many women were unfortunate enough to be branded Gunnarsdatter (Gunnar's daughter) or Eriksdatter (Erik's daughter) or Kristensdatter (Christian's daughter). Thus St. Bridget of Sweden was Birgersdatter and her daughters were all Ulfsdatters. The fairest compromise was struck by the Spanish, who for centuries have named their children after both parents. Consequently, Jose, son of Manuel Rodriguez and Juanita Perez, would be called Jose Rodriguez y Perez. One American who would not compromise was Toni Zimmerman. In 1976, she had her name legally changed to Zimmerwoman!

Mr. Good-Handwriting

The most names in number have been derived from Occupations or Professions as Taylor, Potter, Smith, Sadler. Neither was there any trade, craft, arte, profes-

sion, occupation never so meane but had a name among us.

—William Camden
Remaines Concerning Britain

In the twentieth century, the rush toward modernization and Westernization meant a drive in many underdeveloped countries to provide each and every person with some sort of surname. After Reza Kahn Pahlavi, the father of the reigning Shah, came to power in Iran during the 1920s, he proclaimed that every Iranian must have a last name. The result, wrote Anne Sinclair Mehdevi in 1965, is that "Persia abounds in wonderful last names. There were Mr. Give-Me-Water, Mr. Snowy, Mr. Good-Hand-writing." According to the name-giving decree, each person was allowed to choose any name he or she fancied. As a result, there were quite a number of Mr. Kings and Mr. Emperors and Mr. Bigs. Those who were not terribly imaginative called themselves after the town in which they were born. Thus one finds dozens of Tabrizis, Shirazis and Isfahanis. Others called themselves Mr. Scientist, Mr. Engineer and even Mr. Photographer, in keeping with their occupations.

English surnames based on profession, however, invariably date back several centuries, and are found in hundreds of variations in dozens of languages. There are well over 3 million Smiths in the world, making that the most widely held English surname, but millions more bear its foreign-language counterparts. In French, Smith becomes Lefevre or Faure; in German, Feuer or Schmidt; in Russian, Kuznetsov; in Bulgarian, Kovac; in Syrian, Haddad; in Spanish, Herrera; in Polish, Kowalski; in Italian, Ferraro or Ferrari.

Similarly, the English Baker (or Baxter) becomes Fornari in Italy, Becker in Germany and Boulanger in France. The German Eisenhower, or "iron-hewer," is translated into the common French surname Taillefer, the Italian Taliaferro and the English Tolliver. Carpenter translates into the German Zimmermann, and the French Carpentier. Taylor becomes the French Sartre (tailor) and the German Schneider. Salter's German equivalent: Hitler. When the trades turned to producing the tools of war, they spawned such names as Armour, Boyer ("the man who makes the bows") and Fletcher ("arrow-maker").

The Swedish Hammarskjold ("hammer shield") is curiously related to Molotov, the Russian word meaning "the hammer"— which United Nations Secretary-General Dag Hammarskjold would have found particularly appropriate as he fended off the diplomatic blows of Soviet Foreign Minister Vyacheslav Molotov. (Ironically, Molotov had changed his name from Skriabin in 1906 to escape the Czar's secret police.) The art of war, in fact, has been the source of many other last names, including Archer, Bowman, Castle, Gun, Knight, Shakespeare ("spearman"), Shield(s), Spear(s), Speer and Tower. Even the bureaucracy of the Middle Ages produced numerous names. Among them: Baily (from bailiff), Chancellor, Chamberlain, Clark, Constable, Page, Proctor (an attorney), Reeves (representative of a village), Sargent, Spencer (originally Dispenser), Tollman (toll collector) and Ward.

Nobility was well represented (the French offer Lecomte and Leduc, the Italians Nobile and Conti), as was the church: Pope, Cardinal, Bishop, Archdeacon, Abbott, Pryor, Monk, Nunn, Friar, Cannon, Dean, Vickers, Chaplin, Parsons, Priest, Priestly, Deacon and Church. Royalty is not shortshrifted, either: King, Prince, Duke, Earl, Baron, Lord and Knight. The arts provide enough names for a good-sized orchestra. The string section might include a Harper, a Fiddler and a Luther ("lute player"). Tabor the drummer would lead the percussion section. Providing the wind: Piper, Hornblower and Whistler.

Roots

In the autentical record of the Exchequer called Domes-day, surnames were first found, brought by the Normans, who not long before first took them, but most noted with de, such a place as Godefrides de Maneville, A de Grey, Walterus de Vernoon. . . .

    —William Camden
    Remaines Concerning Britain

Every village and town in the Middle Ages served to name at least one family. In the case of St. Thomas Aquinas, it was the town of Aquino. It is obvious where Jack London's medieval ancestors hailed from, not to mention those of George Washington, Abraham Lincoln, John Hastings, and Felix Frankfurter.

In many cases, however, it is less obvious. At least 75 names derive from the villages of France and Flanders alone, so that Disney owned his name to the village of Isigny, Ashley Montagu to Montauge, Charles Percy to Percy-en-Auge in Normandy, Spencer Tracy to Tracy-sur-Mer and Earl Warren to Le Varenne. Later on, regions, provinces and entire countries lent their names to individuals. The writer Anatole Thibault, for example, formally became Anatole France. Pierre Mendès-France served briefly as premier during the mid-1950s. The Russian playwright Anton Chekhov bore a last name meaning "of the Czechs," and Hermann Hesse's forebears were undoubtedly residents of the German province of the same name.

The famous World War II Admiral Chester Nimitz owed his name to the Slavic word for German, *nemetz*. Charles de Gaulle never doubted his ancestry. Nor does Xaviera Hollander. And it is not uncommon in Eastern Europe for the Slavic patronymic suffix *vich* to be converted into *vitz* and tagged onto a city name, so that many Russians are called Moscovitz, "son of Moscow."

Within the village itself, local landmarks and topographical features were all-important for distinguishing one John or Peter from another. The John who lived on the hill became John Hill or John Hills or John Hillman. The John who lived near the well became John Wells, John Wellman or John Atwell. Winston Churchill's ancestors probably lived near a church on a hill. Gerald Ford's, it may be assumed, lived near a ford in a stream, and might just as well have been dubbed Bridges, Banks, Rivers or Brooks.

The phenomenon, once again, is cross-cultural. Mountain or hill-dwellers were named Depew or Dumont in France, Maki in Finland, Jurek in Poland, Zola in Italy and Kopecky in Czechoslovakia. In addition to the English Rivers and Brooks, streams of various size spawned the Spanish Rio and Rivera, while those who lived near lakes became known as Loch in Scotland, Jarvi in Finland, Kuhl in Germany, and in England, Lake, Pond(s) or Pool(e). The original Dutch Roosevelts lived near a rose field.

Alexander Dumas bore a name meaning "of the little farmstead." John Dos Passos' Portuguese name could either mean "of the steps" or "of the passes," and the Spanish man of letters Garcilaso de la Vega bore a name meaning "of the plains"—the same word that appears in a slightly different form on any map of Nevada: Las Vegas. Many names translate almost exactly. The English version of the French Dubois is Woods, the German, Wald. Calles, an extremely popular Spanish surname, becomes Street or Streeter. Dupont is Bridges. The English Fountain, the Italian Fontana, the Spanish Fuentes and the French la Fontaine all mean the same thing.

As with personal names, surnames were often derived from the physical characteristics of an individual. Names referring to coloring were common in virtually every culture. Dark-skinned people were often dubbed Braun or Schwartz in Germany; Zwart in Holland; Brun, Morin or Lenoir in France; Kara, Karras or Melas in Greek; Fekete in Hungary; Pincus in Hebrew; Cherney in Czechoslovakia; Chernoff in Russia; Czerniak in Poland; Negri or de Negri in Italy and in the English-speaking world, Black, Brown or Gray. From the word Moor, meaning either the marshy wasteland or those dark conquerors of Spain, come the names Moore, Morse, Morrison, Morell, Maurois, Mauriac, Moretti, Mauro and Morelli. To denote light-skinned people, there are Bialas (Poland), Bianco (Italy), Bily and Bilek (Czechoslovakia), Weiss (Germany), Lichter (Holland), Le Blanc (France), and, of course, White.

Often, a man was likened to an animal or even a feature of the landscape. If immense, he might be called Bull or Hill. One who was deemed as cunning as a fox might wind up with Fox as his surname. A pleasant singing voice might earn one the sobriquet—and eventually the family name—Lark, Swallow, Nightingale or Bird. A superb swimmer, Mr. Fish. An exceptionally uncouth person: Hogg. A Beaver or Bee (or Beebe) would be industrious, and long legs would a Crane make. Someone noted for his physical prowess might be dubbed Lion (Lions, Lyon) or Bear. In fact, the bear is probably responsible for more surnames than any other animal; among its permutations are Bahr, Behr,

Baer, Barnhart, Barnhardt, Barnard, Bernard, Barrett and Barnett. Wolf runs a close second, with Wolfe and Wolfson among its many variations. The Arabic translation of wolf, it is interesting to note, is Sirhan—both the given name and the surname of Robert F. Kennedy's Palestinian assassin. Former United States Vice-President Spiro Agnew's adopted English surname (his real name is Anagnostapoulos), curiously enough, means "lamblike."

More ephemeral qualities are also described in thousands of last names. Baruch is "blessed," and Gorky is "bitter." Ming in Mandarin is "bright." Garibaldi means "war bold," Bonaparte is "on the right side" or "good share," and Hungarian Cardinal Mindszenty's surname literally means "all saints." Not so appropriate is the name of the iron-fisted dictator who ruled Spain for nearly four decades. Franco is derived from an old word meaning "free man."

Indeed, surnames are often the source for all sorts of delicious ironies. The original Dutch Vanderbilts, whose name means "at the heap," could not have envisioned how their descendants would wind up on top of it as nineteenth-century America's First Family of Commerce. An Episcopalian minister who has written fiction and a bestselling cookbook (*Supper of the Lamb*) also happens to be the father of six. His name is Robert Capon. Psychologist Michael Fox, author of *Understanding Your Dog,* is perhaps the world's leading authority on animal psychology, and actor Edward Fox was chosen to play the title role in the film *The Day of the Jackal.* Few anthropologists are as aptly named as Dr. Lionel Tiger. H. Head and W. R. Brain became well-known neurologists, while the president of FTD Florists is none other than Don Flowers. The *Washington Post's* horse-loving sports columnist is William Barry Furlong. In Texas, the armless detective who safely recovered Marlon Brando's kidnapped son is a karate black belt, pilot of his own jet helicopter and Rolls-driving proprietor of a private zoo. The flamboyant private eye also fires a .38-caliber bullet from a pistol implanted in one of his hooklike artificial limbs. His incredibly improbable name: J. J. Armes, pronounced—that's right—"arms."

Jewish family names have a bitterly ironic lore all their own. Not until laws enacted in the early nineteenth century forced them to did many Jews drop their traditional patronymic ("David, son of Michael") to adopt a European surname. Many merely took on the name of the town or city where they were born or settled, but some were more creative. "Jews living in crowded, airless and sunless ghettos frequently adopted names which alluded to green woods and fields," claims onomatologist Elsdon C. Smith. The result was names like Rosenblum (rose bloom), Rosenthal (rose valley), Lilienthal (lily valley) and Greenblatt (green leaf).

Many people only find out the truth about their surnames when they begin to trace their family trees. Not all such genealogy buffs like what they find. Typically, they discover that a letter has been added or dropped over the centuries. Often they find out their WASP-sounding name, like Robinson, was at one time Ruebinstein, or that Brock actually started out Brach.

For American blacks, it is widely assumed that surnames were taken from slave owners. In some cases, this was so. But why, then, are there comparatively few blacks bearing the names of such famous plantation owners as the Byrds and the Rutledges, who controlled hundreds of slaves? And if they were also supposed to have taken the surnames of Civil War liberators, why are there relatively few black Lincolns and Grants? In fact, slaves were probably just as likely to adopt the surnames of their overseers as those of their owners, and the most common practice of all was simply to take on the name that was most common to the region among blacks *and* whites. Hence Johnson, now almost even with Smith as the most common name in the United States, is the most widespread among American blacks.

Part of the Language

Many surnames are more than just labels; they have become part of our vocabulary. There are flowers, like the bougainvillea, named after the French navigator and explorer Louis Antoine de Bougainville; Jesuit Georg Josef Kamel's camellia; the dahlia, named after Swedish botanist Anders Dahl; French scientist and governor of Santo Domingo Michel Bégon's begonia; the magnolia, thus dubbed in honor of Pierre Magnol; the zinnia, named after Johann G. Zinn, a professor of medicine at the University of Göttingen; and the poinsettia, discovered in Mexico by the first United States Ambassador to Mexico, Joel Robert Poinsett.

Dozens of articles of clothing are named after people. The mackintosh was created by Charles Macintosh, and knickers were popularized by Washington Irving's Diedrich Knickerbocker; Lord Cardigan's sweater caught on, as did the jacket, so called after the medieval French character who made the short garment popular—*Jacques* Bonhomme. Lord Raglan, commander of the British forces in the Crimean War, is best remembered for a sleeve. The first to wear "pants" was Pantalone, a sort of Italian Renaissance Charlie Chaplin character in trousers. Philip Dormer Stanhope, fourth Earl of Chesterfield, had the unique distinction of lending his name to both a coat and a type of couch.

Food is no exception. It is well-known that the Earl of Sandwich invented the sandwich as a handy way of eating a meal while playing cards, but comparatively few realize that crepes suzette were originated by Edward VII's Monte Carlo chef and named after one of His Highness' favorite flower girls. Melba toast was a staple for the Australian soprano Dame Nellie Melba, and Italian coloratura Luisa Tetrazzini loved chicken cooked her way.

Can a name describe behavior? Absolutely, and with great precision. "Out of his surname they coined an epithet for a knave," wrote Macaulay of Niccolò Machiavelli, "and out of his Christian name a synonym for the Devil." Because of the stringent laws codified by seventh-century-B.C. Greek politician Dracon, even the most trivial offense was punishable by death in Athens. Thus harsh laws are said to be draconian. Napoleon's superpatriotic adjutant Nicolas Chauvin was immortalized in the adjective chauvinistic. Richard Brinsley Sheridan's Mrs. Malaprop and real-life Reverend William A. Spooner evolved into two important "isms" that have a permanent place in our linguistic repertoire. There was no more quixotic soul than Cervantes' own Don Quixote, and the term Shavian pertains to the caustic wit of George Bernard Shaw. Situations and people who are reminiscent of Dickens' *Pickwick Papers* are said to be Pickwickian, while anything harkening to the whole of the great author's work is said to be Dickensian. The Russians even have a word for anything that smacks of their favorite American writer, Mark Twain: *marktvenovsky.*

Shrapnel, silhouette, daguerreotype, the volt, the diesel engine, the watt, the ohm, the galvanometer, the zeppelin, the roentgen, the Bowie knife, the Pullman, the Geiger (or Geiger-Muller) counter, the Bunsen burner, Euclidean geometry, Mesmerism, Calvinism, Buddhism, Lutheranism, Marxism and Christianity all bear the names of their inventors. Therefore it should come as no surprise that the monkey wrench is named after the man who invented it, Charles Monckey. Even Thomas Crapper lent a word to our vocabulary that has something to do with his invention—the modern toilet. Conversely, the guillotine was not, as is widely believed, named after its inventor. The ancient device was merely advocated by Dr. Joseph Guillotin, who opposed the then-prevalent methods of torture. After the terror, Guillotin's family changed its name.

The Record-Holders

Smiths only marginally outnumber Johnsons in the United States. Ivanov is perhaps the most popular name in the Soviet Union. But the most common name in the world by far is Chang, borne by at least 85 million Chinese, or about 10 percent of the Chinese population. Thus there are more Changs in the world—28 times the number of Smiths—than the populations of all but seven of the 145-plus nations in the world.

Nonetheless, a German-born Philadelphian holds the record when it comes to length: Adolph Blaine Charles David Earl Frederick Gerald Hubert Irvin John Kenneth Lloyd Martin Nero Oliver Paul Quincy Randolph Sherman Thomas Uncas Victor William Xerxes Yancy Zeus Wolfeschlegelsteinhausenbergerdorffvoralternawarengewissenhaftschaferswessenschafewarenwohlgepflegeundsorgfaltigkeitbeschutzenvonangreifendurchihrraubgierigfeingdewelchevoralternzwolftausendjarhresvorandierscheinenvandererersteerdemenschderraumschiffgebrauchlichtalsseinursprungvonkraftgestartseinlangefahrthinzwischensternartigraumaufdersuchenachdiesternwelchegehabtbewohnbarplaneten-

kreisedrehensichundwohinderneurassevonverstandigmenschlich-
keitkonntefortpflanzenundsicherfreuenanlebenslanglichfreudeun-
druhemitnichteinfurchtvorangreifenvonanderintelligentgeschopf-
svonhinzwischensternartigraum, Senior. Using only his eighth and
second Christian names, he recently shortened his surname to
Wolfe + 590, Senior.

Rather far behind is the concisely named King of Thailand,
Vajiralongkorn Boromchadrayadisorn Santatiwong Thevettham-
rong Suboribarn Abhigunooprakarnmahitladuldej Phumiphon-
naveretvarangkur Kittosirisom-Booranasawangkawadh Boromkat-
tiyarajkumar. Not to mention an accounting department clerk
in Hawaii named Floyd Kuikealakauaokalani Kealiiwailanamalie
Kamanunuihalakaipo Hoopii.

We Begin Again

Coming full circle, surnames eventually were used as first names.
Begun in England in the seventeenth century, this practice soon
prompted the creation of such given names as Bruce, Chauncey,
Clifford, Courtenay, Darcy, Desmond, Dudley, Hartley, Howard,
Keith, Leslie, Montague, Mortimer, Percy, Rodney, Russell, Sidney, Stanley, Talbot, Vernon, Wallace and Winston—used by the
Churchills since 1620 and, in the case of one illustrious family
member, in combination with another surname-turned-Christian-
name: Spencer. In the eighteenth and nineteenth centuries there
were a few bold additions, as with *Rudyard* Kipling, *Garnet*
Wolseley, *Somerset* Maugham and *Aldous* Huxley.

Patriotism fueled the trend in America. "The meeting of the
first Continental Congress in the fall of 1774," wrote historian
Arthur Schlesinger, Sr., "crystallized the growing sense of na-
tionality. Thenceforth the giving of patriotic names to infants
became a newsworthy event. From the outset John Hancock
proved a prime favorite on baptismal occasions." But as soon as
the fighting began, Washington became the favorite name for
male babies, and Alexander Anderson of New York named his
twins George Washington and Martha Dandridge.

The first legitimate war hero on the continental side was
probably Joseph Warren, killed at Bunker Hill on June 17, 1775.

Hundreds of babies were named after Warren. Loyalists who chose to respond by naming their children for Tory heroes ran a grave risk. In March of 1776, the Edwards of Stanford, Connecticut, christened their son after Thomas Gage, then still the British Governor of Massachusetts. Three days after the christening an army of 170 neighboring women marched on the Edwards' house with tar and feathers for the mother. She narrowly escaped with the help of her dauntless husband.

Over the following decades, thousands were baptized Franklin, Jefferson, Adams, Hamilton, Marshall, Jackson, Harrison, Lincoln, Grant, Lafayette, Madison, Tyler, Scott, Lee, Sherman and Sheridan. Following the Civil War, many admirers of Stonewall Jackson named their children Stonewall, not Jackson, and in this century, Grover Cleveland, Theodore Roosevelt, Franklin Delano Roosevelt and Harry Truman have been popular namesakes. On March 15, 1941, twins in Oklahoma were named Woodrow and Wilson. Five of the 38 presidents were themselves baptized with surnames: Franklin Pierce, Rutherford B. Hayes, Warren Harding, Franklin Roosevelt and Lyndon Johnson.

To distinguish one generation from the next while holding on to the first and last names, some parents turned to middle names, though they were not in common use in England or the United States until late in the eighteenth century. Only three signers of the Declaration of Independence had middle names—Francis Lightfoot Lee, Richard Henry Lee and Robert Treat Paine. Of the first 17 presidents, only John Quincy Adams (middle-named after his father's close friend Josiah Quincy), William Henry Harrison and James Knox Polk had middle names. Often the middle name was a device for preserving the mother's maiden name. Thus Joseph Kennedy and Rose Fitzgerald named their second son John Fitzgerald, and Hannah Milhous and Francis Nixon named their son Richard Milhous Nixon.

The use of middle initials, something of an oddity in Great Britain, has been commonplace in the United States since Ulysses S. Grant. The eighteenth president was originally Hiram Ulysses, but was mistakenly enrolled at West Point as Ulysses Simpson—Simpson was his mother's maiden name—and it stuck. Perhaps it was not such a disaster for the young cadet, who feared that the initials on his trunk, H.U.G. (for the correct Hiram Ulysses Grant), would prompt his peers to nickname him "Hug." By the time he got around to being baptized, Grant chose the form that was already so familiar to the nation: Ulysses S. Another famous S was squeezed between Harry and Truman as a compromise by the thirty-second president's harried parents. They did not want to offend either of Harry's grandparents, Anderson *Shippe* Truman or *Solomon* Young. Since it was far from conventional, the S in "Harry S for Nothing," as he was called, sometimes stood without a period.

CHAPTER 4

The Name Game

The names of women should be easy to pronounce nor implying anything dreadful, possess a plain meaning, be pleasing and auspicious, end in long vowels and contain a word of benediction.
—*Manu-Smriti*, The
Ancient Brahman
Code of Laws

By 1500, the custom of naming a male after his father and appending "the younger"—now Junior—to it had become commonplace. The practice persists, but it has never been widespread in the Jewish community. As with the Islamic belief that one's soul can be "stolen" by, say, a photographic image, Jews have generally accepted the prophet Judah's admonition against naming a child after a living relative. Judah the Pious decreed that a man's soul would be deprived of its rest after death if his name were bestowed on someone else during his lifetime, and expressly forbade any of his immediate descendants to bear his own name or that of his father, Samuel. This custom, according to the *Universal Jewish Encyclopedia*, "still obtains among many Jews at the present day."

The Jewish proscription against Juniors is, say many modern psychologists, advisable on strictly non-religious grounds. "Man does wish to have a link with his ancestors and a child can feel proud to have a relative's name," concedes George H. Pollack of Chicago's Institute for Psychoanalysis. "On the other hand, we all need to be individuals, and parents should not deprive a child of that experience." A nickname distinguishing a son from his father might do the job, but *not* if parents insist on calling him "Sonny" or, worst of all, "Junior." Says Pollack: "His parents are emphasizing a role or kinship identity and may be indicating refusal to give him his own individuality. How one uses a name is frequently how one sees that person on the inside of his head."

Even the most titanic egos may crack under the strain of being known as Junior. Leon Edel reveals that the nineteenth-century novelist Henry James loathed his junior status. His signature was a blur, contends Edel, "over which floated a seemingly inexplicable dot—sole evidence that he intended the small letter 'j' to be there." The dot was dropped suddenly—on the death of James, Sr. From then on, the younger James signed his name "in full, large letters."

The use of Roman numerals, still generally regarded in Great Britain as an invasion of royal prerogative, seems to have begun around 1800. Although John Jones II was originally just an alternative to John Jones, Jr., it later came to indicate not the son of the original, but the grandson. Senator Adlai Stevenson III of Illinois has no complaints. "My father left me a good name," says Stevenson. "No father could do more, and I will try to leave a good name to my son." As for comparisons, Stevenson the Younger insists there has never been any stressful sense of competition with his father. "Not even when my powers as an orator were measured against his," says Adlai III. "And Adlai IV, alias Adlai the Next, shows no signs of stress, either."

Jay Rockefeller, former president of West Virginia Wesleyan College, and governor of West Virginia, was baptized John Rockefeller—a name he kept until he was 21. "As a boy," he explains, "I was told that I should make up my own mind whether I wanted to carry on the full name, which I think stands for public service, a sense of responsibility, and a high standard of demand on oneself. When I turned twenty-one, I moved on my own—with my grandfather's permission, of course —to add the D. and the IV." Why? "Because I was challenged and motivated by the name and its tradition. I've never had anything but positive reactions to carrying it, and, above all, am comfortable with being a person within that name." Just to be fair, Jay and his wife Sharon, daughter of Illinois Senator Charles Percy, have named *their* son John. The D and the V will be added only on request.

People are still naming their kids after each other. In a study of naming patterns among urban middle class and upper class families, Johns Hopkins sociologist Alice Rossi discovered that 83 percent had named at least one child for a relative, compared to 37 percent of the working-class families polled. She also found that, while 78 percent of the first-born sons were named after relatives, only 20 percent of the fourth-born daughters were accorded the honor. Observed Rossi: "Boys are more apt to be named after kin than girls, and first-born children more than later-born children. Sons are of special symbolic significance to the temporal continuity of the family."

If there is scant evidence that Juniors are in any real danger of disappearing, a new practice is in vogue. More and more young parents are naming their children after grandma and grandpa. Probable reason: a longer life expectancy, which enables most people to watch their grandchildren grow to adulthood. Few people are more acutely aware of the impact a grandparent's name can have than journalist Shana Alexander. "I was named after my great-grandmother, or rather, two of them," she writes. "My two grandmothers also shared the same name: Fanny. The double coincidences of those two names—the two Shanas followed by the two Fannys—is a reminder that, only a generation or two back, women were scarcely differentiated one from the next, let alone regarded as people on their own, independent of men."

The Swelling Pool

Over the decades—and the centuries—Americans have tended to remain conservative when playing the Name Game. Wilbur Zelinsky, a geographer at Pennsylvania State University, compiled a list of the names of New Englanders as they appeared in a 1790 census and compared those names to a similar 1968 study of 16 New England counties. Remarkably, of the 94,000 names, John, William and James placed first, second and third in both periods, while George, Thomas and Joseph all placed in the top ten on both lists. For the most part, these names have reigned throughout the English-speaking world—and far longer than a mere 187 years. In the fourteenth century, an estimated 64 percent of all men in England bore one of five names: John, William, Robert, Richard or Henry. One study showed that 6 million Johns and 4 million Marys live in the United States.

Still, the pool of names from which parents can choose has mushroomed dramatically in the past century. In addition to middle-class parents merely searching for the distinctive and the unusual, blacks have added an entirely new dimension in recent years by turning to African tribal or Arabic names.

Until the explosion of black cultural pride in the mid-1960s, practically the only Americans with African names lived in the remote Gullah region that stretches along the Georgia, South Carolina and northeast Florida coasts and includes the offshore islands. According to Dr. Lorenzo D. Turner of Fisk University, most of the 6,000 African words that survive in the Gullah are personal names. "In some families on the sea islands, the names of all the children are African," wrote Turner. "Very few of the Gullahs of today know the meanings of these names; they use them because their parents and grandparents did so."

Generally referring to some circumstance of birth or a personal characteristic, most of the names or nicknames cited by Turner were borrowed from a dozen or so West African tongues. Turner ran across Abeshe and Aditi, the Yoruba words for worthless and deaf; Agali (Wolof for "welcome"); Anika (Vai for "very beautiful"); Arupe (Yoruba for "short"); Ishi (the Kimbundu word for "on the ground"); Tiwauni (Yoruba meaning "it is yours") and Winiwini (Jeiji for "delicate"). The most well-represented language was Mende, spoken in Liberia. Mende accounted for such Gullah names as Boi ("first-born girl"), Hawa ("lazy"), Mandze ("girl born at night"), Mumu ("dumb") and Sanko ("one of triplets").

Now, tribal names like Jomo, Oto, Kwame, Tanisha, Ayanna Kafi, Kai Ayana, Kymer Ashanti, Yesenia, Laisa, Monifa, Camisha, Natine, Mbita and Masika abound among educated middle-class blacks who crave a cultural link with their distant past. The black playwright LeRoi Jones, for example, is now Imamu Amiri Baraka, and Chicago poet Don Lee goes by Haki Madhubuti. Within a few days after the airing of *Roots*, the phenomenally successful television series based on Alex Haley's book, dozens of babies in New York, Los Angeles, Detroit and Atlanta were named after Kunta Kinte, the main character in *Roots*, and after Kunta's daughter Kizzy. In Cleveland, twins were named after the characters.

More popular than African names are Arabic ones such as Abdul, Gamal and Mujib, all found among students in a single elementary school class in Oakland. Perhaps the most famous example is World Heavyweight Boxing Champion Muhammad Ali, who changed his name from Cassius Clay when he converted to Islam in 1965 and became a follower of Elijah Poole, a.k.a. Elijah Muhammed. Upon his release from prison in 1952, another follower of Elijah Muhammed, Omaha-born Malcolm Little, became El-Hajj Malik El-Shabazz. He was better known as Malcolm X, the X signifying his "rebirth" as a Black Muslim. According to the practice, the first member of a Muslim temple named, say, John, would become John X. The next John to join the temple would be dubbed John 2X, and so on. Some temples have gone as high as X to the 17th power. The X is supposed to stand for "ex"— a symbol of what he once was—and for the unknown.

"In short," explained Malcolm X before he was gunned down in 1965, "X is for mystery. The mystery confronting the Negro as to who he was before the white man made him a slave and put a European label on him. That mystery is now resolved. But X is also for the mystery confronting the white man as to what the Negro has become." Basketball's Lew Alcindor, shunning the Black Muslims as too militant, joined the orthodox Hanafei sect in 1968 and changed his name three years later. He chose Kareem Abdul-Jabbar, "generous, powerful son of Allah."

Unlike blacks, more and more American Jews appear to be opting for names that are less readily identifiable with their culture and religion. The trend, which began after the first wave of Jewish immigrants a century ago, stemmed from an understandable desire to meld into the Christian culture of their adopted land. Last names, of course, metamorphosed from Silverstein to Silver, from Bernstein to Burns, and so on. The rise of Hitler made many American Jews acutely conscious of their heritage, and throughout the 1930s many Jews sought to make a personal declaration by giving their children biblical names like David, Emanuel, Miriam, Nathaniel, Elias, Rachel, Rebecca and Ruth. The birth of the state of Israel had a similar effect, and immediately after the 1948, 1967 and 1973 Arab-Israeli wars, there was an upsurge in the numbers of such traditionally named

Jews. The tide, however, has recently been in the opposite direction, so much so that the vast majority of young Jews in the United States have gentile names.

Scanning the Manhattan telephone directory, which lists fully four pages of Cohens, one can find among the Davids and Ruths comparable numbers of Cohens named Alexander, Bruce, Calvin, Camille, Carol, Charles, Chester, Cornelia, Cynthia, Edward, Elaine, Jenny, Jerry, Kenneth, Mark, Marshall, Patty, Paul, Peter, Philip, Richard, Robert, Roberta, Roslyn, Sanford, Stephen, Stuart, Susan, Terry, Theodore, Victor, Walter and—move over, Mr. Erhard—Werner.

Today there is also less inclination on the part of Catholics to name their offspring after saints, a prime source through the ages. Canon 761, promulgated by Pope Benedict XV in 1917, reaffirmed the Vatican's desire to see saints so honored. The Pope instructed the faithful to "take care that a Christian name be given to the one baptized, and if this cannot be accomplished, add to the name given by the parents the name of some saint, and inscribe both names in the book of baptisms." A "Christian name" meant one that was on the Church's list of acceptable saints' names. That many of the saints themselves bore names that are distinctly heathen in origin—the Teutonic Adolph and Charles, the Greek George and even the ancient Roman Caesar were on the list—makes little difference. Strict adherence to Canon 761 is not universal. At the Little Company of Mary Hospital in Evergreen Park, Illinois, it is interesting to note, there were only five Marys and five Josephs out of 388 births in 1972. On the boys' list were names like Brent, Carrol, Curt, Gary, Nedson, Percy, Scott and Troy, while Jennifer showed up among the girls no fewer than 21 times, accompanied by names like Kori, Tara and Tanvia.

Regional patterns may be softening a bit, but geography can still play a major role in the process of naming. Cincinnati-born Ted Turner, millionaire broadcaster, a world champion yachtsman and owner of the Atlanta Braves, is such an unabashed booster of his adopted state of Georgia that he has been called "the Mouth of the South." Turner's the-South-will-rise-again mentality is evident in the names he bestowed on his own children: Robert Teddy, Laura Lee, Rhett, Beauregard and Sarah Jean. To be sure, Beauregards no longer abound in Georgia in the numbers they once did. Nor do every Lars and Sven hail from Minnesota, nor every Priscilla from Boston. But the use of first and middle names essentially as one name—as in Bobby Joe, Jimmy Jack, Terry Sue, Mary Jane and Laura Lee—is almost exclusively the province of the South.

Television's Virginia-based "The Waltons" offers some prime examples: Good night, John-Boy. Good night, Mary Ellen. Good night, Jim-Bob. Any aficionado of country-western music is familiar with dozens of such down-home names. Female singer Bobby Gentry, herself bearing a typically southern name, wrote and sang of the mysterious tragedy that befell a young Mississippi couple in "Ode to Billie Joe." In addition to the likes of Jerry Lee Lewis, Marylou Turner, Jerry Jeff Walker and Jim Ed Brown, the galaxy of country-western stars includes Charlie Rich, Freddy Fender, Willie Nelson, Dickey Lee, Dave Dudley, Sammi Smith, Johnny Rodriguez, Bobby Bare, Jerry Reed, Dolly Parton, Jeannie C. Riley, Charlie McCoy, Freddie Hart, Sonny James, Kenny Starr, Joni Lee, Ed Bruce, Ronnie Milsap, Jessie Colter, Tom T. Hall and Hank Williams—Junior and Senior. Not a Robert (as in Goulet) among 'em.

As for the silver screen, *The Trial of Billy Jack* is one of the biggest moneymakers in film history, and Robert Altman's rhinestone-studded *Nashville* delivers up a cast of characters that includes a troubled C & W superstar named Barbara Jean, a deadhead singer-and-picker called Tom Frank and Hal Phillip Walker, a presidential candidate who capitalizes on the same sort of cozy populism that made Huey Long and country-western music so appealing.

In keeping with the good ole country boy image that is still popular even in the metropolitan areas of the South, many of the region's public officials prefer to be officially listed by their nicknames. When one appropriations bill was ready to be voted on in 1944, H. L. Mencken noted, Sam—not Samuel—Rayburn of Texas, Democratic Speaker of the House for 18 years, was joined by two other Sams, five Freds, four Joes, two Eds, two Wills, a Pa, a Pete, a Ben, a Mike, a Sol, a Thad, a Fritz, a Dan, a Jack, a Nat, a Jed, a Jer, a Jerry, a Cliff, a Newt and a Harve. Even on the rare occasion when the more monied and more decorous Republicans wrested control of the House, as they did during the Eightieth Congress in 1947, there were on the floor five Freds, three Joes, two Sams (including Mr. Rayburn), two Mikes, a Jack, a Wat, an Abe, a Walt, a Si, a Cliff, a Ben, an Ed, a Chet, a Hal, a Pete, a Jay, a Ray, a Toby, a Tom, a Harry, a Sid, a Harve, a Jamie and a Runt.

In 1975, those officially listed in the *Congressional Directory* by nicknames included: Congressmen Jack Edwards and Tom Bevill from Alabama; Arkansas' Bill Alexander; Don Fuqua, Lou Frey and Sam Gibbons of Florida; Senator Sam Nunn and Congressman Jack Brinkley of Georgia; Kentucky's Tim Lee Carter; Louisiana's Joe Waggonner; Mississippi's Jamie Whitten and Thad Cochran; Missouri's Jerry Litton, Gene Taylor and Bill Burlison; Ike Andrews and Roy Taylor of North Carolina; Oklahoma's Tom Steed; Joe Evins and Ed Jones of Tennessee; Texas' Ray Roberts, Bill Archer, Bob Eckhardt, Jack Brooks, Jake Pickle, Bob Poage, Jack Hightower and Bob Casey; Senator Harry Byrd and Congressman Dan Daniel of Virginia, and West Virginia's Ken Hechler.

The list of famous Southerners with nickname names goes on and on, from journalist Willie Morris to evangelist Billy Graham to White House whiz-kid (and now distinguished television commentator) Bill Moyers. Actually, Moyers started out as Billy Don Moyers, but was forced to shorten his name when he became sports reporter for a Texas weekly. "It was an eight-column newspaper, and Billy Don Moyers just wouldn't fit on a byline," recalls Moyers. "William would have been far too formal for the sports page, so I decided on the name Bill—and it stuck." As a Southerner, however, Moyers sees the informality of these names as no more than a facade. "Southern names imply an alleged intimacy," says Moyers, "that often falls apart as soon as two Southerners really get to know one another."

The Top Ten

What are the most popular names today? The United States Census Bureau provides no such statistics, but a wide-ranging sample of hospital records and doctors throughout the country tends to confirm that, with few exceptions, the national pattern conforms to the lists compiled at infrequent intervals by the New York City Bureau of Health Statistics and Analysis. In 1898, the top ten were:

	GIRLS	BOYS
1.	Mary	John
2.	Catherine	William
3.	Margaret	Charles
4.	Annie	George
5.	Rose	Joseph
6.	Marie	Edward
7.	Esther	James
8.	Sarah	Louis
9.	Frances	Francis
10.	Ida	Samuel

"If you should have a boy," John Keats wrote to his brother George Keats in 1820, "do not christen him John. 'Tis a bad name and goes against a man." John may have been a mite too common for the likes of Keats, but it was the first choice of parents through the first half of the twentieth century. Tradition was strong—the names on the 1898 list were just as likely to be found in the Old World as in the New.

Even before the ancient Brahman Code of Laws, there was never a shortage of advice about naming girls. Samuel Taylor Coleridge advocated the two-syllable trochee with the accent on the first syllable, as in Mary, Annie and Sarah. Others argued that the iambus with the accent on the second syllable—Marie, for instance—is dynamic, energetic and strong. Humorist Gelett Burgess favored the accented first syllable in a three-syllable dactyl, as in Valerie, Catherine and Margaret. There is also the three-syllable amphibrach, with the accent on the middle (Patricia, Theresa, Loretta). It has also been suggested that a parent consider the rhythm of the given name in combination with the surname. With family names consisting of one syllable, some onomatologists feel a given name of two or more syllables sounds better. Indeed, Dorothy Clark sounds less harsh than Ruth Clark. Surnames of two syllables may blend better with given names of three syllables (Jonathan Harper, Mirabelle Johnson) and family names of three syllables or more probably sound more lyrical when attached to a Christian name of no more than two syllables. (Betsy Hathaway, John Michaelson). The formula: first and last names are more lilting when unequal in the number of syllables.

When naming a child, it is also advisable to consider first and middle initials in combination with the last name. Many a child has suffered because his parents didn't stop to think that George Irving Kant could be boiled down to G. I. Kant—a little fact schoolmates are not likely to ignore or forget. At Yale University Graduate School, the late professor Richard Foster Flint decreed that all of his geology students would have name signs posted outside their study cubicles—just the first initial and last name, and no exceptions. Not even for Paul Enis.

World War II and the postwar baby boom swept away many of the old standbys that were on the 1898 list. Gone were the ethnic favorites—the Irish Marie, Rose and Annie, the Jewish Esther, Sarah, Ida and Samuel—replaced by 1948 with a list that could only be described as All-American:

	GIRLS	BOYS
1.	Linda	Robert
2.	Mary	John
3.	Barbara	James
4.	Patricia	Michael
5.	Susan	William
6.	Kathleen	Richard
7.	Carol	Joseph
8.	Nancy	Thomas
9.	Margaret	Stephen
10.	Diane	David

Spurred on by the hit song of the same name, Linda came from nowhere and rocketed to the top of the list in the mid-1940s. Mary and Margaret managed to hold on, but the rest among the girls were newcomers. John was deposed by Robert, but the real comer on the boys' list is number four. One of the most popular names among turn-of-the-century English aristocrats, Michael was imitated by upper-class American anglophiles but never reached a prominent position until after World War II. "Michael is popular in England," H. L. Mencken had written just a decade before, in 1938, "but in the United States it is bestowed only rarely."

If the parents of the 1940s sought a return to homespun simplicity, the 1960s saw the suburban ideal carried to its limits in naming. Cutesie-pie was in, exemplified by names like Cindy, Laurie, Candy, Debbie, Patty, Joni and Gary. The Korean War helped popularize Kim, a name latched onto 75 years earlier by Rudyard Kipling. Linda disappeared as fast as it came, replaced at the top by Lisa. Robert managed to stay on in third place, but number one among the boys was that rarity of a generation earlier—Michael. The list for 1964:

	GIRLS	BOYS
1.	Lisa	Michael
2.	Deborah	John
3.	Mary	Robert
4.	Susan	David
5.	Maria	Steven
6.	Elizabeth	Anthony
7.	Donna	William
8.	Barbara	Joseph
9.	Patricia	Thomas and Christopher (tied)
10.	Ann and Theresa (tied)	Richard

The 1970s saw several strong trends—the popularity of French names, a long-suppressed flair for gimmickry and the sudden,

seemingly inexplicable rise of what was a traditional onomatological oddity: Jennifer. The top ten for 1973 were:

	GIRLS	BOYS
1.	Jennifer	Michael
2.	Michelle	David
3.	Lisa	Christopher
4.	Elizabeth	John
5.	Christine	Robert
6.	Maria	James
7.	Nicole	Joseph
8.	Kimberly	Anthony
9.	Denise	Richard
10.	Amy	Brian

And the list for 1974:

	GIRLS	BOYS
1.	Jennifer	Michael
2.	Michelle	John
3.	Christine	Robert
4.	Lisa	David
5.	Maria	Christopher
6.	Melissa	Anthony
7.	Nicole	Joseph
8.	Elizabeth	Jason
9.	Jessica	James
10.	Erica	Jose

Aside from the oddly coincidental pairing of David and Lisa
(the name of a landmark motion picture dealing with two
mentally ill youngsters) in 1974, there are several changes worth
noting. Not one of the girls' names on the 1948 list shows up on
the 1973 or 1974 list, and while six of the top ten boys' names

are on all three lists, William—perhaps tied with John as the most popular English name of all time—has disappeared, along with Richard. Jose, meanwhile, reflects the growth of New York's Spanish-speaking community—a situation not unfamiliar to Los Angeles, San Francisco, Dallas, Houston, Miami and several other major American cities. And in the feminist '70s, five of the most popular women's names are masculine in origin: Michelle, Christine, Nicole, Denise and Erica. By and large, these trends held for 1976:

	GIRLS	BOYS
1.	Jennifer	Michael
2.	Jessica	David
3.	Nicole	John
4.	Melissa	Christopher
5.	Michelle	Joseph
6.	Maria	Anthony
7.	Lisa	Robert
8.	Elizabeth	Jason
9.	Danielle	James
10.	Christine	Daniel

Why the sweeping change in tastes? With the help of Madison Avenue–primed nostalgia, many of the currently popular names have been rescued from the romantic past. Lisa, Amy, Anthony, Christopher, Christine, Melissa, Elizabeth, Jason and Jessica are all relative newcomers to the top ten, but they might well be found in the pages of Charles Dickens or Louisa May Alcott. National heroes and the characters in novels and plays were major sources of names in the last century. Peter, for example, was in vogue following the debut in 1904 of J. M. Barrie's classic *Peter Pan*. "But," notes University of Chicago historian Neil Harris, "we no longer have a defined hero caste and nobody reads Sir Walter Scott anymore."

Movies came along, and the names of characters and stars alike were borrowed to christen the likes of Doris Day, whose star-struck mother named her after silent screen actress Doris Kenyon,

Bette Midler (Midler's mom thought Bette Davis pronounced her name "Bet") and Dustin Hoffman, so named by his mother in honor of silent cowboy hero Dustin Farnum. In the 1950s, Debbie Reynolds as Tammy in *Tammy and the Bachelor* launched both Debbie and Tammy as favorites. "Now," sighs Dr. Robert Appleby, "the days of naming a baby after a movie star, when Shirley Temple or Lana Turner could inspire mothers clear across the land, seem to be over."

Appleby should know. At his family practice in Wilton, Connecticut, Appleby has been all but overrun by the new breed. "Today there is a tendency to be gimmicky to some degree," he observes. "Everybody is trying to be different. They want their child to stand out a little bit. Kimberly is the kind of thing I mean, and Heidi and Holly. And then there is Sean for boys, spelled a hundred different ways." More time is also being taken to name the baby. While a decade ago the name would have been chosen well in advance, more and more parents are waiting several days after the birth to finally settle on a name. Nurses who were used to logging the baby's name within 24 hours after birth are, consequently, becoming increasingly used to playing the waiting game. One patient of Manhattan physician Richard L. Saphir named her son Claude, then over the next few months called him David, Gregg and, finally, Jason.

Trends, it must be remembered, are never created in a vacuum. Sir Walter Scott and Shirley Temple may have been replaced by pop novelists and rock stars. The Beatles' 1967 ballad "Michelle" undoubtedly accounts in large part for Michelle's popularity. Also stemming from the nostalgia craze, Jennifer was helped along by singer Donavan's immensely popular hit, "Jennifer Juniper," as well as by the Camille-like heroine of Erich Segal's blockbuster, *Love Story*, Jennifer Cavilleri. The Jennie Churchill vogue, manifest in Ralph G. Martin's hugely successful biography of Sir Winston's American mom and a well-received television series on the same subject starring Lee Remick, probably didn't hurt, either.

Does this mean that soon every other schoolgirl will be a Jennifer? Not likely. Even though some names are proliferating at a greater rate than others, the fact remains that no single name accounts for more than a tiny fraction of the total. Parents not only have far more to choose from than their parents did, but they are virtually free to make up a name if they so choose.

The phenomenon is not entirely new. During the battle over the Oregon boundary in 1846, one poor soul was named 50°40'. The Hartford, Connecticut, *Courant* reported that local politico K. N. Bill was actually Kansas Nebraska Bill, and that he had a sister christened Missouri Compromise. Two babies born during a flood at about the turn of the century were reportedly named Highwater and Overflow. Also on record: Lingo D. Graham, South Sioux Bickley, Easter Lily Gates, Dew Daley, Erie Canal Jackson, Munsing Underwear Johnson, Eiffel Tower Sutherland, Gold Refined Wilson, States Rights Jones, Jr., Tennessee Iron and Coal Brown, Chesapeake and Ohio Railroad Harry Stringfellow Johnson, Hebrew Hill, Lutheran Liggon, Pictorial Review Jackson, E. Pluribus Ewbanks, Five-Eight Jamieson (named after a friend of the family, no less), Utensil Johnson, Slaughter Bugg and Himself Yubank. There is also the case of a beer drinker who called his three sons, Budweiser, Falstaff, and Michelob. In another instance several illiterate blacks took the names that had been suggested by the wiseacre medical students who delivered them at Johns Hopkins. In addition to Positive Wassermann Johnson, there was a Gonadia, a Placenta and a Gonorrhea.

Depending on the family name, some parents cannot resist the temptation of saddling their child with a running-joke first name. The Florida Bureau of Vital Statistics issued a list in 1973 that included Cherry Pye, Etta Apple, Merry C. Christmas, Mac Aroni and Cigar Stubbs. The Beach Family children were Rocky, Coral, Sandy and Pebble. And in Texas, a very popular governor, James Stephen Hogg, named his only daughter after the heroine of a Civil War poem written by her uncle. She grew up to become a respected philanthropist despite her unseemly name: Ima Hogg.

Most imaginative parents are merely searching for something distinctive yet pleasant-sounding. The romanticism of the post-Civil War period prompted all sorts of rococo concoctions. "The new age was Hellenistic as it was also Tennysonian," wrote Van Wyck Brooks in *New England: Indian Summer*. People "longed . . . for something pretty and were not concerned to scrutinize its source and value. They sometimes invented names that struck them as having associations with the classical world or the world of the poets and romancers . . . one encountered such names as Liverius, Lurella and Lucina, Levina, Zepheretta, Loretta, Zerrilla."

That trend, which has continued unabated throughout the South, spread as poor blacks and whites fanned out across the country and into the cities of the North, Midwest and West. Just as their Jewish counterparts had sought to add color to their lives a century earlier, these lower-class migrants tried to outdo their neighbors with extravagant names. For the girls, some evolved as feminized male names, such as Geraldine, Charlene, Oscaretta, Alburtis, Billye, Lavaughn, Marvee and Frederique. The opposite process resulted in such sexually ambiguous boys' names as Laverne, Levon, Gwendel, Hollene, Omae and Dorotha.

Combination plates appealed to other imaginative parents, resulting in such blends as Bethene (Elizabeth and Christine), Romiette (Romeo and Juliette), Pearline (Pearl and Eilene), Therica (Theodore and Erica) and Lunette (Luna and Nettie). Evangelist-turned-actor Marjoe Gortner says he owes his first name to the fusion of Mary and Joseph.

Yet another category defies any explanation beyond a basic craving for attention. Among those attention-getters that have graced birth certificates over the years (many of which caught Mencken's eye and wound up in his *American Language Supplement II*) : Ace, Alfa, Amer, Anvil, Aola, Arrow, Arson, Australia, Avon, Boscoe, Brownelle, Brunetta, Capitola, Cash, Cementa, Chick, Cletis, Cloret, Comma, Cyclone, Dartanyun, Dawnette, Denver, Deoda, Dial, Dude, Echo, Esso, Euzelle, Fairy, Faucette, Finis, Glamora, Hexachlorophene, Human, Jackaline, Jaycee, Junian, Kewoie, Kiwanis, Lalabelle, Lethal, Lincolna, Lush, Madame, Manila, Mazola, Mecca, Merdelle, Mert, Momma, Monk, Monzelle, Mydol, Necco, Oder, Ogalallah, Ova, Oval, Payola, Phalla, Phygenia, Pink, Pleasantina, Poke, Romaline, Roudy, Roumaine, Rozetta, Satira, Satis, Tangerine, Texola, Thaine, True, Twitty, Ureatha, Utis, Vaseline, Vetta, Vital, Wazell, Winola, Xylophone, Yale, Zee, Zenna and Zippa. However ludicrous Cloret, Kiwanis and Vaseline may be as names, there is no denying that they are pleasing to the ear.

Fame has made some of these fanciful creations rather familiar.

There are singers Eartha Kitt, Etta James and British-born Petula Clark, not to mention comedian Clerow (Flip) Wilson, sports figures Cleon Jones, Elgin Baylor and Kyle Rote, actors Gig Young, Lovelady Powell, Zena Bethune, Zasu Pitts and Cloris Leachman, avant-garde choreographer Twyla Tharp, composer Hoagland "Hoagy" Carmichael, folk balladeer Burl Ives and United States Supreme Court Judge Thurgood Marshall. Sammy Davis' current wife is named Altovise, while George Wallace's late wife, herself at one time the Governor of Alabama, was named Lurleen.

The Beautiful People are not exempt. As far back as 1934, the *New York Social Register* listed an Ambolena, an Adgurtha, an Anzonetta, an Armella, a Helentzi, a Theotistie, a Belva Dula, a Chancie, a Daisette, a Columbia Maypole, a Melroe Abbey, an Edelweiss, a Nopie, a Velvalee, and an Isophene. Things haven't changed all that much. In the 1975 *Social Register* we find a Gilmar, a Dimitra, a Benedicta, an Avon, a Hulbert, a Derby, a Fargo, a LeGrand, a Flavia, a Julester, a Candida, a Zina, an Ila, a Fal, a Harald, a Petrea, a Cyrena, a Jodee Bel Isle, a Bukk, a Tolede, a Bramman and sisters named Cree and Starr.

Not surprisingly, show business folk continue to provide some of the most conspicuous examples of the bizarre. James and Pamela Mason became pioneers of sorts when they decided to name their daughter after a favorite city: Portland. Actress Barbara Hershey named her child by David Carradine Free, then changed her own name when she tossed a rock on the beach and inadvertently killed a seagull. Jarred by the experience, she changed it to—what else?—Barbara Seagull. When perpetually spaced-out rock diva Grace Slick gave birth to a daughter, she declared that she would name the child god, "with a small 'g.'" Later, Grace reneged. China, she decided, was more suitable.

In a characteristically kinky move, activist Abbie Hoffman went the patriotic route, naming his son america (with a small "a"). John Lennon and his wife Yoko threatened to commemorate Lennon's long-running battle with United States immigration authorities by naming their son George Washington United States of America Citizen Lennon. Frank Zappa's boy is nothing less than Moon Orbit Zappa, Neil Sedaka's daughter is the mysterious Dara, and Diana Ross has named two of her children Tracee and

Chudney. Actor Tony Perkins and his wife Berry Berenson named their first child Ozzie, then christened their second son Elvis. Jimmy Seals of Seals and Crofts has a son named Sutherland, while his partner Dash Crofts has a son named Faizi and a daughter, Lua. Obviously not wanting him to suffer from a lack of attention, Ringo Starr (Richard Starkey) named his son Zak. Mick and Bianca Jagger, meanwhile, overlooked Rudy and Sapphire and Opal to dub their daughter Jade. Cher has Chastity. Tiny Tim has his daughter Tulip. Bisexual superstar David Bowie (pronounced Boo-ee) named his boy Zowie (pronounced Zoo-ee). That's right: Zowie Bowie.

All of which simply delights name expert Dick Neff. Chronicling the misfortunes of oddly named people for two decades, he has uncovered a father of 11 named Peter Rabbit; a millionaire oilman, Carbon Petroleum Dubbs; and the father of a famous Harvard anthropology professor, Newton Hooton. Others listed in the Neff archives: Stanley Zigafoose, Wilhelmina Wetter, Irmgard Quapp, Douglas A. Unfug, Gretchen Stubblebean, Milton Leathers, W. Nelson Bump, Magdakeba Babblejack, Hung Gum, Liselotte Pook, Appelonia Pica, Lester Chester Hester, H. Whitney Clapsaddle, Arkady Leckyn, Solite Arbib, Philomena Fonetaminglio, Ladorise Quick, Effie Bong, Twila Delilah Blonigan, Tulip Chestman, Sividous Stark, Deadato J. Flicker, Luther Orange Lemon, Dillon C. Quattlebaum and, appropriately enough, Sir Horace Smirk.

CHAPTER 5
Knowing How to Play

As more and more students of human behavior delve into the meanings of our names, we may eventually see the kind of "name counselors" that have existed in the Orient for centuries take hold here.

Until then, you must play the Name Game anyway. So why not become a champion? First, assess your own attitudes. How do you feel about your name? How do you instinctively react when you are introduced to someone else by name? Are you proud, do you enjoy hearing your name spoken in an introduction? Or do you experience a vague sense of uneasiness, or perhaps even embarrassment? How do you feel when you see your name in print—on a passport, a driver's license, a birthday card? Do you sign your name boldly, or do you blur your signature? Which is the healthier of these two attitudes and why? How do you react to the other person's name when you are first introduced? Do you pay close attention, and size people up accordingly, or do you tend not to focus on a person's name at first?

Do you find yourself calling some people by name more or less often than others? Why do you suppose this is? Become *consciously* aware of your likes and dislikes when it comes to names, and how these prejudices affect your relationships. Understand that you feel superior to some people and inferior to others in part because of the images you associate with their names. Do your friends tend to have names you've always liked? This is not just a coincidence. In the cases where you feel superior to someone else, do you find yourself using that person's name frequently in a subconscious effort to put him in his place? Do you sometimes use unwelcome nicknames as weapons to belittle others or to maintain a psychologically superior position? Do your friends and acquaintances conform to the characteristics described by various name studies? Have you ever stopped to observe how appropriate or inappropriate a person's name seems —that your sexy college roommate doesn't "look" or "sound" or "act" like an Agatha? When you are irritated with your spouse or your children, do you skip the abbreviations and go straight to the seldom-used formal names? "Jonathan, go to your room!"

Once you have gotten in touch with your feelings about names, sit down and determine just what it is *you* want from a name. Are you looking for an authoritative name to give you unseen leverage at the office? Perhaps you want to be better liked, create a sexier image, or get better grades. Or maybe you are out to land that stevedore's job that the foreman is not about to give to someone named Lubertus.

You may, once you have assessed all the factors, be perfectly happy with your name. Your primary concern, then, may be perfecting your Name Game technique to analyze those around you. People's names, you are discovering, can tell you quite a bit about their backgrounds, intentions, motivations and how they handle relationships. Knowing that, in turn, makes it easier for you to cope with others—or to avoid them if that is the message their names transmit.

If you are about to become or are considering becoming a parent, there is yet another main objective—to insure that your child's name will afford him numerous advantages in his relations with others, and not constitute a handicap.

Whether your objective is one or all of the above, you will find that you have a sizable advantage when you can recognize and utilize the socio-psychological powers—both positive and negative—harnessed in our names. The stakes of the game? The rewards for winning are virtually limitless, since names can help to either free or frustrate human potential. Having done your homework and set your objectives, you are now ready to play.

CHAPTER 6

Your Name Is Your Fortune

J. Pierrepont Finch
All capitals!
Yes, block letters.

J. Pierrepont Finch
There is Wonderful Music
in the very sound of your name.
    —Frank Loesser
        How to Succeed in Business
        Without Really Trying

J. Pierrepont Finch knew it, and every executive knows it: in many ways, your name is your fortune. It can affect your chances of being hired, fired or promoted. It can add to your weight in the boardroom, at the sales conference or across the bargaining table. Or it can undermine your standing in the eyes of your peers—and your superiors. It can help you get into the clubs that count—or it can keep you out. It can, in short, make all the difference in the world.

From the outset, many personnel agencies give preference to certain names over others. Some agencies even make a practice of asking applicants to change their names to improve their chances of getting a job. Employers avoid applications with names that make them uncomfortable. All other factors being equal, a hiring officer will choose a strong, distinctive or aristocratic-sounding name over one that is negative, anemic or too common. Once hired, a man or woman will find that his or her name will definitely help to determine the degree of respect and attention accorded by co-workers. A memo from Lulu Butts is easier to ignore than a memo from Jennifer Mayhew Adams.

Name prejudice at the top of the corporate ladder is blatant.

In choosing a vice-president from four equally qualified people, the head of one California firm picked the one who "sounded" right for the job. The lucky fellow's name was the best possible combination: a lone first initial (preferably a consonant), followed by a three-syllable middle name (his mother's maiden name, thereby insinuating that one has descended from two dynasties merged by marriage) and a WASP family name. Anyone who wishes to rise to the top in business could make the trip a lot easier by dumping his first name in favor of his first initial and using his full middle name. This is, for all intents and purposes, *the* most desirable type of name for anyone aspiring to the executive suite. There are several reasons. There is a certain attractive arrogance attached to such names, a sense of self-importance that demands attention. In effect, the name itself is a declaration of where the individual intends to go. No man chooses to be known as P. Jamieson Burke or T. Symington Braithwaite or some other such name unless he is ambitious. A person who believes he is special from the outset and tries to separate himself from the rest of the pack with a distinctive and aristocratic-sounding name stands a better chance of making it. He has already pronounced himself superior to those around him. Because his name conveys the message that he wants to be taken seriously, he usually is.

Names that merely *imply* the best family background, an Ivy League education, trust funds and memberships in the right clubs cannot and do not go unnoticed. In much the same way that a hyphenated name is viewed by the British as a sign of inherited wealth and influence—"I love hyphens," says Katharine Hepburn in *Love Among the Ruins,* "they inspire confidence" —Americans have their own aristocracy of names. The first initial– middle name–last name is the most effective. The chief require-ment, however, is that a name be utterly unforgettable.

Once a person has somehow managed to get through child-hood with an attention-grabbing first name, he may well find that what was a handicap on the playground is a decided asset in the business world. Certainly, most top business executives have names like John, James and David. But the number of captains of industry with the unlikeliest of names is out of all proportion.

Not long ago, the Big Three auto makers were guided by a Lynn (Townsend of Chrysler), a Lido (Ford President Lee Iacocca) and an Oscar (Vice-Chairman Lundin of General Motors). If Ford Chairman Henry Ford II has a tame-sounding name, consider his predecessor Edsel and his likely successor, son Edsel II—not to mention Henry II's wealthiest relative (worth over $150 million), brother Benson Ford.

There sits on the board of directors of Brown-Forman Distillers a man whose first name is Robinson, as well as a Henning, a Mason and two Owsleys. Cessna Aircraft is directed by a Delbert and a Duane, and has vice-presidents that answer to Shelby and Pierre. The three top men at the $2.49-billion-a-year multinational conglomerate TRW are Horace Shepard, Simon Ramo and Ruben Mettler.

The president of Borden is Augustine Marusi, while Russian-born Plato Malozemoff serves as chairman and chief executive officer at Newmont Mining. Barron Hilton, son of Conrad, runs the Hilton Hotel chain. The president of the Equitable Life Assurance Society is Coy Ecklund. At one time, key niches in the empire built up by California financier Norton (Norton?) Simon were occupied by a Gustav and a Graham on the finance committee, a Raymond Rich (then chairman of a Norton Simon subsidiary, the McCall Corporation), and an Arnold LaForce (the president of Swift and Company, the meatpacking giant that is also part of the Norton Simon conglomerate). Evans Products Chairman Monford A. Orloff, whose company merged with Simon's in the 1960s, perpetuated the cycle by handpicking C. Calvert Knudsen as Evans' president.

Golden Initials: One Key to Your Success

J. Pierpont Morgan, J. Paul Getty, J. C. Penney, H. L. Hunt, N. Bunker Hunt, H. Ross Perot, M. L. Annenberg, W. Clement Stone, J. Seward Johnson, Henry C. Frick, J. S. McDonnell, H. J. Heinz, S. Mark Taper. Their names, bespeaking matchless wealth and financial power, are as shiny as freshly minted coins. Why are certain names more formidable-sounding than others in the corridors of corporate power? The seeds of the great American fortunes were sown in the early 1800s by men with such forceful and distinctive titles as Junius Spencer Morgan, Cornelius Vanderbilt, Asa Whitney and John Jacob Astor. As dynasties merged through marriage, the offspring acquired the names of both branches. Thus the son of Junius Spencer Morgan and Juliet Pierpont became John Pierpont Morgan. Others were given middle names that paid homage to more distant but financially significant relatives, each syllable a reaffirmation of lofty social and economic status. Witness Alfred Gwynne Vanderbilt, Harold Sterling Vanderbilt, John Hay Whitney, William Waldorf Astor and William Backhouse Astor. In the distinguished history of America's wealthiest family, the DuPonts, major roles were played by family members christened Lammot, Pierre, and Coleman.

In no segment of society is the initial put to better and more frequent use than among the very rich. Sprinkled through the pages of *Standard and Poor's* and *Who's Who* like so much gold dust, initials are freely employed to enhance the stature of the individual. Thus John Jones either becomes J. Doe Jones, J. D. Jones, or at the very least John D. Jones. The practice, if somewhat obvious, at least fulfills one chief requirement: distinctiveness. Once heard, such a name is rather difficult to forget.

Elite Names

When F. Scott Fitzgerald told Ernest Hemingway, "The very rich are different from you and me," Hemingway replied, "Yes, they have more money." Perhaps Fitzgerald was right, if for no other reason than the names of the rich tend to be quite extraordinary. American literature in general and F. Scott in particular did their best to advance that notion. At one of Gatsby's parties, for example, the guests include the Chester Beckers, Doctor Webster Civet, Hubert Auerbach, Edgar Beaver, Clarence Endive, the O. R. P. Schraeders, S. B. Whitebait, Maurice A. Flink, Cecil Roebuck, Cecil Schoen, Newton Orchid, Eckhaust and Clyde Cohen, G. Earl Muldoon and S. W. Belcher. As for the women, there were Mrs. Ulysses Swett, Ardita Fitz-Peters, Claudia Hip, Faustina O'Brien—and the four girls that always came with

Benny McClenahan. "I have forgotten their names," recalls Fitzgerald's Candidelike narrator Nick Carraway. "Jacqueline, I think, or else Consuelo, or Gloria or Judy or June, and their last names were either the melodious names of flowers and months or the sterner ones of the great American capitalists whose cousins, if pressed, they would confess themselves to be."

All of which provides ample opportunity for satire. One of the most entertaining take-offs on upper class names was executed by Shepherd Mead, whose hilarious book, *How to Succeed in Business Without Really Trying*, was transformed into a hit Broadway musical. The story involves young J. Pierrepont Finch, who rises from window washer to head of the World Wide Wicket Company. Finch does so by tricking the president of the company, J. B. Biggley, into firing Benjamin Burton Daniel Ovington as Vice-President in Charge of Advertising and replacing him with a fresh young newcomer—namely, Finch. Throughout, Biggley and Ovington are known as J.B. and B.B.D.O. respectively, while the bumbling head of the mailroom is saddled with a name that suitably reflects his sorry lot in life: Bud Frump.

A quick scan of *Fortune, Forbes, Business Week* or *The Wall Street Journal* often proves as entertaining as the antics portrayed in *How to Succeed*. Meshulam Riklis, whose father operated a citrus exchange in Tel Aviv, was always at odds with the elder Riklis for giving him the name Meshulam after his long-dead grandfather. In current Hebrew, it means "paid up," but Riklis' father insists that it is only a variation of "Mushalam," meaning "perfect." After Meshulam Riklis migrated to the United States, he taught Hebrew for a time at Talmud Torah School in Minneapolis. His salary was a meager $4,500, and the school secretary would sympathize when he came into the office asking for advances. "Don't worry," he assured her. "Before I leave Minneapolis, I'll have a million dollars." Riklis was not far off. In 1955, "Rik," as he was known to close friends, founded the Rapid-American Corporation. After years of merging, acquiring and exchanging securities, the oddly named entrepreneur pyramided Rapid-American into a conglomerate with such subsidiaries as B.V.D. and McCrory Corporation, racking up world-wide yearly sales of around $2.7 billion. In 1975, Riklis was the highest-salaried executive in the country, earning $916,000 in salary and bonuses.

The retail business has its own memorable examples of peculiar names. J. C. Penney was a retail giant, as were competitors S. S. Kresge and F. W. Woolworth. San Francisco-based Prentice Cobb Hale's Broadway-Hale chain has gobbled up a number of top-flight department stores, from Dallas' Neiman-Marcus to Bergdorf Goodman in New York. Heading up the Kenton Corporation (owner of Cartier and Mark Cross, among other stores), young S. Roger Horchow in one year turned Kenton around from a $2 million loss to a $1 million before-tax profit.

Oddball yet formal-sounding names—usually with lots of initials—are of immense help in scaling the heights. Graphic evidence is provided by *Forbes'* extended roster of the highest-paid men in America. Fully one-quarter were standouts in the name department. It is quite apparent from this sample that a distinctive name—whether it features initials, numerals, a lengthy middle name, or what-have-you—has sizable rewards. Among those who have placed in the top 130 over the past three years: *Meshulam* Riklis of Rapid-American, *C. Peter* McColough of Xerox, *Rawleigh* Warner, Jr. of Mobil Oil, *B. R.* Dorsey of Gulf, *W. H. Krome* George of Alcoa, *Willibald H.* Conzen of Schering-Plough, *W. Paul* Thayer of LTV, *O. Pendleton* Thomas of B. F. Goodrich, *Derald H.* Ruttenberg of Studebaker-Worthington, *R. Burt* Gookin of *H. J.* Heinz, *C. Gordon* Murphy of Cerro, *H. Everett* Olson of Carnation, *I. John* Billera of U. S. Industries, *E. Mandell* de Windt of Eaton, *E. Burke* Giblin of Warner-Lambert, *Andrall E.* Pearson of PepsiCo, *R. Nelson* Shaw of Mercantile Stores, *C. William* Verity, Jr., of Armco Steel, *John B. M.* Place of Anaconda, *S. Bruce* Smart, Jr., of Continental Can, and *J. Robert* Fluor of Fluor Industries, *J. Edward* Lundy of Ford, *J. Peter* Grace of *W. R.* Grace, *J. Stanford* Smith of International Paper, *J. Mark* Hiebert of Sterling Drug and *J. Paul* Austin of Coca-Cola.

Had they possessed common, unmemorable names, would they have risen to become the best-paid men in the country? Perhaps. But there is no question that their distinctive names played a significant role in shaping the way they perceived themselves, the way others saw them, and the way the two combined to influence their attitudes, actions and the course of their lives. Anyone seeking the same degree of success should take note: such names are the onomatological equivalent of the pinstriped suit. Among the corporate movers and shakers, they are evidently a standard piece of attire.

Now, see if your banker fits the pattern. When First National City Bank, the nation's second largest, officially changed its name to Citibank, it announced the change in a series of television commercials. In one of the TV spots, a Citibank officer proudly identifies himself as Stanley Benjamin Hubbard, Jr. The commercial is most revealing, since the intent is to earn the viewers' trust and confidence. Obviously, one way of doing that is to introduce this archetypal representative of the banking community with the elaborate Harvard-to-Wall Street name. The head of the world's largest banking institution, the Bank of America, is another gentleman with a penchant for initials— A. W. Clausen. Not to be ignored are Chairman Gaylord Freeman of the First National Bank of Chicago, Chemical Bank President Norborne Berkeley, Jr., Marriner S. Eccles of Salt Lake City's First Security Corporation, Ellmore C. Patterson of J. P. Morgan and the First National Bank of Denver's Montgomery Dorsey.

"People expect bankers to look like bankers," contended the president of the National Bank of Washington, who also happened to be a former U.S. Ambassador to Switzerland, assistant secretary of the U.S. Treasury and unsuccessful candidate for the Senate. Accordingly, the banker wore pinstriped suits, shiny black shoes and a green satin tie on a white shirt. On the wall of his office at 14th and G Streets N.W. was an oil painting of several wooden barrels filled with cash. Still, the banker's name —True Davis—sounds above reproach, as does Davis' chief competitor for the banker with the most-honest-sounding name: Fulton National Bank Chairman Pope F. Brock.

No less suitably named for her work is Tecla M. Virtue, who presides at the Phillips Foundation in Beverly Hills. Indeed, foundations are also a magnet for impressive names. J. Cib Barton heads the Doss T. Sutton Charitable Foundation of Fort Smith, Arkansas, while Thorwald J. Fraser directs the activities of the Anderson Foundation of Boise, Idaho. Some others: F. Paschal Gallot of the Miranda Lux Foundation in San Francisco; Royce H. Heath, Allen-Heath Memorial Foundation, Chicago; Cason J. Callaway, Jr., Pine Mountain Benevolent Foundation of Columbus, Georgia; and E. Blois du Bois of the du Bois Foundation of Phoenix, Arizona. Still, the prizewinner is probably the head of the Ford Foundation, former presidential advisor in the John F. Kennedy and Lyndon B. Johnson administrations, McGeorge Bundy.

Curiously, the men who populate the upper echelons of academia in many cases have first, middle and last names that are interchangeable. Once again, this conjures up the image of melded family fortunes, yacht clubs, Harvard and trust funds. As NBC commentator Edwin Newman points out in his best-selling book, *Strictly Speaking*, "If you examine the names of American university and college presidents, past and present, you find this circular quality to a remarkable degree."

Drawing from the *Yearbook on Higher Education 1974–75*, it is not at all difficult to find the names of university and college presidents that sound just as correct—in some cases more so— when read back-to-front: Tilghnan Aley, Casper (Wyoming) College; Hudson T. Armerding, Wheaton College; Kingman Brewster, Yale University; Imon E. Bruce, Southern State College (Arkansas); J. Whitney Bunting, Georgia College; Leadie Clark, Los Angeles Southwest College; Lambuth M. Clarke, Virginia Wesleyan College; Dero G. Downing, Western Kentucky University; Powell A. Fraser, King College (Tennessee); Brage Golding, California State University at San Diego; T. Felton Harrison, Pensacola Junior College; Ferrel Heady, University of New Mexico; J. Renwick Jackson, St. Mary's College of Maryland; Gibb R. Madsen, Hartnell College (California); Fount Mattox, Lubbock Christian College; Culbreth Y. Melton, Emmanuel College (Georgia); Mahlon A. Miller, Union College (Kentucky); Placidus H. Riley, St. Anselm's College (New Hampshire); Prezell Robinson, St. Augustine's College; Ferebee Taylor, University of North Carolina at Chapel Hill; Dolphus Whitten, Jr., Oklahoma City University; Harris L. Wofford, Jr., Bryn Mawr (Pennsylvania).

Even professions as disparate as the military and the clergy have the elite-name syndrome. An informal study by William Gaffney showed that West Point graduates tend to have unusual and distinctive-sounding names. The church seems to have specialized in initial-laden names that sound too important ever to be reduced to the monosyllabic nicknames of lesser mortals. They are to be remembered—and memorable they are —in toto. The Episcopalians have long held the title. Among their bishops are: C. Kilmer Myers and G. Richard Millard of San Francisco; H. Coleman McGehee, Jr., of Detroit; New York's J. Stuart Wetmore; W. Moultrie Moore, Jr., of Raleigh, and Houston's J. Milton Richardson. Even the Reformed Episcopal Church boasts the likes of the Rev. Theophilus J. Herter, Presiding Bishop, and D. Ellsworth Raudenbush, who serves as Secretary.

The United Methodist Church is catching up fast. Their roster of bishops includes Bishop L. Scott Allen of Knoxville; A. James Armstrong of Aberdeen, South Dakota; Seattle's Wilbur W. Y. Choy; F. Gerald Ensley of Columbus; Nashville's H. Ellis Finger, Jr.; Richmond's W. Kenneth Goodson; O. Eugene Slater of San Antonio; W. McFerrin Stowe of Dallas; San Francisco's R. Marvin Stuart; W. Ralph Ward of Rye, New York, and D. Frederick Wertz of Charleston.

Like their secular counterparts, these men have risen to power and prestige in their respective churches. Their names, distinguished and powerful-sounding, probably helped make it possible for them to assume positions of spiritual leadership. Nowhere is pomp and symbolism more highly valued than in the church. As important as their vestments, these clergymen's names are full of sound and fury and signify plenty—chiefly their vaunted social position in the community.

Your Name Can Spell Success

Anyone wishing to climb up the organization—whether in business, academia or government—should assess the power inherent in his name. How does it look on your stationery? On a contract, a check, a letter, a business card, an interoffice memo—alongside your colleagues' (and competitors') on a management chart? As a rule, nicknames do not fare well in this formal atmosphere.

The chairman of the board of Acme Industries may be known as Bud to his friends, but on the annual report T. Braithwaite Boggs carries the necessary weight. Anything innocuous or negative can only do damage.

Charged as it is with covering the business world, Time Inc.'s *Fortune* boasts its share of onomatological curios: Gurney Breckenfeld, Harold Burton Meyers, A. James Reichley, Wyndham Robertson, A. F. Ehrbar, Rush Loving, Jr., Aimée Morner and Bro Uttal, not to mention two Sanfords—Sanford S. Parker and Sanford Rose. On the corporate side, the editor-in-chief answers to the name of Hedley Donovan. J. Richard Munro is one of four group vice-presidents and there are regular vice-presidents named Clifford J. Grum, N. J. Nicholas, Jr., E. Gabriel Perle, J. Garry Valk, Barry Zorthian, even Kelso F. Sutton. P. Peter Sheppe is assistant secretary, while J. Winston Fowlkes serves as assistant treasurer. Time Inc.'s forest products executives include Felix M. Hammack, W. Ray Frye and Gex (Gex!) P. Condit.

There are things you can do to enhance your name. If you have an exceedingly bland first name—Irving, for example—combined with a common last name—say, Smith—there are several steps you can take to remedy the situation. You can change your name completely, from stem to stern, or you can substitute for your real first name something more authoritative and ear-catching. Short of that, try replacing your first name with golden initials. I. J. Smith is as far away from Irving Smith as you can get. Or try using your first initial with your middle name. Thus Irving Smith becomes I. Jacob Smith. If you are not willing to go quite that far, there is the very common practice of merely dropping your first name entirely and replacing it with your middle name, as in Jacob Smith. You may also want to try using the entire name (Irving Jacob Smith), or at the very least including your middle initial on all formal correspondence. Even Irving J. Smith is a notable improvement.

Women face a very special problem when it comes to the executive name. They must sound authoritative but retain some femininity. Unfortunately, Fifi and Peggy are not names generally designed to promote a woman's career. Noted financial columnist Sylvia Porter wrote for years under the name S. F. Porter because her editors feared that readers would not take financial advice from a woman. It was the male editors themselves that novelist Taylor Caldwell feared. That's why she dropped her first name—Janet—when she began submitting manuscripts. Oddly, only a handful of the most accomplished female mystery writers were allowed to use their own names, and then almost exclusively in England. British authors like Josephine Tey, Margery Allingham, Dorothy Sayers and of course Agatha Christie took full credit for their work as women, but American Dorothy Tillett was forced to hide behind "John Stephen Strange."

For the most part, however, sexual ambiguity in a name does little more than promote hostility from men and women—not to mention the seemingly warranted suspicion that the female executive may be trying to conceal her sex behind a neuter name. If a woman has a strong, positive name (see Chapter 10), that should suffice. If she does not, she may opt for a change. Again, short of changing her name completely, a woman does have alternatives. The principal options are highly effective in raising the woman in the eyes of her colleagues and her superiors. Peggy Mae Santos may wish to become P. M. Santos, though she can expect to encounter some mystification and perhaps even some irritation when the vice-president who was impressed by her memos discovers that P. M. is a woman. No one likes a surprise—least of all a vice-president.

There is always the highly flexible option of putting one's middle name into action. This tends to work best when the middle name is a surname. Peggy Haynes Santos is memorable, strong, authoritative. Peggy Mae Santos, on the other hand, sounds like a cocktail waitress or a country-western singer. If married, the woman's maiden name may do the trick, as in the case of Mary Wells Lawrence, the $400,000-a-year advertising tycoon married to Braniff Airlines President Harding Lawrence. Once again, the lone middle initial works wonders. Peggy Santos would not be regarded as a threat to J. Pierrepont Finch, but Peggy M. Santos might give the wizard of World Wide Wickets a run for his money.

Clothes make the man? To some extent, certainly. No less valid is the contention that a strong, positive name makes the man—and the woman. Again, there is no substitute for talent, ability or luck. But among the subtle devices we all use to advance in our chosen sphere, a name can be among the most effective tools of all. The evidence, as we have seen, is found in the unusually large number of top businessmen, foundation heads, bankers, educators, administrators and clergymen who brandish bold Excalibur names that deserve attention and command respect. You can give yourself the same edge by taking one of the steps outlined in this chapter and putting your good name to use.

Elmer Jacobson discovered the career value of a name on his own. For the eight years he worked as a junior marketing consultant for a New York-based clothing manufacturer, Elmer was known among his peers and immediate superiors as imaginative and hard-working. Yet whenever his boss recommended him for a promotion to management level, a memo came back from the office of senior vice-president D. Rutherford Miles saying that the time was not quite right. Meanwhile, Elmer added up those who leapfrogged over him. Looking at the Ivy League names, he could only bitterly surmise that they were hired and promoted because of old school ties.

While he weighed the possibility of resigning, Elmer stumbled upon the answer to his dilemma at a formal dinner party. At the table, he was surprised to find himself a center of attention—one role he had never become accustomed to. He was also treated with a certain deference that had eluded him in the past. As he rose to leave toward the end of the evening, he checked his place card to make sure everybody else hadn't mistaken him for someone more important. The name on the place card was his all right, but with a difference. Instead of Elmer Jacobson, the card read E. F. Jacobson.

Elmer submitted his resignation and took his new resumé—the one describing the background and talents of one E. F. Jacobson—to an executive personnel agency. Within two weeks, he signed on with his former company's chief competitor as a full-fledged marketing executive, and for 50 percent more than his previous salary. From that point on, Jacobson has been known solely as E. F.—and that is the way he signs every memo, letter and note. Five years later, E. F. Jacobson is vice-president of the firm. He is also convinced that old Elmer probably never would have made it.

CHAPTER 7

Names and Nicknames

You jig, you amble and you lisp, and nickname God's creatures.

—Shakespeare

The time was when men were had in price for learning; now letters only made men vile. He is unbraidingly called a poet, as if it were a contemptible nickname.

—Ben Jonson

More than any other, ours is a nation of nicknames. Nearly everyone has at one time or another during his lifetime been known by something other than his formal name—whether he liked it or not. That makes nicknames an important factor in the Name Game. Nicknames may, of course, simply be contractions of given names—Jim for James, Sandy for Alexandra, etc. While most of these seem simple enough, the evolution of, say, Margaret to Peggy is anything but direct. In between lie Marge, Margery, Marjorie, Margot, Mag, Meg and Peg. Elizabeth runs the etymological gamut from Eliza to Liza to Lisa to Liz to Lizzie to Libby to Bess and Betsy and Beth.

Surnames supply nicknames as well, so that John Smith becomes not Johnny or Jack but "Smitty" to his friends. As we Andersens and Andersons know all too well, few can resist the urge to try to label us "Andy." Nicknames may also derive from physical characteristics, as in Fats Domino and Red Skelton. They may also reflect some trait (Smiley, Swifty) or some unusual circumstance. Because they acceded to the White House on the death of a president, Millard Fillmore, John Tyler, Andrew Johnson and Chester A. Arthur were all called "His Accidency," among other things.

Whatever the reasons behind them, nicknames are crucially

important in determining how one is viewed by others and how one views oneself. The lore of nicknames is rich indeed. Egyptian pharaohs were accorded nicknames, as well as the ancient Greeks. Aristocles, a Greek philosopher, is certainly more recognizable as Plato, the nickname he was given because of his broad shoulders. Sophocles was nicknamed "The Bee" for his stinging observations, while the Athenian philosopher Chrysostom was dubbed "The Light." Yet it was the Rome of the Caesars that went so far as to formalize a nickname by legally appending it to one's surname. Thus corpulent Quintus Horatius (more easily recognized as the poet Horace) became Quintus Horatius Flaccus—or Quintus Horatius the Flabby. It is not terribly hard to imagine what another Roman poet, Ovid, probably looked like once his appended name is known: Naso, meaning "long-nosed."

Nicknames blossomed with the Renaissance. Had "Big George" Giorgione and "Bad Tom" Masaccio met, they would not have talked Mafia business. Both noted Italian Renaissance painters, they, like many of their contemporaries, were widely known by their nicknames. The practice has carried over into modern Italian politics. Feisty 5-foot-4-inch Amintore Fanfani was premier three times in his thirty-year career in Italian politics. His nicknames included "The Tuscan Pony," the "Pint-sized Napoleon," "Little Caesar" and "Il Padrino" ("the Little Godfather").

Nowhere have nicknames flourished more than in America, from George Herman "Babe" Ruth to supersocialite Barbara "Babe" Paley. There are enough celebrated "Docs" to staff a small hospital. Playwright Neil Simon is known as "Doc," as are TV trumpeter Carl "Doc" Severinson and basketball's "Dr. J," Julius Erving. Medich of the Pittsburgh Pirates follows such illustrious baseball Docs as outfielder Roger "Doc" Cramer and infielder Edward Stephen "Doc" Farrell, a dentist by profession. Even the Lord of the Loafers, designer Aldo Gucci, prefers to be called *Dottore*.

There is a plethora of Reds: Red Skelton, Red Buttons, Red Grange, Red Barber, Redd Foxx, Red Nichols, artist Red Grooms, sportswriter Walter "Red" Smith. Even Sinclair Lewis was known to his close friends as Red. And though the British provided an early example with Benjamin Disraeli, a dizzying number of American "Dizzys" have popped up over the years, including legendary pitcher Jay Hanna "Dizzy" Dean, who allegedly made everyone that way when he played the game, and jazz trumpeter John Birks "Dizzy" Gillespie. Noteworthy childhood names range from Charles "Sparky" Schulz, creater of Charlie Brown and the rest of the "Peanuts" gang, to writer Clifton "Kip" Fadiman, who owes his monicker to an extended attack of the hiccups that befell him as a youngster.

Fittingly, occupants of the White House have had scores of epithets and nicknames heaped upon them over the past two centuries. George Washington alone was accorded at least 13 appellations. Thomas Jefferson was affectionately called Long Tom. Andrew Jackson proved himself tough as hickory commanding troops during the War of 1812, and thus became Old Hickory—a nickname he very much enjoyed. Martin Van Buren was called Mat as a child and later Little Van. For his frontier toughness, James Knox Polk earned the sobriquet Young Hickory. Zachary Taylor was always known as Zack, and James Buchanan as Buck in boyhood. Buchanan became Ten Cent Jimmy for advocating low tariffs and low wages during his presidency. Abraham Lincoln was Abe and then Honest Abe, and Andrew Johnson was dubbed King Andy. Ulysses S. Grant was U.S., and Rutherford B. Hayes' fussy manners prompted some to call him Granny. Smooth Chester Arthur was Prince Arthur, and Benjamin Harrison's short legs made Little Ben inevitable. William McKinley sometimes seemed so pure he was snidely labeled the Virgin Male.

Theodore Roosevelt was Teddy and T.R., and his successor William Howard Taft, weighing in at over 300 pounds, became Jumbo Bill. Woodrow Wilson, as mentioned earlier, grew up Tommy, and redheaded Calvin Coolidge joined the ranks of Reds everywhere. Coolidge was Silent Cal to the nation.

Whereas no one was ever heard to call Herbert Hoover Herb or Herbie, Franklin Delano Roosevelt, always Franklin to his family, was called Frank by cronies early in his political career —long before he evolved into F.D.R. Truman's full first name —Harry—obviated the need for a monicker, but Dwight Eisenhower went through Little Ike and Ugly Ike before everyone settled on just plain Ike. Jack Kennedy's initials—J.F.K.—are instantly recognizable, yet few know that the young hero of PT-109 was known to his wartime buddies as Shafty because he was shaft-thin. Lyndon Johnson was probably referred to as L.B.J. more often than anything else, and Richard Nixon was branded Tricky Dick and Tricky Dicky long before Watergate. As long as anyone can remember, Gerald Ford has been called Jerry. Jimmy Carter, who fought and won a battle to be listed as Jimmy (and not James Earl) on presidential ballots in all 50 states, became the first President in history to abandon his formal name completely. That includes being sworn in and signing all bills into law as Jimmy .

In the best fraternity tradition, all the President's men have had their nicknames, as well. In the Nixon White House, Chief of Staff H. R. ("Bob the Brush") Haldeman referred to Transportation Secretary John Volpe as "The Bus Driver," Defense Secretary Melvin Laird as "The Bullet," and Postmaster General Winston Blount as "The Postman." On the rare occasion when he was referred to at all, Vice President Spiro Theodore Agnew was called by his lifelong nickname, Ted. Martha Mitchell, meanwhile, was known as "The Account"—an advertising term for a client. Nixon himself was apparently above such monickers. In memos and at meetings, he was always "The President," "RN," or "Searchlight"—his military code name.

At the Ford White House, the nicknames continued. Alexander Haig's successor as Chief of Staff, Donald Rumsfeld, liked to call Congressional liaison man John Marsh "Jackson" and Press Secretary Ron Nessen "Tiger." Rumsfeld, later Secretary of Defense, had his own nickname: "Rummy."

If there is any doubt that the trend will continue, it should have been dispelled not only by the field of candidates in the 1976 presidential campaign, but by the winner himself. While a Jerry (Ford) battled a Ronnie (Reagan of California) for the Republican nomination, the contenders on the Democratic side included a Jimmy (Carter of Georgia), a Scoop (Jackson of Washington), a Mo (Udall of Arizona), a Terry (Sanford of South Carolina), a Frank (Church of Idaho), a Fred (Harris of Oklahoma) and another Jerry (Governor Brown of California) . On the sidelines, a Rocky (lame duck Vice President Nelson

Rockefeller) sat out his party's battle, as a Teddy (Kennedy of Massachusetts) lay low at the Democratic Convention. When he was nominated by the Democrats, Jimmy Carter picked as his running mate Walter "Fritz" Mondale.

Old Yellowstain

Nicknames abound in the sports world, from Lawrence "Yogi" Berra to Cornelius "Connie Mack" McGillicuddy to Charles "Casey" Stengel. George Herman Ruth was not only the "Babe," but also the "Mighty Bambino" and the "Sultan of Swat." The gutsy football coach at the University of Alabama may have been baptized Paul, but generations have known him as "Bear" Bryant. Besides the Docs and Dizzies, there are dozens of Mickeys, Hanks, Joes, Mikes, Jimmys, Billys, Willies, Tommys, Bobbys and Jerrys.

Big George Giorgione and Bad Tom Masaccio notwithstanding, the mobster's world is rife with colorful aliases and sobriquets. The list of gangland greats includes "Scarface Al" Capone, "Ma" Barker, "Lucky" Luciano, "Bugsy" Segal, "Legs Diamond," "Three Finger" Brown, "Pretty Boy" Floyd, "Baby Face" Nelson, Sam "Momo" Giancana and "Crazy Joey" Gallo. Even the lesser lights in the underworld are accorded titles. One recent West Coast investigation into alleged mob activities actually ran into a "Rat" and a "Cheese." Antonio Corallo, arrested 15 times but convicted only twice, was dubbed "Tony Ducks" because he successfully ducked conviction so often.

Hollywood had its King (Clark Gable) and Duke (John Wayne), and the royalty of American music had names like Duke Ellington (Edward Kennedy Ellington), Count Basie (William Basie), Nat "King" Cole. There are a few "Fats," like Waller and Domino, and Earl "Fatha" Hines, a Julian "Cannonball" Adderly, a Huddie "Leadbelly" Ledbetter, a "Blind Lemon" Jefferson, a Charlie "Bird" Parker, not to mention a Benny (Goodman, "King of Swing"), a Woody (Herman), a Cab (Calloway), a Harry (James), a Ted (Lewis), a Guy (Lombardo), a Red (Nichols), a Buddy (Rich) and Dorseys named Tommy and Jimmy.

Members of one famous family act were known exclusively by their wacky nicknames. Julius Henry Marx got the monicker Groucho in a poker game because he always carried his money in a "grouch bag"—a g-string. Carrot-topped Arthur, a virtuoso harpist, became the zanily mute Harpo, while Leonard emerged as the wise-cracking Chico. Two other brothers, Gummo (Milton) and Zeppo (Herbert) dropped out of the team by 1935.

It is more than just coincidence that television talk show hosts have sported endearing boy-next-door nicknames: Johnny (Carson) and his sidekick Ed (McMahon), Merv (Griffin), Joey (Bishop), Mike (Douglas), Steve (Allen), Dick (Cavett), Jack (Paar), Phil (Donahue), Tom (Snyder). In Chicago, *Sun-Times* columnist and syndicated talk show host Irv Kupcinet reigns as Kup. Is it any wonder that John Bartholomew Tucker has never quite made it as a national talk show host? Meanwhile, the only woman to really make it on the small screen in that capacity has a very homey name indeed: Dinah Shore. Interestingly enough, the exceptions to this rule are two somewhat more cerebral fellows who happened to share a first name that, according to studies, is thought to convey achievement and authority. That name is David, as in Frost and Susskind.

The art of nicknaming has reached new heights with the cult of the long-haul trucker. Linked to one another by their Citizen's Band radios, the drivers know each other by anything but what their mothers intended. Number One Nose Picker tears by good buddy Squirrel. Woodpecker passes with his co-driver Stogie. At a grimy roadside diner, Popper Stopper, Silver Fox and Rubber Duck listen to Mule Skinner tell about his latest encounter with Smokey Bear, the name for any highway patrolman or state trooper. One Smokey Bear who ticketed a driver for urinating on the side of the road earned an additional title. He is known to the truckers as Fly Inspector. Even the women— mostly waitresses at greasy spoon diners, truckers' wives and some female drivers—get into the act with names like Lovey Dovey, Blondie, Squirt, Granny GoGo, Sugar Britches, Truckin' Mama, and, in the case of CB operator Betty Ford, First Mama.

Military men thrive on monickers. In Herman Wouk's Pulitzer Prize-winning novel *The Caine Mutiny*, cowardly, psychotic Captain Queeg is known to shipmates as "Old Yellowstain." All in the best tradition of the Navy, of course. Admiral David Glasgow Farragut was called the "Old Salamander," and Admiral William Frederick Halsey earned his nickname—"Bull"—on the football field before becoming one of the best-loved military figures of World War II.

The Army, meanwhile, turned out the likes of "Light-Horse Harry" Lee, leader of light cavalry troops against the British during the Revolutionary War, "Stonewall" Jackson, William Tecumseh "Old Billy" Sherman, "Uncle Robert" E. Lee, Ulysses S. "Unconditional Surrender" Grant, "Boy General" George Armstrong Custer, "Black Jack" Pershing, Omar "Doughboy's General" Bradley, Creighton "Abe" Abrams, "Vinegar Joe" Stilwell, "Old Blood and Guts" George Patton and Douglas "Dugout Doug" MacArthur.

But the United States Marine Corps, with its passion for grit, probably holds the record among the services. Dozens of leatherneck nicknames blossomed during World War II alone. In 1942, "Manila John" Basilone became the first enlisted Marine to win the Congressional Medal of Honor. Major Gregory "Pappy" Boyington also won the Medal of Honor, voted by Congress when he was in the hands of the Japanese and presumed dead. The Corps also boasted the likes of General Lewis B. "Chesty" Puller, so named because of his bulldog stance, mercurial Holland M. "Howling Mad" Smith, Martin J. "Stormy" Sexton and Frederick "Dopey" Wise. Scrappy as a wire-haired terrier, five-foot-four-and-three-quarters-inch-tall Lt. General Victor H. Krulak was nicknamed "Brute."

The Nickname Set

For all its imagination, the roster of military nicknames pales in comparison to the New York Social Register. The guest list for one Park Avenue party, for example, included Tootie, Bitsy, Bubbles, Laddie, Babe, Bunny, Toddie and Happy. A reunion of Walt Disney characters? Not at all. Tootie's birth certificate reads Ella Widener (of the wealthy Philadelphia Wideners). Bitsy is actually Joan Connell Field, daughter of Marshall Field IV and heiress to the Chicago department store fortune.

Bubbles is wealthy Leonora Hornblow (Bubbles Hornblow, that's right) . Laddie is Financier Steven Sanford. Babe is Barbara, wife of former CBS Chairman William S. Paley. That Bunny could either be Rachel (Mrs. Paul) Mellon or Genevieve du Pont. Toddy (Mary Toddhunter Clark) , was Nelson Rockefeller's first wife, replaced by Margaretta, better known as Happy .

Anyone who wants to make it socially, whether in Manhattan or Minneapolis, can start by cultivating a nickname. If you are a man, initials of the type that help you get to the top should do the job nicely. P.J. is just as effective in the ballroom as in the boardroom. Avoid the weekend jock names that tend to pop after a game of golf or handball. They invariably sound banal outside the locker room. Women can apparently afford to sound silly, however, if their chief aspiration is social success. At the very top of the heap are regal, cultured and intelligent women who prefer to be known by names they wouldn't bestow on their Shih Tzus.

The reasons for this are complex. "A nickname has a certain cachet," says one syndicated society chronicler. "Society folk do go in for that sort of thing." She should know. Although the columnists's real name is Aileen Mehle, she is simply Suzy to her millions of readers. Another internationally read columnist, Eugenia Sheppard of the *New York Post,* thinks the Beautiful People's love of nicknames runs far deeper. "Nicknames are a great security blanket for these people," claims Sheppard. "Many of them grew up together in a tight, intimate little world. When they call each other by their childhood nicknames, they show their enduring affection for one another." Whatever the reason, one thing is important: Nicknames serve as passports, the failure to use which immeditely alerts the BPs to the presence of an outsider. A person who shows up at a chic dinner party and refers to the guest of honor as Barbara instead of Babe loses points.

Thus it is of vital importance to find out just what the nickname-passwords are. One name to know is Bobo Sears. The daughter of Lithuanian immigrants who settled in the Pennsylvania coal country, she was christened Jievute Paulekiute—a name she anglicized to Eva Paul. When she became a model and bit-part stage actress, she changed her name again, this time to Barbara Paul. She soon moved up into the chic New York social set, which redubbed the bubbling blonde "Bobo." Bobo's place was secure by the time she met and married the late Winthrop Rockefeller, onetime governor of Arkansas. When the pair divorced, Bobo's settlement was well in excess of $6 million.

Rose Kennedy's father, longtime Boston Mayor John F. Fitzgerald, went from being called Fitzie as a child to Johnny Fitz and finally Honey Fitz for his charm and eloquence. The reigning queen of society, known to the tabloids as Jackie O, was the daughter of a dashing gambler called "Black Jack" Bouvier, the wife of an Ari (tanker tycoon Aristotle Onassis), the mother of a John-John, the sister-in-law of a Stash (Prince Stanislaw Radziwill), the stepdaughter of a Hughdie (Hugh D. Auchincloss), the distant cousin of a Didi (Mrs. Diane Auchincloss) and of a Gore (Vidal, who was voted class hypocrite in high school when he changed his name from Eugene to honor his uncle, Senator Thomas Gore of Tennessee). In the White House, the then-First Lady was assisted by social secretary Tish (Letitia) Baldridge, one of Washington's top hostesses.

That all this smacks of self-parody does not deter the ardent social lion. To be sure, *Auntie Mame*'s insufferably snooty Bunny Bixbie would feel right at home on the social scene today. Mrs. William Randolph Hearst, Jr. (Austine) prefers to be called Bootsie. A simple Boots will do for Catharine Treat, who, along with Sister Parish (real name: Dorothy), is one of the Palm Beach crowd's most in-demand interior decorators. It was Dorothy who helped Jackie redo the White House in 1961. Presumably Boots and Bootsie get together every now and then with Feets (Mary) Monell for lunch at Toots Shor's. Over cracked crab, these ladies who lunch might well discuss the furniture made by Dobbie (Susan) Bassett's super-rich husband, Teddy.

Jievute Paulekiute is not the only Bobo around. Moneyman Laddie Sanford's niece Bokhara Legendre also goes by Bobo. Among the Minnies are Minnie (Mary) Cushing, ex-wife of photographer Peter Beard, and Minnie Cushing Astor, whose real name is also Mary. Could anyone keep a straight face watching heiress Bumpy (Elizabeth) Rogers and her husband Beans (Richard) being introduced to Prune (Priscilla) St. George

Duke Ryan of New York? "Prune, meet Bumpy and Beans. Bumpy, Beans—Prune."

Muriel Pershing prefers Momo. Lehman Brothers' Joseph Thomas calls his wife Martha Paula by her chosen nickname— Poppi. Melissa Bancroft of the Wall Street Bancrofts answers to Missy, and her much-sought-after stepdaughter Margaret to Muffie. One mother and daughter even share the same monicker. Chesbrough Patcevitch and her daughter Chesbrough Raynor, heirs to the Ponds cold cream fortune, are both called Chessie. The younger Chessie runs a booming decorator business with Mica Ertugen, wife of bearded Atlantic Records founder Ahmet Ertugen. Actress Lauren Bacall also ranks high in these circles. To her close friends, Bogie's widow is not Lauren at all. Instead, she goes by her real first name, Betty.

Among the fellows, perhaps the best-known is the ubiquitous Jock (John Hay) Whitney, followed by Sonny (Cornelius) Vanderbilt, Stash Radziwill and Buzzie (Barclay) Warburten. Some of the most coveted invitations come from literary agent extraordinaire Swifty (Irving) Lazar, who maintains lavish residences on both coasts. Dashing, Saville Row-clad Indian Prince Rajsingh of Rajpiela is known as Pippy in London circles. St. George Biddle Duke, protocol officer Angier Biddle Duke's oldest son, owns and runs the Duke Ranch in Wyoming. Fittingly, he still goes by his childhood nickname: Pony. Now Pony Duke need only invite Oatsie (Mrs. Robert) Charles of Washington for a visit. Meanwhile, Mrs. Anthony Drexel Duke, the former Maria de Lourdes Alcebo, is Luly. Her daughter is Lulita.

Some society nicknames bespeak an uncharacteristic economy. Voted the best-dressed woman in America when she was only 21, Amanda Burden, daughter of Babe Paley and ex-wife of Manhattan publisher and society princeling Carter Burden, is known only as Ba. That's the closest her brother could come to "baby" when referring to his little sister. Dorinda Dixon Ryan insists on D.D. Her mother-in-law is none other than Nin (Margaret) Ryan. Mrs. Winston F. S. Guest, Lucy, is emphatically C.Z. (or Cee Zee), though nobody seems to know precisely why. Even with all this to choose from, few upper-crust nicknames compare with that of Princess Hohenlohe-Ingelfingen, the former Patricia

Ann Wilde of Tennessee. To friends, the Princess is Honeychile.

One outsider who quickly caught on to the nickname set was Laura, the ambitious Cleveland-born wife of a young lawyer transferred from the Midwest to New York. No sooner had they moved into their Upper East Side co-op than Laura anxiously made her plunge into the social whirl. But at her first function— a charity luncheon—she was unable to connect the socially prominent faces with the names. Not these names, anyway. Her hostess, who insisted on being called Bubbles, started out by introducing her to Poppi. Bubbles and Poppi, it seemed, could not remember if it was Chessie, Sister Parish or someone else who had decorated Swifty's New York place. And after Babe, Ba and Bobo joined in the conversation, well, it was decided that somebody would have to ask Cee Zee the next time they saw her. She'd know. By the way, had anyone seen Pippy lately?

Thoroughly confused, Laura turned to the society columns the next day to find out just who it was she had met, and what in the hell all those people were talking about. Later, she called Bubbles, only to discover that her hostess had all but forgotten her. Bubbles repeatedly called her "Dora," and kept confusing her with another hapless young newcomer in a Halston ultrasuede suit who had also wandered about the previous day's festivities in a daze.

It was quite clear to Laura what the Bubbleses and the Bitsys and the Cee Zees had in common besides money. At the next party, she introduced herself not as Laura, but as "Poppsy" —the name of a dog she had as a little girl. And since she had boned up, Poppsy dropped all the right nicknames, whether she actually knew the person involved or not. After all, wasn't it just assumed that only the most *intimate* friends used each other's outrageously silly childhood names? The next morning, there was Poppsy in the columns alongside all the others.

Your Nickname Can Mean Trouble

Nicknames can be valuable tools for getting into certain social circles, and for simply endearing oneself to others. If such is your situation, hang on to your nickname. Unfortunately, most people have precious little to say about the nicknames they may be forced to carry through life. Certainly, the damage a nickname can do is self-evident. The seven-year-old who is branded Dumbo for his failure to pass a second grade spelling test may find himself living up to that popular conception of his intellectual abilities. A Fats or a Pudgy will in all likelihood do the same. The opposite may also occur. In trying to overcome his or her nickname, the individual may be driven to extremes. A fat child may become a scrupulously weight-conscious adult. But that is a bittersweet victory at best; the emotional scars remain.

On balance, it is probably desirable for parents to discourage all descriptive nicknames. A simple contraction is perfectly permissible, so long as the suffix "y" or "ie" is not applied. A Richard may become a Rick or a Dick, but Ricky or Dicky robs a boy of a certain amount of dignity and self-worth that is especially important during the formative years. One should opt for Bill or Will over Billy or Willy, for Tom over Tommy and Bob over Bobby. Timmy and Mickey are unconscionable. Girls should be treated no differently, except in those cases where the full formal name ends in "y" or "ie," as in Sally, Betty, Marjorie or Valerie. When weighing nicknames, choose Sue over Suzie, Liz over Lizzie, Fran over Frannie.

The most important thing one can do is be aware. If your son Bill is being called Billie, tell him to correct his friends and, if need be, his teachers. Politely but firmly, of course. There should be no hesitation. His future sense of self hangs in the balance.

There is also hope for the adult who has lugged an unwanted nickname through life. If you have been called Red or Smitty and never liked it, start telling people so. For many, the problem never arises until later in life. A Chrissy who never minded being known by that nickname before may, as she approaches middle age, start to feel a bit silly. If that is the case, she should start referring to herself as Chris or Christine verbally as well as in writing. When the opportunity arises, she should ask others to start calling her by her new, more mature-sounding name. A 40-year-old Billy may sound only slightly strange, but a 60-year-old Billy is hard to take seriously. Before your childhood nickname starts sounding ludicrous, get rid of it.

CHAPTER 8

Don't Be the Victim of Your Name

The name which is given a child at birth or shortly thereafter may constitute a psychological hazard.
—F. Teagarden

Well, my daddy left home when I was three,
And he didn't leave much to Ma and me,
Just this old guitar and an empty bottle of
  booze.
Now, I don't blame him because he run and hid,
But the meanest thing that he ever did was
Before he left, he went and named me Sue.
—"A Boy Named Sue"

Your Name and Your Health

As if our careers weren't vulnerable enough to the effects of our *first* names, one British physician has gone so far as to suggest that one's health as well as his personality is influenced by the alphabetical standing of his surname. Dr. Trevor Weston, a London general practitioner and hospital consultant, declared at a British Medical Association meeting in 1967 that he had investigated the mortality statistics for Great Britain over the preceding decade and had discovered that people whose last names began with the letters S through Z averaged a life expectancy fully 12 years shorter than the national average. He also carried out a survey at a London hospital that revealed members of what he called the "S–Z Club" were three times more prone to coronaries and twice as likely to contract ulcers. The number of neuroses was 50 percent higher in the group, as well.

"Alphabetical Neurosis" is, says Weston, due in large part to what transpires in the classroom. "It is clear," he states, "that the strain of all this waiting for our names to be reached—or always being last—renders us much more liable to become morose and introspective." Not only are children in the S–Z group usually the last to get examination results—"which leaves them still waiting for their names to be reached, sick with apprehension to hear the worst while others are noisily congratulating each other"—but the last to read or make speeches, with the result that what they have to say has "usually been said earlier by someone else." The final insult: being the last to have lunch. "And therefore," continues Weston, "last to escape the stuffy, starchy supervision of the dining room to the freedom of the playground."

However valid Weston's theory, the statistics relating to "Alphabetical Neurosis" are startling. A review of the "Death Roll" of prominent people who died between Nov. 1, 1973, and Nov. 1, 1974, upholds Weston's findings. From astrophysicist Charles Greeley Abbott, 101, to 35-year-old actor-singer Bruce Yarnell to astronomer and jet propulsion pioneer Fritz Zwicky, 74, the A–R group averaged 76 years and 4 months old compared to 68 years for the S–Z group—a difference of 8 years and 4 months.

Undoubtedly, first *and* last names have an impact not only on our health, but on our self-image. We tend to picture ourselves the way others see us, and behave in a way to help fulfill those expectations. A Brunhilde Funch may be made to feel homely, and consequently may try to live up to that image by dressing shabbily and generally neglecting her appearance.

For losers at the Name Game, the penalties can be far worse than being locked out of the executive washroom and not getting invited to the right parties. We now have the evidence to prove that your name is an important factor in your emotional development. Thus, by understanding the relationship between names and behavior, both good and bad, you can better deal with this all-too-often neglected facet of your life. You can also act to rectify the situation by changing or altering your name, if the situation warrants it. As for the next generation, *you can take steps to avert such problems by naming your children wisely.*

The first authority to direct the attention of the psychiatric community to the possibility of a connection between a peculiar name and personality problems was the German psychologist E. Kraepelin, who in 1909 decried the "absonderliche Vornamen" that made normal adjustment "difficult at best."

Names begin to take on their uniquely all-pervasive powers in the cradle. The ego starts to develop during the first two years of life, when an infant begins to label everything—including himself. Thus ego, name and identity are inexorably intertwined, and the individual is set on a given course of behavior. Declares psychologist A. D. Clifford: "That names are of much importance can be easily appreciated when one thinks of the fact that many people are known only by their names."

The Criminally Misnamed

The most startling evidence of this comes from Dr. Robert C. Nicolay, A. Arthur Hartman and Jesse Hurley, all of Chicago's Loyola University. Over a five-year period, they studied the cases of 10,000 white delinquent boys, teenagers and men at the Cook County Psychiatric Institute. One group with such bizarre names as Oder, Lethal and Vere was compared to the rest. The findings: Criminal misdeeds were *four times* as frequent among those with unusual names. With the exception of the difference in names, both groups were remarkably alike. Their families and social backgrounds were comparable, as were their employment histories, marital records and the frequency of alcoholism. Nor were there significant differences in the types of crimes they tended to commit—the oddly named men were just four times as likely to pile up arrests for drinking, assaults, sex offenses and attempted suicide.

Your son or daughter may have to pay the price for a damaging name. "When a child is given a name," observed Nicolay, "that is an object of ridicule (such as Precious) or connotes snobbery (such as Throckmorton) or provokes embarrassment (Looney) or confusion as to sex (Marion), he is placed on the defensive and may have to fight for it." In fact, defamation ranks second only to assault as the primary cause of homicides in America.

"There's something to living up to a name," noted Nicolay. "A child tends to identify with the strength or weakness in his name. One with a mild name such as Carroll tends to adopt a mild personality. Some names tend to promote a mental picture of intelligence, others of stupidity. People react to the name in the same way." The marriage between name and identity is reflected in the tendency of schizophrenics to forget their names or adopt new ones. At the Cook County Psychiatric Institute, recalled Hartman, one patient would identify himself only as God Almighty. "The need to record his name temporarily for the official files produced a minor crisis," claimed Hartman, "because the clerk could not decide which name to indicate as first or last."

Such disorientation was frighteningly evident among the hippies and drifters who made up the Manson Family. Fittingly, their leader, the illegitimate son of a 16-year-old girl named Kathleen Maddox, was born "no name Maddox." Eventually, his mother settled on Charles as a first name for her boy. One of the several men she lived with, William Manson, married her and provided Charlie with his surname.

Once a potential convert stumbled onto the Spahn Ranch, Charles Manson's base in the Hollywood Hills, Manson would begin his brainwashing process by renaming the newcomer. Of course, this provided handy aliases for eluding police, but it also served to weaken the identity of each newcomer and to affirm Manson's godlike authority. Appropriately, Manson himself went by such unassuming titles as Jesus Christ, God, Soul and the Devil, as well as by the more pedestrian alias of Charles Milles.

The first girl to join the Manson clan was Mary Theresa Brunner, a.k.a. Mary Manson, Christine Marie Euchts, Linda Dee Moser, Marioche, Och and Mother Mary. Lynette Alice Fromme, later convicted of trying to assassinate President Gerald Ford in Sacramento and sentenced to life imprisonment, became Squeaky, as well as Elizabeth Elaine Williamson. Family member Maria Alonzo was known as Crystal. Susan Denise Atkins, involved in the grisly Tate-LaBianca murders that rocked the country in 1969, was told by Manson on her arrival at the ranch to change her name to Sadie Mae Glutz. Also involved in the Tate-LaBianca slayings was Patricia Krenwinkel, also known as Marnie Reeves, Katie, Mary Ann Scott and Big Patty. Yet another accomplice was Leslie Sue Van Houten, dubbed LuLu, Leslie Sankston, Louella Alexandria, and Leslie Owens.

Manson was not the only master of such manipulation. Another was Donald DeFreeze, a.k.a. "Cinque," the ex-convict and Symbionese Liberation Army leader whose efforts at brainwashing Patty Hearst included changing her name. His choice— "Tania," the name of an African revolutionary—was an exotic number that served to reinforce Patty Hearst's identity as a machine-gun-toting guerrilla.

A direct cause-effect relationship between a name and behavior at first seems difficult to establish scientifically. The parents who give children strange names may be the real problem. "You often discover," says leading child expert Lee Salk, "that parents who give their kids weird names are weird themselves." Yet the fact remains that there were few differences in the backgrounds of the people studied at the Cook County Psychiatric Institute. Nicolay's strongly worded conclusion: "There is without doubt a significantly higher frequency of psychosis leading to criminal behavior in the peculiar-name group."

The notion that oddly named people are four times as likely to commit crimes is supported by evidence outside the Nicolay-Hartman-Hurley Report. Prisons and psychiatric hospitals as a whole appear to have extraordinarily large numbers of such people confined within their walls. One excellent case in point is the 33-year-old Californian who was sentenced in 1976 to ten years in prison for robbing five Long Island banks. The defendant, who had commuted between California and New York to carry out the robberies, was named Gaylord Anguish.

While odd names frequently pop up on the FBI's 10 Most Wanted List, perhaps even more revealing are those federal fugitives with ordinary names. At one point in 1976, for example, Number One on the FBI hit parade was Benjamin Hoskins Paddock, an escaped federal prisoner. Benjamins, according to studies, are widely thought to be dishonest.

Names in the Classroom

In 1945, Spelman College Psychology Professor Oran Eagleson was prompted by his own experience coping with a bizarre name to study 334 black women students at Morris Brown College in Georgia. Almost a quarter of the women studied were openly dissatisfied with their names, and one-fifth felt strongly that they had been influenced to a significant degree by their names. All of those who were openly dissatisfied claimed that their names made them feel sensitive, embarrassed and shy when they were being introduced to strangers—an event that invariably sets the tone for the remainder of any relationship. But several of those with uncommon names expressed an uncommon pride, claiming that they were motivated to "live up to" their names by behaving in an exceptional manner. One woman said, for example, that her name was mispronounced so often that she would strive to pronounce each word distinctly. The vast majority of the dissatisfied women, however, made it clear that they would rather switch than fight. Among the changes requested by the students themselves: from Arlisha to Elizabeth, from Robbie to Dolores and from Burnease Estella to Mary Elaine.

At Harvard, B. M. Savage and F. L. Wells set out to discover whether the kinds of names that made Eagleson's black Southern co-eds "sensitive, embarrassed and shy" had any impact in a rarefied Ivy League atmosphere. In their study, Savage and Wells pored over the records of 3,320 men who attended Harvard from 1941 through 1944. Heading the first-name sweepstakes for those four years were: John, which appeared on the rolls 273 times; Robert, 227 times; William, 219; Richard, 138; George, 122, and James, 100. Since many bluebloods bestow surnames on their Harvard-bound sons—Cranston, Harrison, Alden, to name a few —only 4 percent of the total 3,320 could be deemed to have names that were *prima facie* eccentric. That 4 percent accounted for 15 percent of the students treated at one time or another during their stay at Harvard for "psychoneurotic" illness and for fully 17 percent of the total who flunked out over those four years. "These figures," declared Savage, "point to a statistically significant occurrence of academic and psychological maladjustments in those students with singular names."

If we adults are influenced to such a degree by our names, the impact on our children can be described as nothing less than enormous. Examining 1,682 case histories at the Northern New Jersey Mental Hygiene Clinic, psychologists Albert Ellis and Robert M. Beechley culled the 144 most peculiar-sounding names and compared their records to the remainder of the group. With names like Zenko, Carmello, Arend, Rockwell, Allerton, Barrett, Pinkney and Freeling, the boys in the group tended to be far more psychologically disturbed than the rest. But the girls, saddled with such burdensome names as Glenneth, Philomena, Lauris, Alverna and Enis were only slightly more disturbed than the norm—a difference that indicates a wider tolerance of girls' names. Since female names generally cover a wider and more idiosyncratic range, Ellis and Beechley suggested, "girls' names seem to be given less social spotlighting."

Perhaps. But a Susan, it can be safely stated, is likely to have an easier time of it in the classroom and on the playground than a Philomena or an Enis. The capacity for cruelty among youngsters is sizable, and it is during childhood that most people first realize their names count for a great deal in determining popularity. Kindergarteners, third-graders and sixth-graders were asked in one experiment to answer the following questions about five names: "Who runs? Who sits?" The kindergarteners did not share adult opinions that Baxter, Bruno, Otto, Sargent, and Shephard were active while Aldwin, Alfred, Milton, Wendell and Winthrop were passive. But the older children concurred with the adult sample, indicating that they had either learned the stereotypes from adults or met people who fit those stereotypes.

During their tenure on the faculty of the University of Miami in the mid-1960s, psychologists Herbert Harari and John McDavid discovered that 10- and 12-year-olds care very much about the sound of their friends' names. Asked to rate the popularity of their fellow students, these young subjects put an inordinately large number of their oddly named classmates at the bottom of the list.

To begin with, the psychologists asked the children to rate

49 names according to their personal likes and dislikes. A month later, they were asked to rate their peers as people. "Think of all the boys and girls in the class in which you are now sitting," the children were instructed. "Try to think of several whom you like as friends better than all the rest in the class. These would be people you would like to sit next to at school if you could, that you would like to go to the movies with, or that you would like to play with."

The children selected the three classmates who best fit this criterion, then were given the task of picking their least favorite classmates. "Now in the same group of boys and girls," they were told, "there must be some people you don't really like as well as the rest. Although you may not actually dislike them, everybody likes certain people less than they do others. Try to think of several people whom you don't really like very much as friends. These would be people that you wouldn't much like to sit next to at school, that you wouldn't especially care to go to the movies with, or that you don't like much to play with."

The students whose names were rated as most popular were also the most well-liked children in their group. "This pattern in itself is striking," said Harari. "Despite the difference between the two tasks presented a month apart (evaluating *names* as opposed to evaluating *people*), there is evidence of confusing the label with the thing, the name with the person."

Does that confirm that each child's regard for names is much influenced by his own direct experience, or vice versa? The answer to that appears to lie in Part II of the Harari-McDavid study. When they asked the youngsters to rate the names of children outside their class, *the children whose names were given high marks by virtual strangers were also the most popular in their respective classes.*

Disturbingly, name prejudice, subconscious or otherwise, is particularly prevalent among those adults who exert the most influence on a child's behavioral development outside the home—teachers. In an experiment involving 80 elementary school-teachers in San Diego, Harari, now a full professor of psychology at San Diego State College, and McDavid, a Georgia State psychologist, asked the teachers to grade compositions by eight fifth- and sixth-graders on "What I Did All Day Last Sunday."

All the papers were judged to be of about the same quality before they were submitted to the teachers. The researchers merely removed the students' real names and substituted four popular ones—Michael, David, Lisa and Karen—and four unpopular ones—Elmer, Hubert, Adelle and Bertha.

The results were alarming. Michael and David came out a full grade higher than Elmer and Hubert. Karen and Lisa did a grade-and-a-half better than Bertha. Concluded Harari: "Teachers know by previous experience that students with unusual names haven't been their best students. So when a Sanford or an Elmer or a Rufus comes along, they don't demand much from him. If a teacher has a low expectation of a student, she is likely to get less out of him. A self-fulfilling prophecy."

Why do teachers appear to attach academic significance to a student's name? The teachers in the Harari-McDavid study appeared to pick up their prejudice from the students themselves. The bias that was so flagrantly evident when seasoned teachers graded the essays was less extreme when the papers were evaluated by teacher trainees.

Prejudice of this sort among teachers can make a lasting impression. A recent study by S. Gray Garwood of Tulane compared desirably named 11-year-olds (Craig, Gregory, Jeffrey, James, John, Jonathan, Patrick and Richard) with boys named Bernard, Curtis, Darrell, Donald, Gerald, Horace, Maurice, Jerome, Roderick and Samuel. The results showed that children with names teachers liked scored higher on tests and were better adjusted.

The interaction between name and personality is, as studies indicate, complex and circular. If a youngster is saddled with a bizarre name, it often means that he is also saddled with psychologically disturbed parents who will continue, perhaps unknowingly, to throw obstacles in his path toward emotional maturity. To make things even more difficult, he must often defend himself against taunts from peers and be forced to buck an unfair disadvantage in the classroom. As Dr. Harari observes, "He reacts by becoming belligerent, aggressive and antagonistic toward his teachers—and he doesn't study."

Nonetheless, the effect of a negative name can, in some instances, be *positive* in the long run. Just about everyone can reach back into his collection of childhood memories and re- trieve a Malcolm or a Hubert or a Prissy whose name was the seemingly endless butt of merciless taunts. Yet many people overcome this handicap of early years to lead normal—and in some cases outstanding—lives.

It can even be argued that such emotional scars may have changed history. French schoolboys chided one of their peers and even beat him up because of his unusual first name. The little Corsican's last name was Bonaparte. At Harrow, young Winnie Churchill was mocked when his father, Lord Randolph Churchill, succumbed to syphilitic insanity in the House of Commons. The other boys took up the chant, "Randolph Churchill lost his head, Winnie Churchill pissed his bed." Whether or not his name was a major cause of his miserable loneliness at Harrow, he conceded two world wars later that the taunts and jeers of his fellow students would haunt him until the end of his long life.

Dwight Eisenhower was known as "Ugly Ike" and "Little Ike" throughout his rough-and-tumble boyhood in Abilene, Kansas. He and his older brother Edgar, who also had to con- tend with being the poorest children in school, were always ready for derision. Fights were a daily occurrence for the two. "It made us scrappers," Edgar Eisenhower said later. "Any time anybody walked on us they learned from us. It didn't make any difference how big or how little he was, if he did something that infringed on our rights he got a punch right then and there." By the time he reached West Point, Eisenhower's biog- rapher Peter Lyon observed, "Ugly Ike" was better prepared for the rigors of military life because "he had had the unnecessary vanities kicked out of him."

Lyndon Johnson, on the other hand, never fought over his name. He relished its uniqueness, and it served to set him apart from—and in his mind above—his peers. As a result, he was always a superb student who was regarded by his schoolmates with no small degree of awe.

For three months, however, Johnson had gone with no name at all. One morning Rebekah Johnson refused to make breakfast for her husband Sam until they decided on a name for their baby son. "Now you suggest names and I'll pass judgment," she ordered. First Sam proposed Clarence, the name of his favorite brother-in-law. "I know how much Clarence hated his name. No boy of mine is going to be stuck with it," she snapped. Then came Dayton, after Austin District Attorney Dayton Moses. Finally, Rebekah Johnson agreed to name the baby after Sam's friend W. C. Linden—but only if she could spell it the way she liked. "Spell it as you please," Sam growled. "He will still be named for my friend Linden." Almost 56 years later, Lyndon Johnson would pick a running mate who also claimed that his less-than-popular name was a source of strength and character: Hubert Horatio Humphrey.

In the case of industrialist Armand Hammer, the problems surrounding his name persist. Ever since attending grade school in Brooklyn at the turn of the century, the wheeling-and-dealing founder of Occidental Petroleum has grown weary of explaining that he was named after the hero in Dumas's *Camille* and not off a box of baking soda.

Had they been fully familiar with the incredible properties of names, the parents of these famous figures might have named them differently. These giants perhaps would have acted on their own, as young Sigismund Freud did, to minimize any foreseeable difficulties and make the best possible use of their names. How might this have changed history? What Napoleon and Churchill could not have known about the all-encompassing psychological influence of these words we call names, we are at last beginning to comprehend. As future generations use this knowledge, the impact on events is all but inevitable.

CHAPTER 9

How to Win the Name Game

If you don't like it—change it!

At one point in his life, nearly everyone has considered what it would be like to live with another name. For many, it goes beyond idle speculation. Every year thousands of Americans change their names, not counting the roughly 3 million who do so through a change in marital status. Many are trying to escape something in their pasts, or the law. Some want to disguise their ethnic background, or simply make their name easier to pronounce and less difficult to spell. Still others want to revamp their image for career purposes.

Whatever the reasons, few actions you will ever take in your lifetime will have the all-pervasive influence of a name change. Once a person has changed his or her name, he or she "becomes" the new name. As most married women who have adopted their husbands' surnames well know, people grow into their new names with incredible speed, and the old ones soon seem alien. Once she achieved stardom as Marilyn Monroe, Norma Jean Mortenson obstensibly ceased to exist, except as a dim and unpleasant memory. EST's Werner Erhard said he wanted to "get as far away from Jack Rosenberg as I could get," viewing Rosenberg as a being entirely separate and apart. More than a "Feudian rejection of Jewishness and a seizure of strength," the creation of Werner Erhard represents the forging of a new personality. Past influences remain, as one might expect, but indications are that, when a person sheds a name, he sheds an identity. Before you decide for or against, consider the following.

Their names are as familiar to us as our own. There were the silent stars, like good-as-gold Gladys Smith, sultry Theodosia Goodman and lovably earthy Leila Koeber. Then came the talkies and magnificent ladies like Lucille Le Sueur, Maria

Magdalena von Losch and Sarah Jane Fulks. They acted opposite larger-than-life leading men: Melvyn Hesselberg, Frederick
Bickel, Muni Weisenfreund and Emanuel Goldenberg. There
were great funny men like William Claude Dukenfield, and
musical stars like Zelma Hednick. And unforgettable couples.
Frances Gumm and Joe Yule, Jr. Doris von Kappelhoff and
Archibald Leach. Frederick Austerlitz dancing cheek-to-cheek
with Virginia McMath. Or with Margarita Cansino. Or Tula
Finklea.

In Hollywood, nothing—and no one—was quite what it seemed.
Few understood the value of a good name better than the Sam
Goldwyns and the Louis B. Mayers. As soon as a new contract
player stepped onto the lot, his or her name was tailored to fit
a screen image. It began with Gladys Smith, worshipped as
America's Sweetheart, Mary Pickford—a name that had actually
been picked out by Broadway producer David Belasco. He took
an altered form of her middle name, Marie, and combined it
with the last name of one of her cousins. Theodosia Goodman
vamped across the screen as Theda Bara. In such films as *Min
and Bill, Tugboat Annie* and *Dinner at Eight,* hefty Leila Koeber
achieved star status as Marie Dressler. Lucille Le Sueur started
out with a sexier name than the one she was given by the studio:
Joan Crawford. Deeming her real name too theatrical, MGM
sponsored a contest awarding $500 to the person who came up
with a name "simple to pronounce," "euphonious," and fitting
the personality of a girl who was "energetic, ambitious and
typically American." The winning name was Joan Arden, but
it turned out that was already taken by an MGM actress. Miss
Le Sueur had to settle for the second-place entry. "I started out
hating 'Joan Crawford,' " she conceded. "Now I love the name."

Maria Magdalena von Losch, blitzing onto the screen in *Blue
Angel,* insured her million-dollar legs with Lloyds of London.
The name on the policy—and on the marquee—read Marlene
Dietrich. Sarah Jane Fulks won an Oscar playing a deaf mute
in *Johnny Belinda* under the name Jane Wyman. Melvyn Hesselberg became Melvyn Douglas, and since the name Frederick
Bickel somehow lacked authority, Bickel was presented to the
filmgoing public as Fredric March. Muni Weisenfreund managed to preserve part of his real name in Paul Muni, and Emanuel

Goldenberg, an urbane gentleman off the screen who amassed an impressive art collection, tough-guyed his way through scores of movie roles as Edward G. Robinson. W. C. Field's stage name, meanwhile, was a little easier to handle than the real one: William Claude Dukenfield.

Zelma Hednick, a.k.a. Kathryn Grayson, sang countless duets with Howard Keel in movie musicals of the 1940s and 1950s. No adolescent boy-girl team ever matched Joe Yule, Jr. and Frances Gumm, known to three generations as Mickey Rooney and Judy Garland. As for the romantic duos, Doris von Kappelhoff and Archie Leach teamed up in *That Touch of Mink*, calling themselves Doris Day and Cary Grant. Day also made several films with another tall, dark and handsome leading man, Roy Scherer, Jr. His Hollywood name was Rock Hudson. Fred Astaire, born Frederick Austerlitz, went through several partners in an unparalleled career, beginning with Ginger Rogers (Virginia McMath) in the 1930s, following through with Rita Hayworth (Margarita Cansino) in the 1940s and Cyd Charisse (Tula Finklea) in the 1950s.

Why Suffer? They Changed Theirs

Long before Hollywood, people changed or altered their names to suit their ambitions. The Italian lyric poet Dante Alighieri chose to drop his last name, and in so doing made his two-syllable first name a symbol of the netherworld. The fourteenth-century poet and humanist Petrarch started out as Francesco Petrarca. Dutchman Gerard Gerards became a great scholar and humanist under the name Desiderius Erasmus. Both the Latin Desiderius and the Greek Erasmus mean "beloved"—the rough equivalents of the Dutch Gerard. One modern cleric more easily recognized by his adopted name was christened Peter Sheen after his birth in El Paso, Texas. Sheen replaced Peter with John, then added his mother's maiden name, Fulton. Few religious figures have achieved the kind of celebrity status accorded silver-tongued Bishop Fulton J. Sheen.

It would surprise many an Englishman to learn that the Duke of Wellington's family name was not really Wellesley, but Colley. His grandfather, Richard Colley, had assumed the name borne by a more illustrious branch of the family. The Swedish botanist who established the binomial system of nomenclature and originated the modern method of classifying plants and animals was formally Carl von Linné. His Latinized pseudonym, Carolus Linnaeus, is immortal.

As a teenager, Stephen G. Cleveland replaced his first name with the middle, and Grover Cleveland was twice elected President of the United States. Again, Thomas Wilson also found his middle name—Woodrow—far more distinctive. Modern politicians still enjoy toying with their names. Born out of wedlock in Liinbeck, Germany, as Herbert Ernst Karl Frahm, one young man who was destined to be Chancellor took the pen name Willy Brandt when he was a fiery young left-wing newspaper columnist in pre-Hitler Berlin. One of the most famous encounters in history might have involved John Rowlands and Livingstone if Rowlands had not taken the name of his adoptive father, Henry M. Stanley.

Politics and war have spawned many name changes. During World War I, there was a wholesale effort among Britons to sever all cultural and historic ties with the Germans. Leading the way was King George V, who changed his surname and that of the entire royal family from Wettin to Windsor by proclamation on July 17, 1917. The Battenbergs translated their name into the less Germanic Mountbatten, and Queen Mary's family, the Techs, became Cambridges. Another for whom World War I meant a change of name was flying ace Eddie Rickenbacker. He dropped the Germanic spelling under which he had grown up: Richenbacher.

To elude authorities, the Bolsheviks hid behind a wide variety of aliases. These, ironically, are the names that survive in the history books. Vladimir Ilich Ulyanov led the revolution as Nikolai Lenin, and Joseph Stalin is the name assumed by Iosif Vissarionovich Dzhugashvili. Lev Davydovich (Leon) Trotsky was actually a Jewish Bronstein.

The history of art and literature is rife with examples of great figures who discarded their old names for bright new ones. Rembrandt was actually born a Geretz, but he changed to the more dignified Van Rijn about the time he embarked on his career as an artist. Voltaire, the great French philosopher and writer, was a pseudonym for François Marie Arouet. The French playwright Molière was really a Poquelin. Honoré de Balzac's ancestors were actually named Guez, meaning "beggar," until his great-grandfather decided it was no longer a fitting surname. Balzac, which he formally adopted (Honoré himself later added the "de"), was the name of a family estate. Marc Chagall's father, a Jewish herring merchant in Russia, changed his name from Segal to Chagal, and Marc added the second "l" for panache. William Somerset Maugham was only one of many twentieth-century writers who did away with excess baggage—in his case, the William.

Among American writers, few have doubted the importance of a proper name under the title. Samuel Langhorne Clemens borrowed a term from his days as a riverboat pilot on the Mississippi. To denote a depth of two fathoms, Clemens and the other pilots would call out "Mark Twain." Charles F. Browne wrote under a name that belonged to a Revolutionary War general, Artemus Ward.

As an undergraduate, the novelist who would go on to become the first American to win the Nobel Prize for Literature was an unimpressive Harry S. Lewis. Dropping his first name and spelling out his second gave him what writer and friend Brendan Gill calls "a bright battle-flag of a name": Sinclair Lewis. Early on in their friendship, Gill, then Brendan M. (for Michael) Gill, received a note from Lewis that changed his life. "My letterhead," recalls Gill, "read 'Brendan M. Gill,' and Lewis, knowing by then that I intended to become a writer, circled the 'M.' on a letter of mine and returned it with a scrawled inquiry in the margin: 'Brendan *M.* Gill? Rudyard *J.* Kipling?' Then and there, I dropped the 'M' forever. Lewis was shrewd about names." Indeed, there are, as Gill further points out, writers remembered not for their work but for their names: Mazo de la Roche, Ouida, Warwick Deeping. Isaac Asimov was told to change his name because no one would buy a book by an Isaac Asimov. He has since written well over 180. Rooted in the South, playwright Thomas Lanier Williams took his pseudonym from one of its states—Tennessee. Theodore Seuss Geisel writes his children's books under the name Dr. Seuss, and Frank Morrison Spillane's pen name, Mickey, fits his hard-as-nails Mike Hammer image. Joseph Conrad was infinitely more palatable to the American reader than Teodor Józef Konrad Korzeniowski. Replacing his unfortunate first, Jerome, with his two distinctive initials, J. D. Salinger created an aura of mystery that persists today. James B. Taylor and James B. Matthews were shrewd enough to write under the names Bayard Taylor and Brander Matthews, jettisoning the commonplace James. Likewise, Jacob W. Reid is not nearly so grabby as Whitelaw Reid.

For a few writers, one pen name is not enough. Frederick Schiller Faust published serious essays and poetry under his own name and pulp novels under a dozen different pseudonyms, including David Manning, Martin Dexter, Max Brand, Nicholas Silver, Hugh Owen and George Owen Baxter. One pulp magazine carried three stories by Faust, each under a different byline. The tradition is continued by David Slavitt, who has written poetry under his own name and such bestsellers as *The Exhibitionist* under Henry Sutton. Children's author L. Stremeyer has admitted to over 20 pseudonyms. Among them: Harrison Adams, Jim Daley, Spencer Davenport, Allan Chapman and Arthur M. Winfield. Some publishers have gone so far as to copyright names, then farm them out to writers. There have been at least four Bertha M. Clays and W. B. Lawsons, while no fewer than seven separate people turned out dime novels under the byline Nick Carter. Nearly all gothic novels are written under women's names, even when they are the work of male authors. Ann Landers is a pseudonym that has been used by two Chicago-based advice columnists, the last of whom is now the world's most widely read columnist. There is considerable doubt that she would have had similar success under her own name: Esther "Eppie" Friedman Lederer. Her twin sister Pauline "Popo" Friedman Phillips has cornered the rest of the market writing the syndicated "Dear Abby" column as Abigail Van Buren.

Names in Lights

As the 1920s theatrical producer Winthrop Ames pointed out, "A good stage name is a valuable trademark. It should sound good, be easy to remember without seeming tricky or invented, and be short enough to display in electric lights. It should also fit the player's personality." Despite its inherent egocentricity, show business is the one profession where just about everyone is willing to be known by something other than his real name. Herman Wouk's heroine in *Marjorie Morningstar* is in fact a Morgenstern. In the 1936 version of *A Star Is Born,* Esther Victoria Blodgett becomes an Oscar-winning actress as Vicki Lester. The way she obtains her new name is fairly typical. A producer takes Vicki from her middle name, then toys with Esther. "Let's see, what rhymes with Esther? Chester, Hester, Lester. That's it! You'll be Vicki Lester."

The greatest names of the acting world are largely cosmetic concoctions. They are no less a part of the actor's camouflage than his costumes and make-up. Rosine Bernard adopted the stage name Sarah Bernhardt to enhance her dramatic appeal, and Oscar Wilde immortalized her as "The Divine Sarah." So much more impressive than "The Divine Rosine." Henry Irving, the first actor to be knighted, ruled the English stage during the latter half of the last century. He had been christened John Henry Brodribb. Although her real name seems theatrical enough, it apparently did not satisfy British-born Sarah Frances Frost, who emigrated to the United States in 1871 and in 1887 made her New York stage debut as Julia Marlowe. She went on to become a leading Shakespearean actress of the age. Herbert Blythe took a law degree at Cambridge, but changed his name to Maurice Barrymore so as not to embarrass his upper-class family when he decided to give up the law for amateur light-weight boxing and the theater. Blythe plucked his new name out of thin air, guided only by the fact that its gentlemanly ring was equally well-suited to boxing and the stage. His children—Lionel, Ethel and John—went on to make the name Barrymore, not Blythe, synonymous with great acting.

Even opera has its representatives, dating back to the great eighteenth-century Italian castrato Farinelli (Carlo Broschi). Australian soprano Helen Porter Mitchell was somewhat better known as Dame Nellie Melba, having shed her Anglo-Saxon surname for one that was a modified form of her hometown, Melbourne. Baritone Moishe Miller went from Morris Miller to Merrill Miller, then tried out Merrill Morris before settling on

Robert Merrill. Reuben Ticker became Richard Tucker. Jacob Pincus Perelmuth metamorphosed into Jan Peerce, while Maria Anna Sofia Cecilia Kalogeropoulos trimmed down to Maria Callas. Belle "Bubbles" Silverman lights up the Met as Beverly Sills. Ballet also has its examples, from choreographer Jerome Rabinowitz (Jerome Robbins) to dancer Jacques d'Amboise, born an Ahearn.

The practice reached its zenith with the arrival of the silver screen. Fittingly, Sam Goldwyn led the way. It was the Master of the Malaprop, born Gelbfisch, who established a legal beachhead for legions of people dissatisfied with their names. He changed his to Goldfish soon after migrating from Warsaw to the United States, and in 1918 made the formal change to Goldwyn—the name by which he rose to fame as one of the greatest movie moguls ever. Goldwyn lost control of Goldwyn Picture Corporation relatively early in his career, and found himself slapped with a court injunction when he resumed making movies on his own. Ordered to credit his new productions to "S. G. Inc.," Goldwyn went before Judge Learned Hand—a jurist who, understandably, knew the impact of a name. "A new name, when honestly assumed and worn," ruled Judge Hand, "may well be of as much or nearly as much consequence to its bearer as though it were familial. Our names are useful or dangerous to us according to the associations they carry among those who hear them. If we have by our past conduct established a good name, that is an interest, pecuniary or honorific, of which we may well object to being deprived. A self-made man may prefer a self-made name." Goldwyn could use the name, Hand ruled, so long as he agreed to add "not connected with Goldwyn Pictures Corporation" to his new ventures. From then on, Goldwyn took a keen interest in the labels people are known by. He complained when a friend told him the name he had given his new son. "Now why did you name him John?" Goldwyn asked. "Every Tom, Dick and Harry is named John."

The job of coming up with just the right pseudonym for Stockholm-born Greta Luisa Gustafson bedeviled director Mauritz Stiller. At first he toyed with the notion of calling her Greta Gabor. In the end, of course, the last few letters were transposed. Joe Yule, Jr., had a similar close call. Already the star of many "Micky McGuire" comedy shorts when it came time for him to start acting in feature-length films, six-year-old Joe was almost dubbed Mickey Looney by his overeager stage mom. Fortunately, Rooney prevailed.

Benjamin Kubelsky launched his comedy career as "The Admiral's Disorderly, 'Izzy There'" in a World War I service show. In vaudeville, he was billed Ben K. Benny, but changed it to Jack Benny when another fiddle-playing comic, Ben Bernie, complained. Benny married actress Mary Livingstone, whose real name was Sadye Marks, in 1927. Songwriter Sammy Cahn began as Cohen, then tried Cohn, Kahn and finally Cahn. Leslie Townes Hope was "Les" in school, and opted for Bob Hope when his classmates started calling him "Hope-Les." Seven-year-old Harry Lillis Crosby liked the Sunday comic strip "Bingville Bugle" so much his parents called him Bing. The Old Groaner's first wife, Tennessee-born Wilma Winnifred Wyatt, was under contract at Fox under the name Dixie Lee when he first met her. Crosby's second wife, television actress Kathryn Grant, was born Olive Kathryn Grandstaff.

A great black performer, Ray Charles Robinson, dropped his surname to avoid being confused with boxer Sugar Ray. Comedian Clerow Wilson was flip enough to achieve fame with that name, and Redd Foxx started out as John Elroy Sanford—the last name being the same as that of the character he plays in television's *Sanford and Son*. The comic got his professional name from baseball great Jimmie Foxx and the character he used to identify with when he was a kid—the red fox in children's books.

Comedian-author-filmmaker Woody Allen remembers all too well what it was like growing up as Allen Stewart Konigsberg. "When the other kids learned my name," he cracks, "they beat me up. So I'd tell them my name was Frank, but they'd still beat me up." Samuel Joel Mostel was given his unique name in honor of his academic achievement—Zero—or so the story goes. If Allen and Mostel think they had a tough time growing up, Richard Jenkins was the twelfth of thirteen children born to a Welsh coal miner. Jenkins borrowed a new surname from his mentor Philip Burton, and before graduating from Oxford made his theatrical debut as Richard Burton.

The daughter of an English Army officer who died before she was born, Tasmanian Estelle Merle O'Brien Thompson went on the London stage under the music hall name of Queenie Thompson. After being discovered by Sir Alexander Korda, she combined one of her middle names with that of Shakespeare's King of the Fairies in *A Midsummer Night's Dream*. The result: Merle Oberon. Christened Virginia Katherine McMath in Independence, Missouri, Fred Astaire's most famous dance partner acquired the nickname Ginger as a moppet, then added it to Rogers when her stage mother moved to Texas and remarried. The first of Ginger Rogers' five husbands was vaudeville hoofer Edward Culpepper, billed as Jack Pepper. Joan de Beauvoir de Havilland arrived in Hollywood on the heels of her sister Olivia, and chose her stepfather's last name—Fontaine—to avoid confusion. While working as a dancer at the Capitol Theater in New York, Ann Leppert took headliner Frank Faye's name. "I thought if I took that name," recalls Alice Faye, "it might bring me success."

Brooklyn native Ruby Stevens thought her name too pedestrian. She took her new one from a playbill listing the role of *Barbara* Fritchie played by Jane *Stanwyck*. For years, the marriage of Barbara Stanwyck to Spangler Arlington Brugh (Robert Taylor) was a Hollywood dream match.

Thelma Booth Ford became Shirley Booth because her father did not want her using his good name on the stage. Frances "Fanny" Rose Shore became Dinah after she got her own radio show in Nashville. A disc jockey dubbed her Dinah because of her penchant for singing the old Ethel Waters favorite of the same name. Doris von Kappelhoff, who owed her first name to her mother's fondness for silent screen actress Doris Kenyon, was singing "Day by Day" at Barney Rapp's Little Club in Cincinnati when Rapp changed her last name to Day. "I'm glad," says the eternal virgin who was America's top box office draw for nearly a decade, "that he didn't catch me singing the *Götterdammerung*."

Others have not been so lucky. Piper Laurie rightfully hates the name her studio gave her to replace her own Rosetta Jacobs. Susan Kerr Weld was born on a Thursday, but her mother thought she "looked like Tuesday." Two months after christening her daughter Susan, Mrs. Weld began calling her Tuesday. The blonde starlet changed her name to Tuesday legally on Oct. 19, 1959.

Rock Hudson, Tab Hunter, Chad Everett and, of course, Rip Torn (whose favorite musician should be "Alley Cat" pianist Bent Fabric) are all studio or agent concoctions. The rough-and-tumble breed of western star produced demands for similar names. Few moviegoers would recall the image of Leonard Slye riding into the sunset, though Slye's professional name could hardly be more fitting: Roy Rogers.

Who's Not Who

For many performers, the route to a star-charged name is a meandering one. Many actors and actresses are now able to see themselves on the late, late show wearing not only outdated fashions and hairdos, but outdated names as well. Ellen Drew, for example, made more than 20 films under the name Terry Ray. Harriet Lake acted in several movies before becoming Ann Sothern. A rising starlet named Phyllis Isley appeared in B films like Republic Pictures' *New Frontier* and *Dick Tracy's G-Men*. By the time she won a best actress Oscar for *The Song of Bernadette*, Phyllis Isley had become Jennifer Jones. The Eunice Quedens of one or two 1930s flicks is the same actress who played "Our Miss Brooks" on television, Eve Arden.

Bud Flanagan appeared in 50 movies, including *I Am a Fugitive from a Chain Gang,* before hitting the jackpot as Dennis O'Keefe. Donna Adams was eventually transformed into the wholesome Donna Reed. The actress who played Barbara Stanwyck's pampered daughter in *Stella Dallas,* Ann Shirley, was billed in movies for years as Dawn O'Day, while Depression ingenue Marjorie Moore re-emerged during World War II as Marjorie Reynolds, leading lady to Bing Crosby and Bob Hope. Bernard Schwartz, who uttered the famous lines "Yonder lies duh castle of my faddah" in one of his early movies, was billed as Jimmie Curtis in 1949's *Criss Cross.* Then, remembering his hungry childhood, he considered changing his name to Anthony Adverse. He compromised on Tony Curtis.

Happy Land's Natasha Gurdin climbed to the top as Natalie

Wood in dozens of movies. Clara Lou Sheridan of *College Rhythm* blossomed into wartime "Oomph Girl" Ann Sheridan. Handsome tenor Stanley Morner, a supporting player in *The Great Ziegfeld*, became Dennis Morgan in time to play the love interest opposite Ginger Rogers in *Kitty Foyle*. Constance Keane of *All Women Have Secrets* peered from behind her trademark hair years later as Veronica Lake. Rita Cansino stuck to a version of her real name, Margarita, in such stinkeroos as *Charlie Chan in Egypt* before Rita Hayworth was born.

Some have to go through several incarnations. On her way to becoming Cyd Charisse, leggy Tula Finklea was billed as Lily Norwood in movies like *Mission to Moscow*. Helen Koford, who first appeared in 1941's *The Howards of Virginia*, acted under the name Judy Ford in *My Gal Sal* and Jan Ford in *The Devil on Wheels* before she fluttered out of her cocoon as Terry Moore, aspiring wife of Howard Hughes. Ellen Burstyn, who won a Best Actress Oscar for her performance in *Alice Doesn't Live Here Anymore*, was born Edna Rae Gillooly. She modeled and was on TV's "Jackie Gleason Show" under the name Edna Rae, danced in the chorus line in a Montreal nightclub as Keri Flynn, did a screen test for producer Gregory Ratoff under the name Erica Dean, then acted on Broadway as Ellen McRae. Eventually, she married her third husband, Neil Burstyn, and settled on Ellen Burstyn. Carole Bishop acted for months as one of the leads in the Pulitzer Prize-winning musical *A Chorus Line*, but picked up a Tony as Kelly Bishop. With film work likely in her future, she was required to change her name when the Screen Actors Guild found it already had a member named Carole Bishop.

"Whaddya mean, 'When did I change my name?' " asks movie and television star Cloris Leachman. "Do you think I'd actually change it *to* Cloris Leachman?" Josh Logan got her to change it to Amy Clairborne. Tallulah Bankhead suggested April Claiborne. Elia Kazan begged her to change it to anything at all. Desperate, she pulled out the Manhattan telephone directory and picked out a name at random: Leavitt. Cloris' reaction was predictable. "Right then," she shrugs, "I said the hell with it."

When someone asked Ann Miller what she thought of then-newcomer Cloris Leachman, she supposedly said, "I really don't know. Mother takes care of the laundry." Cloris Leachman is not the only celebrity whose name sounds like a detergent soap. One housewife confided to her neighbor that she was thinking of switching from Tide to Vida Blue.

Picking just the right stage name is a knack that few possess. Justin de Villeneuve (whose real name is Nigel John Davies) scored in the 1960s when he turned a scrawny model named Lesley Hornby into Twiggy. In the pop music field, Gordon Mills has an unmatched record. He turned a pigtailed Welsh rock singer stage-named Tommy Scott into a Sinatraesque dandy known as Tom Jones. The *nom de chanson,* a boiled-down version of his real name—Thomas Jones Woodward—capitalized on the movie that was popular at the time. Later, Mills signed a new singer, darkly handsome Arnold Dorsey, and borrowed the name of a nineteenth-century German composer, Engelbert Humperdinck. And in 1972, Svengali Mills added yet another find to his string of Trilbys with an Irish ex-postal clerk named Raymond O'Sullivan. Before changing O'Sullivan's image, Mills changed the singer's name. Since then, Gilbert O'Sullivan has sold millions of records, including such chartbusters as "Alone Again (Naturally)" and "Claire." For pure inspiration, however, it is difficult to beat top blues-rock singer Phoebe Loeb, who borrowed her show biz name—Phoebe Snow—from the side of an Erie Lackawanna train that used to pass by her home in Teaneck, New Jersey.

Taylor-made Names

Ironically, Hollywood actors whose very names would come to symbolize strength and character on the silver screen often bore the scars of being raised under "sissy" names. Spangler Arlington Brugh (who did well to change his name to Robert Taylor after launching his movie career) and little Humphrey Bogart were quiet, introspective youngsters—partly because of the incessant kidding from their less-than-understanding peers. Already thought of as being sedentary and effeminate because of his terribly unpopular name, little Humphrey's problem was aggravated by his mother's insistence that he wear long curls and

Little Lord Fauntleroy suits to school. Those who regarded Humphrey Bogart as a sissy would never have imagined him cast as the Hollywood tough guy par excellence.

Weightier still was the cross born by John Wayne. The Duke's real name: Marion Morrison. More than once, recalls Wayne, teachers assigned young Marion to sit with the girls on the first day of class before looking up to see that Marion was a boy.

In the case of the Hollywood tough guys, it would appear that having sissified names made all three of the above actors hell-bent on vindication. While many others who bear the same pressure from derisive peers bend and become the Casper Milquetoasts they are supposed to be, there are always the individualists who, like "Ugly Ike" and Napoleon, overcompensate in their efforts to prove everyone wrong. Ironically, "sissy" names that put psychological pressure on the bearer force him to choose between one of the two extremes. You will find that few of these people emerge as strictly middle-of-the-road when it comes to temperament.

One-Name Legends

"Last names have a way of falling away," observes novelist and critic Judah Stampfer. "The world kept yanking away the last name from Marilyn Monroe. It wanted her to finish life by saying, 'Call me Marilyn.' " Oddly enough, great fame is exemplified by the ultimate reduction of one's name to a single word so recognizable as to be a trademark. People, in short, become "brand names" in the same way that we refer to tissue as Kleenex, talk about Xeroxing instead of photocopying and thirst for Coke rather than cola. We even reduce a public utility to an anthropomorphized brand name: Ma Bell.

There is a certain unique form of intimacy that comes with knowing a person chiefly by a first name. For symbols like Marilyn Monroe, surnames just get in the way; they are excess baggage that we would just as soon discard to get at the essence of Marilyn. Only a handful of individuals have so captured our imagination in such a spectacular way. They became one-name legends: Liz, Garbo, Judy, Lucy, Liza, Brando, Harlow, Bogie, Chaplin,

Streisand, Dinah, Sammy, Dino, Tracy and Hepburn, Gable and Lombard, Frank, Elvis and, yes, Marilyn.

Each of these legendary characters brought his or her own peculiar brand of magic to the screen or onto the stage, and each transcended simple stardom. In so doing, they became more than just glamorous performers to their millions of fans. Their private lives, without exception, were exposed for all to see— like the Lizas and Judys and Franks next door. As a phenomenon, the one-name legend offers proof that a single name, stripped to its essentials and conveying as it does a multitude of images, is a powerful force indeed.

It Worked for Them—It Can Work for You

It was the bucktoothed comic's first big break—a vaudeville act on Broadway opposite Elizabeth Kennedy. But the team of "Berlinger and Kennedy" was almost impossible to squeeze on a marquee. Hence Milton Berle was born. In fact, as soon as Milton Berlinger became Milton Berle, the entire Berlinger family—Milton's mother, three brothers and a sister—went along. The story is part and parcel of the Hollywood legend, and it applies just as broadly to first names as it does to surnames. A Rock or a Tab is certainly easier to envision as the romantic lead in a motion picture than, say, a Howard or a Theodore. The practice of shedding or changing a name is by no means restricted to the acting profession, however. An abbreviated list drawn from the past and the present:

Bud Abbott (William Abbott)
Maude Adams (Maude Kiskadden)
Eddie Albert (Edward Albert Heimberger)
Fred Allen (John Florence Sullivan)
Woody Allen (Allen Stewart Konigsberg)
June Allyson (Jan Allyson)
Don Ameche (Dominic Felix Ameche)
Dame Judith Anderson (Frances Margaret Anderson)
Julie Andrews (Julia Wells)
Ann-Margret (Ann-Margret Olsson)

Eddie Arcaro (George Edward Arcaro)
Elizabeth Arden (Florence Nightingale Graham)
Harold Arlen (Hyman Arluck)
Beatrice Arthur (Bernice Frankel)
Fred Astaire (Frederick Austerlitz)
Mary Astor (Mary Lucile Langhanke)
Brooks Atkinson (Justin Brooks Atkinson)
Charles Aznavour (Varenagh Aznaourian)
Lauren Bacall (Betty Joan Perske)
Kay Ballard (Gloria Katherine Balotta)
Honoré de Balzac (Honoré Guez)
Anne Bancroft (Annemarie Italiano)
Theda Bara (Theodosia Goodman)
Red Barber (Walter Lanier Barber)
Ethel Barrymore (Ethel Blythe)
John Barrymore (John Blythe)
Lionel Barrymore (Lionel Blythe)
Maurice Barrymore (Herbert Blythe)
Count Basie (William Basie)
Orson Bean (Dallas Frederick Burrows)
Warren Beatty (Warren Beaty)
David Ben-Gurion (David Green)
Tony Bennett (Anthony Dominick Benedetto)
Jack Benny (Benjamin Kubelsky)
Polly Bergen (Nellie Paulina Burgin)
Ingmar Bergman (Ernst Ingmar Bergman)
Milton Berle (Milton Berlinger)
Irving Berlin (Israel Baline)
Sarah Bernhardt (Rosine Bernard)
Yogi Berra (Lawrence Peter Berra)
Joey Bishop (Joseph Abraham Gottlieb)
Georges Bizet (Alexandre César Léopold Bizet)
Amanda Blake (Beverly Louise Neill)
Dirk Bogarde (Derek Niven van den Bogaerde)
Sonny Bono (Salvatore Bono)
Pat Boone (Charles Eugene Boone)
Shirley Booth (Thelma Booth Ford)
Botticelli (Alessandro di Mariano Filipepi)
Willy Brandt (Herbert Ernst Karl Frahm)

Fanny Brice (Fannie Borach)
Vanessa Brown (Smylla Brind)
Yul Brynner (Taidje Kahn, Jr.)
George Burns (Nathan Birnbaum)
Ellen Burstyn (Edna Rae Gillooly)
Richard Burton (Richard Jenkins)
Red Buttons (Aaron Chwatt)
John Cabot (Giovanni Caboto)
Sammy Cahn (Sammy Cohen)
Michael Caine (Maurice Joseph Micklewhite)
Taylor Caldwell (Janet Taylor Caldwell)
Maria Callas (Maria Anna Sofia Cecilia Kalogeropoulos)
John Calvin (Jean Chauvin)
Eddie Cantor (Edward Israel Iskowitz)
Kitty Carlisle (Catherine Conn)
Hoagy Carmichael (Hoagland Howard Carmichael)
Scott Carpenter (Malcolm Scott Carpenter)
Vicky Carr (Florencia Bisenta de Casillas Martinez Cardona)
Diahann Carroll (Carol Diahann Johnson)
Lewis Carroll (Charles Lutwidge Dodgson)
Marc Chagall (Marc Segal)
Cyd Charisse (Tula Ellice Finklea)
Ray Charles (Ray Charles Robinson)
Charo (Maria Rosario Pilar Martinez Molina Baeza)
Paddy Chayefsky (Sidney Chayefsky)
Cher (Cherilyn La Piere)
Chubby Checker (Ernest Evans)
René Clair (René Chomette)
Ina Claire (Ina Fagan)
Eldridge Cleaver (Leroy Eldridge Cleaver)
Grover Cleveland (Stephen Grover Cleveland)
Van Cliburn (Harvey Lavan Cliburn, Jr.)
Buffalo Bill Cody (William Frederick Köthe)
Claudette Colbert (Lily Chauchoin)
Colette (Sidonie Gabrielle Claudine Colette)
Dorothy Collins (Marjorie Chandler)
Perry Como (Pierino Como)
Joseph Conrad (Teodor Józef Konrad Korzeniowski)
Bert Convy (Bernard Whalen Patrick Convy)

Alice Cooper (Vincent Damon Furnier)
Gary Cooper (Frank James Cooper)
Alex Cord (Alexander Viespi)
Joan Crawford (Lucille Le Sueur)
Bing Crosby (Harry Lillis Crosby)
Marie Curie (Marja Sklodowska Curie)
Tony Curtis (Bernard Schwartz)
Jacques d'Amboise (Jacques d'Amboise Ahearn)
Vic Damone (Vito Farinola)
Rodney Dangerfield (John Cohen)
Dante (Dante Alighieri)
Denise Darcel (Denise Billecard)
Bette Davis (Ruth Elizabeth Davis)
Doris Day (Doris von Kappelhoff)
Dizzy Dean (Jay Hanna Dean)
Yvonne De Carlo (Peggy Yvonne Middleton)
Dolores Del Rio (Lolita Dolores Martinez Asunsolo Inez
   Negrette)
Jack Dempsey (William Harrison Dempsey)
Patrick Dennis (Edward Everett Tanner III)
John Denver (Henry John Deutschendorf, Jr.)
Marlene Dietrich (Maria Magdelena von Losch)
Phyllis Diller (Phyllis Driver)
Isak Dinesen (Karen Dinesen Blixen)
Kirk Douglas (Issur Danielovitch)
Melvyn Douglas (Melvyn Hesselberg)
Mike Douglas (Michael Delaney Dowd, Jr.)
Billie Dove (Lillian Bohaney)
Marie Dressler (Leila Koeber)
Patty Duke (Anna Marie Duke)
Bob Dylan (Robert Allen Zimmerman)
Buddy Ebsen (Christian Ebsen, Jr.)
Samantha Eggar (Victoria Louise Eggar)
George Eliot (Mary Ann Evans)
Duke Ellington (Edward Kennedy Ellington)
Mama Cass Elliot (Ellen Naomi Cohen)
Desiderius Erasmus (Gerard Gerards)
Werner Erhard (Jack Rosenberg)
Dale Evans (Frances Octavia Smith Rogers)

Chad Everett (Raymond Lee Cramton)
Tom Ewell (Yewell Tompkins)
Farinelli (Carlo Broschi)
Alice Faye (Ann Leppert)
José Ferrer (José Vicente Ferrer de Otero y Cintrón)
W. C. Fields (William Claude Dukenfield)
Eddie Fisher (Edwin Jack Fisher)
Barry Fitzgerald (William Joseph Shields)
Rhonda Fleming (Marilyn Louis)
Joan Fontaine (Joan de Beauvoir de Havilland)
Dame Margot Fonteyn (Margaret Hookham)
Ford Madox Ford (Ford Madox Hueffer)
Glenn Ford (Gwllyn Samuel Newton Ford)
Whitey Ford (Edward Charles Ford)
Redd Foxx (John Elroy Sanford)
Anatole France (Jacques Anatole François Thibault)
Anthony Franciosa (Anthony Papaleo)
Arlene Francis (Arlene Francis Kazanjian)
Connie Francis (Concetta Franconero)
Joe Frazier (Joseph Frazier)
Carlton Fredericks (Harold Casper Frederick Caplan)
Clark Gable (William Clark Gable)
Zsa Zsa Gabor (Sari Gabor)
Greta Garbo (Greta Luisa Gustafson)
Judy Garland (Frances Gumm)
James Garner (James Baumgardner)
Ben Gazzara (Benjo Antonio Gazzara)
Lou Gehrig (Henry Louis Gehrig)
Genghis Khan (Temujin)
Geneviève (Ginette Marguerite Auger)
Geronimo (Goyathlay)
Dizzy Gillespie (John Birks Gillespie)
Samuel Goldwyn (Samuel Gelbfisch)
Maxim Gorky (Aleksei Maksimovich Peshkov)
Billy Graham (William Franklin Graham)
Red Grange (Harold Edward Grange)
Stewart Granger (James Lablache Stewart)
Cary Grant (Archibald Leach)
Lee Grant (Lyova Haskell Rosenthal)

Ulysses S. Grant (Hiram Ulysses Grant)
Barry Gray (Bernard Yaroslaw)
Kathryn Grayson (Zelma Hednick)
El Greco (Domenico Teotocopulo)
Joel Grey (Joel Katz)
Lefty Grove (Robert M. Grove)
Sacha Guitry (Alexander Guitry)
Buddy Hackett (Leonard Hacker)
Haile Selassie (Ras Tafari Makonnen)
Halston (Roy Halston Frowick)
Walter Hampden (Walter Hampden Daugherty)
Jean Harlow (Harlean Carpenter)
Bret Harte (Francis Brett Harte)
Laurence Harvey (Larushka Skikne)
June Havoc (June Hovick)
Susan Hayward (Edythe Marrener)
Rita Hayworth (Margarita Carmen Cansino)
Heinrich Heine (Harry Heine)
O. Henry (William Sydney Porter)
Audrey Hepburn (Audrey Hepburn-Ruston)
William Holden (William Franklin Beedle, Jr.)
Billie Holiday (Eleanora Fagan)
Judy Holliday (Judy Tuvim)
Bob Hope (Leslie Townes Hope)
Harry Houdini (Ehrich Weiss)
John Houseman (John Haussmann)
Leslie Howard (Leslie Stainer)
Rock Hudson (Roy Scherer, Jr.)
Engelbert Humperdinck (Arnold Dorsey)
Kim Hunter (Janet Cole)
Ross Hunter (Martin Fuss)
Tab Hunter (Arthur Gelien)
Walter Huston (Walter Houghston)
Betty Hutton (Betty Thornburg)
Rev. Ike (Frederick Joseph Eikerenkoetter II)
Sir Henry Irving (John Henry Brodribb)
Kareem Abdul-Jabbar (Ferdinand Lewis Alcindor, Jr.)
Al Jolson (Asa Yoelson)
Jennifer Jones (Phyllis Isley)

John Paul Jones (John Paul)
Tom Jones (Thomas Jones Woodward)
Louis Jourdan (Louis Gendre)
Al Kaline (Albert William Kaline)
Garson Kanin (Gershon Labe)
Boris Karloff (William Henry Pratt)
Danny Kaye (David Daniel Kominsky)
Nora Kaye (Nora Koreff)
Buster Keaton (Joseph Francis Keaton)
Patsy Kelly (Sarah Veronica Rose Kelly)
Kemal Ataturk (Mustafa Kemal)
Deborah Kerr (Deborah Kerr-Trimmer)
Sidney Kingsley (Sidney Kirshner)
Serge Kossevitzky (Sergei Kossevitzky)
Sandy Koufax (Sanford Koufax)
Elsa Lanchester (Elsa Sullivan)
Ann Landers (Esther "Eppie" Pauline Friedman Lederer)
Frankie Laine (Frank Paul Lo Vecchio)
Lily Langtry (Emily Charlotte Le Breton)
Mario Lanza (Alfredo Arnold Cocozza)
Lao-Tzu (Li Erh)
Ring Lardner (Ringgold Wilmer Lardner)
Stan Laurel (Arthur Stanley Jefferson Laurel)
Piper Laurie (Rosetta Jacobs)
Gertrude Lawrence (Gertrud Alexandra Dagmar Lawrence
   Klasen)
Steve Lawrence (Sidney Leibowitz)
Leadbelly (Huddie Ledbetter)
John Le Carré (David John Moore Carnwell)
Gypsy Rose Lee (Rose Louise Hovick)
Peggy Lee (Norma Egstrom)
Janet Leigh (Jeanette Morrison)
Vivien Leigh (Vivian Mary Hartley)
Nikolai Lenin (Vladimir Ilich Ulyanov)
Benny Leonard (Benjamin Leiner)
Jerry Lewis (Joseph Levitch)
Shari Lewis (Shari Hurwitz)
Sinclair Lewis (Harry Sinclair Lewis)
Liberace (Wladziu Valentino Liberace)

Jenny Lind (Johanna Maria Lind)
Carolus Linnaeus (Carl von Linné)
Carole Lombard (Jane Alice Peters)
Julie London (Julie Peck)
Jack Lord (J. J. Ryan)
Sophia Loren (Sophia Scicolone)
Myrna Loy (Myrna Williams)
Clare Boothe Luce (Anne Clare Booth Luce)
Bela Lugosi (Bela Lugosi Blasko)
Leonard Lyons (Leonard Sucher)
Connie Mack (Cornelius Alexander McGillicuddy)
Gisele MacKenzie (Marie Marguerite Louise Gisele La Fleche)
Shirley MacLaine (Shirley MacLaine Beaty)
Guy Madison (Robert Moseley)
Marjorie Main (Mary Tomlinson Krebs)
Karl Malden (Mladen Sekulovich)
Fredric March (Frederick McIntyre Bickel)
Marie Antoinette (Josèphe Jeanne Marie Antoinette)
Julia Marlowe (Sarah Frances Frost)
Dean Martin (Dino Crocetti)
Chico Marx (Leonard Marx)
Groucho Marx (Julius Henry Marx)
Gummo Marx (Milton Marx)
Harpo Marx (Arthur Marx)
Zeppo Marx (Herbert Marx)
André Maurois (Émile Herzog)
Paul McCartney (James Paul McCartney)
Alec McCowen (Alexander Duncan McCowen)
Fibber McGee (James Edward Jordan)
Marshall McLuhan (Herbert Marshall McLuhan)
Butterfly McQueen (Thelma McQueen)
Steve McQueen (Terence Stephen McQueen)
Dame Nellie Melba (Helen Porter Mitchell)
Peter Mennin (Peter Mennini)
Melina Mercouri (Maria Amalia Mercouri)
Ethel Merman (Ethel Zimmerman)
David Merrick (David Margulois)
Robert Merrill (Moishe Miller)
Ray Milland (Reginald Truscott-Jones)

Ann Miller (Lucy Ann Collier)
Mitch Miller (Mitchell William Miller)
Joni Mitchell (Roberta Joan Anderson Mitchell)
Molière (Jean Baptiste Poquelin)
Marilyn Monroe (Norma Jean Mortenson)
Yves Montand (Ivo Livi)
Robert Montgomery (Henry Montgomery, Jr.)
Garry Moore (Thomas Garrison Morfit)
Rita Moreno (Rosita Dolores Alverio)
Grandma Moses (Anna Mary Roberts Moses)
Zero Mostel (Samuel Joel Mostel)
Bill Moyers (Billy Don Moyers)
Wolfgang Amadeus Mozart (Johannes Chrysostomus Wolfgangus
    Theophilus Mozart)
Paul Muni (Muni Weisenfreund)
Ken Murray (Don Court)
Pola Negri (Appolonia Matias-Chalupez)
Ozzie Nelson (Oswald George Nelson)
Ricky Nelson (Eric Hilliard Nelson)
Pablo Neruda (Ricardo Eliezer Neftali Reyes Basoalto)
Bob Newhart (George Robert Newhart)
Mike Nichols (Michael Igor Peschowsky)
Red Nichols (Ernest Loring Nichols)
David Niven (James David Graham Niven)
Kim Novak (Marilyn Paul Novak)
Merle Oberon (Estelle Merle O'Brien "Queenie" Thompson)
Hugh O'Brien (Hugh J. Krampe)
Margaret O'Brien (Angela Maxine O'Brien)
Pat O'Brien (William Joseph O'Brien, Jr.)
Frank O'Connor (Michael O'Donovan)
Maureen O'Hara (Maureen FitzSimons)
Gilbert O'Sullivan (Raymond O'Sullivan)
Peter O'Toole (Seamus O'Toole)
Patti Page (Clara Ann Fowler)
Satchel Paige (Leroy Robert Paige)
Lilli Palmer (Maria Lilli Peiser)
Drew Pearson (Andrew Russell Pearson)
Gregory Peck (Eldred Gregory Peck)
Jan Peerce (Jacob Pincus Perelmuth)

Pelé (Edson Arantes do Nascimento)
S. J. Perelman (Sidney Joseph Perelman)
Bernadette Peters (Bernadette Lazarra)
Petrarch (Francesco Petrarca)
Mary Pickford (Gladys Marie Smith)
Plato (Aristocles)
Jane Powell (Suzanne Burce)
Stefanie Powers (Stefania Zofia Federkiewicz)
Paula Prentiss (Paula Ragusa)
Robert Preston (Robert Preston Meservey)
J. B. Priestley (John Boynton Priestley)
William Proxmire (Edward William Proxmire)
Emilio Pucci (Emilio Pucci di Barsento)
Ellery Queen (Frederic Dannay and the late Manfred Bennington
    Lee)
Raphael (Raffaello Santi)
Martha Raye (Margie Yvonne Reed)
Della Reese (Delloreese Patricia Early)
Pee Wee Reese (Harold Henry Reese)
Régine (Regina Zylberberg)
Max Reinhardt (Max Goldmann)
Lee Remick (Ann Remick)
Debbie Reynolds (Mary Frances Reynolds)
Richelieu (Armand Jean du Plessis)
Eddie Rickenbacker (Edward Vernon Richenbacher)
Harold Robbins (Francis Kane)
Jerome Robbins (Jerome Rabinowitz)
Edward G. Robinson (Emanuel Goldenberg)
Buddy Rogers (Charles Rogers)
Ginger Rogers (Virginia Katherine McMath)
Roy Rogers (Leonard Slye)
Gilbert Roland (Luis Antonio Damasco de Alonso)
Jules Romains (Louis Farigoule)
Mickey Rooney (Joe Yule, Jr.)
Lillian Russell (Helen Louise Leonard)
Babe Ruth (George Herman Ruth)
Mort Sahl (Morton Lyon Sahl)
Buffy Sainte-Marie (Beverly Sainte-Marie)
Yves Saint Laurent (Henri Donat Mathieu)

Soupy Sales (Milton Hines)
J. D. Salinger (Jerome David Salinger)
George Sand (Amandine Aurore Lucie Dupin, Baronne
   Dudevant)
Dr. Seuss (Theodore Seuss Geisel)
Artie Shaw (Arthur Arshowsky)
Bishop Fulton J. Sheen (Peter Sheen)
Toots Shor (Bernard Shor)
Dinah Shore (Frances "Fannie" Rose Shore)
Jean Sibelius (Johann Julius Christian Sibelius)
Simone Signoret (Simone-Henriette-Sharlotte Kaminker)
Beverly Sills (Belle "Bubbles" Silverman)
Phil Silvers (Philip Silversmith)
Nina Simone (Eunice Kathleen Waymon)
O. J. Simpson (Orenthal James Simpson)
Red Skelton (Richard Bernard Skelton)
Bubba Smith (Charles Aaron Smith)
Kate Smith (Kathryn Elizabeth Smith)
Red Smith (Walter Smith)
Dick Smothers (Richard Smothers)
Tom Smothers (Thomas Bolyn Smothers III)
Duke Snider (Edwin Donald Snider)
Phoebe Snow (Phoebe Loeb)
Ann Sothern (Harriet Lake)
Sissy Spacek (Mary Elizabeth Spacek)
Mickey Spillane (Frank Morrison)
Joseph Stalin (Iosif Vissarionovich Dzhugashvili)
Stanislavski (Konstantin Sergeevich Alekseev)
Sir Henry Morton Stanley (John Rowlands)
Kim Stanley (Patricia Reid)
Barbara Stanwyck (Ruby Stevens)
Kay Starr (Kay Starks)
Ringo Starr (Richard Starkey)
Rod Steiger (Rodney Steiger)
Stendhal (Marie Henri Beyle)
Casey Stengel (Charles Dillon Stengel)
Stepin' Fetchit (Lincoln Theodore Perry)
Connie Stevens (Concetta Ann Ingolia)
Irving Stone (Irving Tennenbaum)

Sly Stone (Sylvester)
Barry Sullivan (Patrick Barry Sullivan)
Tamerlane (Timur)
Robert Taylor (Spangler Arlington Brugh)
Terry-Thomas (Thomas Terry Hoar Stevens)
Danny Thomas (Amos Jacobs)
Tintoretto (Jacopo Robusti)
Tiny Tim (Herbert Buckingham Khaury)
Titian (Tiziano Vecelli)
Marshall Tito (Josip Broz)
J. R. R. Tolkien (John Ronald Reuel Tolkien)
Toulouse-Lautrec (Henri Marie Raymond de Toulouse-Lautrec
   Monfa)
Leon Trotsky (Lev Davydovich Bronstein)
Gene Tunney (James Joseph Tunney)
Lana Turner (Julia Jean Turner)
Mark Twain (Samuel Langhorne Clemens)
Twiggy (Lesley Hornby)
Rudolph Valentino (Rodolpho d'Antonguolla)
Rudy Vallee (Hubert Prior Vallée)
Abigail Van Buren (Pauline Esther "Popo" Friedman Phillips)
Gore Vidal (Eugene Vidal)
Pancho Villa (Doroteo Arango)
François Villon (François de Montcorbier)
Bobby Vinton (Bobby Vintula)
Voltaire (François Marie Arouet)
Jersey Joe Walcott (Arnold Raymond Cream)
Nancy Walker (Ann Myrtle Swoyer)
Mike Wallace (Myron Wallace)
Bruno Walter (Bruno Walter Schlesinger)
Artemus Ward (Charles Farrar Browne)
Muddy Waters (McKinley Morganfield)
Alec Waugh (Alexander Raban Waugh)
John Wayne (Marion Michael Morrison)
Clifton Webb (Webb Parmelee Hollenbeck)
Robert Weede (Robert Wiedefeld)
Tuesday Weld (Susan Kerr Weld)
Nathanael West (Nathan Wallenstein Weinstein)
Rebecca West (Cicily Isabel Fairfield)

E. B. White (Elwyn Brooks White)
Tennessee Williams (Thomas Lanier Williams)
Flip Wilson (Clerow Wilson)
Woodrow Wilson (Thomas Woodrow Wilson)
Shelley Winters (Shirley Schrift)
Stevie Wonder (Steveland Morris Hardaway)
Natalie Wood (Natasha Gurdin)
Jane Wyman (Sarah Jane Fulks)
Ed Wynn (Isaiah Edwin Leopold)
Cy Young (Denton True Young)
Loretta Young (Gretchen Young)

The Americanization of Spiro Anagnostopolous

Closet Ethnic?
*Film maker seeks 2nd genrtn, Italn or Armenian, who
changed names to avoid discrim and now proud to come
out.*
—Ad in *The New York Times*

For most of us, the name-changing process is not strictly career-oriented. The vast majority of those who shed their old name and don a new one are motivated by a desire for cultural assimilation. The first immigrants to undergo wholesale name changes in the United States were the Germans. Even before immigration officials at Ellis Island began randomly bestowing names on the illiterate arrivals from Eastern Europe at the end of the last century, German peasants were often at the mercy of English-speaking bureaucrats who found it difficult if not impossible to discern their true names and record them. Compromises were struck. The *ch* ending in names like Bech and Bloch would become a *ck*, turning future generations into Becks and Blocks. From Rauch came Rock; from Sänger, pronounced "senger," came Sanger. George Westinghouse, inventor of the air brake and founder of an industrial empire, was descended from Westinghausens. Buffalo Bill Cody's real surname was Köthe, and the Rockefellers began as Roggenfelders. General "Black

Jack" Pershing could trace his ancestors back to the tongue-twisting Pfoerschings. Herbert Hoover was descended from the Huber family, and boasted cousins named Hover, Hoofer and Hoeber.

Far more than any other ethnic group, Jews have been willing to drop their names and adopt fresh ones. Forced as they were by government fiat to adopt surnames in the 1800s, many Jews felt no strong allegiance to them. With good reason, since the whole business was often downright degrading. To avoid being branded by gentile officials with such insulting names as Wanzenknicker (louse-cracker) and Ochsenschwanz (ox tail), Jews sometimes resorted to bribery. Once the proper palm was greased, they could count themselves the proud possessors of such lilting surnames as Lilienthal (valley of the lilies) and Edel (noble).

Russian Jews were doubly accustomed to switching names. Since the eldest son of a Jewish family was exempt from military service, it was customary for younger sons to buy themselves a new name so they could pass as the firstborn sons of nonexistent families. As they came up in the world, Russian Jews often exchanged their names for distinctly Russian ones.

Jewish immigrants to the United States soon learned that there were dozens of ways to anglicize their names. Weinstein could be transformed into Winston, Lowenthal into Lowell, Cohen into Cone, Rosenthal into Rose, Greenblatt into Green.

The Poles came next, reacting to the fact that most Americans had severe problems with the spelling and pronunciation of Polish names. Among Polish-Americans, names like Leon Jaworski, Roman Polanski and Jerzy Kozinsky have survived, but Bobby Vintula became pop singer (and Polish patriot) Bobby Vinton. Actress Loretta Swit of television's "M*A*S*H" was told that her Polish name "sounded like a bad nose job looks. They wanted me to change it to Starr," says Swit, "as in Brenda. I ran."

Similarly, the Czechoslovakians, Lithuanians, Ukrainians, Russians and other Slavic peoples living in the United States more often than not feel compelled to make modifications. With the renewed emphasis on ethnicity, some young people are reverting to their original family names. Listed as co-authors of the bestselling *People's Almanac* are prolific novelist Irving Wallace and son David Wallechinsky, who has an obvious preference for the original family name.

While Italian- and Spanish-speaking immigrants have had little trouble because they tend to settle in areas where their language and culture predominate, Greeks who come to this country frequently dump several syllables, turning, say, a Pappadopulos into a Pappas. Former Vice-President Spiro T. Agnew started out an Anagnostopolous. As in the case of Mr. Wallechinsky, a Greek storekeeper in Chicago who had been known for years as Harris legally reverted to Haralampoulas. Since he did business in a Greek neighborhood, his customers found Haralampoulas easier to handle than Harris.

How to Change Your Name

Although many nations make it extremely difficult for the individual to change his name, an American can make the change in any state without petitioning a court for permission—so long as there is no fraudulent or criminal intent.

Most people who do change their names—movie stars and writers included—never bother to go through the formality of having the change decreed by a court. The best way to go about it is simply to drop the old name and start using the new one whenever and wherever possible. Register to vote, apply for a driver's license or a credit card, open a bank account under your new name. Once again, as long as you are not out to elude your creditors or the law, it is perfectly legal to call yourself Mickey Mouse or Queen Victoria if that's what you really want.

Still, there are certain advantages to having a court formally approve a switch. When he was criticized for using the adjective "painless" to describe his technique, a San Francisco dentist named Parker applied to have his first name changed. He became Dr. Painless Parker. On a more serious note, a California judge has ruled that if a person signs an affidavit of registration as a voter, he must use the same name he uses on passports and other federal papers, or face conviction on charges of perjury. In some jurisdictions, the right of a woman divorced or separated from her husband to revert to her maiden name is not recognized, while others have gone so far as to allow a transsexual to change his/her name to a female/male one. And in New York, a homosexual law school graduate barred from marrying his boyfriend changed his name from Jack Baker to Pat McConnell, obtained a marriage license and went through with the ceremony.

Pat McConnell notwithstanding, more and more people are questioning the practice of having the husband's surname stand for both parties in a marriage. Lucy Stone, an early suffragist, would not adopt her husband Henry Blackwell's name when she married in 1855 because, as she then put it, "My name is the symbol of my identity." Until the feminist movement took hold once again over a century later, few women had the courage to follow Lucy Stone's defiant example. One notable exception was Katharine Hepburn, who married Ogden Ludlow Smith in 1928 and requested that he drop his last name so she wouldn't be known as "Kate Smith." He did. They were divorced in 1934. Now, however, perhaps as many as one out of every dozen women who marry refuses to submerge herself completely in her husband's name.

One such woman is San Francisco author and former talk show hostess Pat Montandon. Taking the name of her husband, millionaire businessman Alfred Wilsey, she soon suffered "a very serious loss of identity. I was just not as active any more." She changed back, and her sense of self returned. "What is important about your own name," she observes, "is the psychology of being yourself instead of living through someone else."

The same decision was reached by Mary Ann "Mazie" Livingstone Delafield Cox, sister of Edward Cox and sister-in-law of Tricia Cox. Married to Brinley Stimson Thorne, an architect, Mazie Cox chose to retain her maiden name while teaching architectural design at Smith College. Susan McGovern Rowen, daughter of the 1972 Democratic presidential contender George McGovern, went back to Susan McGovern. Pamela Howard, daughter of retired Scripps-Howard President Jack Howard, stayed a Howard after she wed book publisher Clarkson N. Potter. "I'm contributing to a partnership, and partners don't take each other's names," said Pamela, a freelance writer.

As a compromise, some women merely hold on to their maiden

names as middle names. Other couples hyphenate their last names, as in Jane Doe-Smith. Such democratization can be carried to extremes. "My husband-to-be refused to get married unless he also got a new name out of the union," says Carolyn Snyder-Stonebreaker of Boulder, Colorado. "After much arguing and discussion, we combined his name with my maiden name to make Snyder-Stonebreaker. Lest our mothers be forgotten, we each dropped our middle names and inserted our mothers' family names. Alphabetical order, of course, for the four family names." The ungainly result: Carolyn Holub Sands Snyder-Stonebreaker.

Though many women believe that they are required by law to adopt a husband's name, only Hawaii has such a statute on the books. Under English common law, a woman may select any name as long as she uses it consistently. If a woman wants to keep using her name after marriage, all she has to do is just that—keep using it. She should continue calling herself by that name whenever the opportunity arises, and never use her husband's. (If she wants to use both her name and her husband's, she runs a sizable risk of government interference. Government agencies, for example, have the right to choose which name will be used on official documents.) A woman who is known by her husband's name but wants to go back to her maiden name should start by using her maiden name as much as possible, since in most cases no court petition is necessary. In addition to informing her friends and relatives, she should tell her employer, creditors, Social Security, the Motor Vehicles Department, the Board of Elections and anyone else who might be interested. She should go to her bank and change the name on her accounts. If a bank refuses to cooperate fully, she should withdraw her money and deposit it elsewhere, under the name of her own choosing.

What happens to the children when a mother is known by her maiden name? Usually, they take the father's name anyway. But VISTA volunteers Cornelia Ann Miller and Albert Henry Norman came up with their own solution. They gave their daughter, Winter, Daddy's surname as a middle name, and followed it up with Mommy's last name. Their daughter, then, is Winter Norman Miller. Massachusetts Attorney General Robert

Quinn upheld the name. "Giving Winter my wife's last name," claims Norman, "symbolized the equality of our relationship."

Minors, in general, may have their names changed only when a petition is co-signed by both parents or guardians. If a divorced woman wants her child to take the name of her second husband, for instance, the courts tend to be reluctant to overrule the objections of the natural father. As is the case in New York, most states recognize a father's "primary right to have his children bear his name."

While most people have little difficulty getting approval when they do go to the trouble of petitioning the courts, a few have not been so lucky. There was a great uproar in Boston over 50 years ago, when a Russian Jew named Kabotchnick tried to change his name to Cabot. The Cabots, then Boston's most powerful clan, prevented Kabotchnick from going ahead with his plan. Several years ago, a man with an Irish name legally changed to a Jewish-sounding one, then wanted it changed again to a Protestant-sounding one so he could take a Middle East vacation without fear of being harassed. The court refused to grant the change. A New Yorker who wanted his name changed to Arindam in honor of a spiritual leader in India was denied his request on the grounds that "judicial approval of the use of a single name would be retrogressive to antiquity, cause havoc and chaos in the proper identification and location of persons, cause serious disruption of official records and lead to all kinds of complications in an economy largely dependent upon credit of easily identifiable persons."

The most important case, however, was that of Robert Lee Middleton, a student at Brooklyn's New York City Community College, who applied to have his name changed to Kikuga Nairobi Kikugis so that he could feel more comfortable teaching African culture after his graduation. Finding that Kikuga and Kikugis are meaningless in any African language, New York Civil Court Judge Irving Smith denied Middleton's petition. The Judge pointed out that other black Americans were teaching African culture "without resorting to such subterfuge." Ironically, Judge Smith's own Polish ancestors had changed their family name when they migrated to the United States.

Anyone who is seriously contemplating a full-fledged legal

name change should fully realize that he is changing far more than just his name. To some extent, he is altering his personality. Just as Woodrow Wilson adopted a new, more confident attitude when he dropped Tommy for a more dignified first name, and as "Tiger Woman" Judd changed her pattern of behavior as she switched from Winnie to Ruth to Marion Lane, most people who change their names undergo some discernible psychological evolution.

To be sure, the change in personality may be slight. But it can be and often is significant. "A Seymour Schlumpf who has always hated his name and felt defensive about it might *feel better* if he changes his name to Steve Jones," says psychologist Albert Ellis, "but that doesn't mean he'll *get better*. Still," he continues, "if you are made to feel better by changing your name, then your behavior may change for the better."

Singer Bobby Darin became Robert Darin as he neared middle age, and his songs, dress, manner—both onstage and off—mellowed. Garrison Morfit gained renewed confidence and the public responded accordingly when, while performing as a comedian on the "Club Matinée" radio show in the 1940s, a contest was held to give him a new name. A woman in Pittsburgh sent in the winning suggestion: Garry ("very, very popular, masculine and diligent") Moore.

Something of a bumbler in her young life, international nightclub owner Regina Zylberberg changed her name by dropping the Zylberberg and replacing the "a" in Regina with an "e." Régine is the French word for queen, and she has been acting like one ever since. Once down-to-earth, designer Roy Halston Frowick began acting like a one-name legend when he jettisoned all but his aristocratic-sounding middle name.

Singer Clara ("dull but very feminine") Ann ("ladylike and honest, but not pretty") Fowler, second youngest of a railroad section foreman's 11 children, was singing at a radio station in Tulsa when she was given a new, more upbeat name: Patti ("a winner—dynamic, feminine, very popular") Page. Her surname came from the radio show's sponsor, the Page Milk Company. Bernice ("sedate") Frankel brought her forbidding presence to the stage as Vera Charles in the musical *Mame* and to television as "Maude." Her regal stage name, Beatrice Arthur, bolstered her standing in her own eyes as well as ours, and the heightened self-esteem made her more confident and aggressive. Better than anyone, Amos Jacobs knows the power of a name. Born to Lebanese immigrant parents on January 6, 1914, Jacobs considers his "second birthday" August 12, 1940—the day he stood up at the 5100 Club in Chicago and, borrowing the names of his two brothers, introduced himself as Danny ("a nice guy") Thomas.

How to Keep on Winning

To remain on top in playing the Name Game, here are some basic rules to memorize:

- Recognize the fact that a name is a living, changing thing. The name that fits you today may not fit tomorrow. What is good for the football hero may be lousy for the chairman of the board. A slight modification may someday be necessary, or a complete overhaul. If you don't like your name, seriously consider changing it.
- Whether naming a child or picking a new name for yourself, stay away from fads and gimmicks.
- Once you have landed on a name, don't be afraid to enforce its use. Don't allow others to corrupt your name or your child's name with incorrect pronunciation and spelling. It's well worth setting straight, and others will appreciate you for it.
- In general, avoid nicknames—unless you want to score some social points with the Bunnys and Tooties. Straight abbreviations—Sue for Susan or Tom for Thomas—are acceptable, as are most other more or less standard forms. But stay away from the "ie" and "y" endings. Don't hesitate to lay down the law when the neighborhood kids insist on calling your son David "Davey." His sense of self is at stake, and that's at least as important as seeing that he brushes his teeth.
- If you are interested in legally changing your name, refer to pages 221–235 and check out the laws in your state.

Now, look at those around you. How do they fit their names? How does your child fare in school? Your friends' children? Do the underachievers in your child's school tend to have "loser" names? Do the children you know with out-of-the-ordinary names have emotionally troubled parents? Are they themselves headed for trouble? Has your son been taunted as a sissy because of his feminine-sounding name? Has your daughter been graded unfairly because hers is not a name associated with intelligence? Is she also having difficulty adjusting socially because her name is blatantly unattractive?

Have you been discriminated against while job-hunting because employment agencies and personnel officers are subconsciously turned off by your name? If you are already employed, do you think you have been helped or hampered by your name? Do the top executives in your company have distinctive names or "golden initials"? Are the fast-rising stars, not so coincidentally, people with the kinds of elitist names described in Chapter 6? Are those people you know who have made it despite a "loser" name overly aggressive super-achievers, indicating that they have had to overcome much in transcending the image of their name? Is your coworker with that unfortunate handle suffering for it at the office? Are the people who show up in the society pages of your local newspaper the owners of unbearably cute nicknames? Should that fiftyish neighbor of yours who has always been called Suzie respectfully request that her friends start calling her Susan or Sue? Does that friend of your spouse's live up to the Casper Milquetoast image conveyed by his name? Or does he overcompensate for it? Do others not respect you because they do not respect your name?

The Name Game is serious business. Like any breakthrough in the area of human behavior, what we are now learning about the way in which names influence the development of our personalities and the paths of our lives is loaded with exciting possibilities for your future. We already know now that a name can be a boost or an obstacle in the office, in the classroom and at home. It can improve your chances of going to jail, or to the top of your field. It can give you special insight into the psychological makeup and motives of others. Working relations, marriage, love affairs and parent-child relationships can be better understood, improved and, yes, successfully manipulated by those who understand the subtleties and intricacies of the Name Game. Use what you have learned to improve yourself and your children. Use it to better fathom your friends and your enemies. Whatever you do with this knowledge, one thing is certain: You will never again underestimate what's in a name.

CHAPTER 10

894 Names
and What
They Really Mean

Here is the key to mastering and winning the Name Game—the first and only index for understanding the psychological vibrations that our names set forth. This list draws on the raw data from a wide variety of studies and sources to come up with the characteristics most often linked with our names. Among the many primary sources of raw information: the Winsome Poll of 1,100, Barbara Buchanan and James Bruning's Ohio University studies, E. D. Lawson's research and the David Sheppard poll.

To more accurately reflect reality, commonly used names—both formal and informal—are included. Elizabeth and Charles were monarchs, and a child whose mother insists she or he should be called Elizabeth or Charles lives an entirely different life from children known as Beth and Chuck, while Betsy and Charlie are different creatures still. Refer to the name by which the subject is best known, since one's formal name often bears scant resemblance to that which he has lived by. As mentioned earlier, many people who dig up their birth certificates are flabbergasted at what they find.

Check the following list and see how close the people you know and have known come to fitting their names' descriptions. Think of famous names, too. Arlenes Dahl and Francis are certainly "comely and brisk," as the glossary indicates an Arlene should be. Actors Anthony Perkins, Anthony Hopkins and Anthony Quayle join with entertainer Anthony Newley and former British Prime Minister Anthony Eden to lend credence to the belief that Anthonys tend to be "tall, wiry and elegant."

Douglases from MacArthur to Fairbanks support their super-masculine reputations, just as Sophia Loren, Natalie Wood and

Brigitte Bardot promote the sexy image of Sophias, Natalies and Brigittes. Does Mark Spitz fit the picture of all Marks as spoiled? "Gutsy" is the adjective used to describe Roy, as exemplified by handicapped baseball great Roy Campanella and civil rights leader Roy Wilkins. Journalist Sally Quinn. Actress Sally Struthers. Legendary San Francisco madam Sally Stanford (who got her last name for serving the lads at that prestigious place of learning). Fan dancer Sally Rand. Do all Sallys *have* to be sassy and blonde? These ladies make one wonder.

Girls List

A

Abigail	feminine, proper and staid
Ada	lethargic
Adelaide	unexciting
Adele	not very active, but womanly
Adeline	girlish
Adrienne	sexy
Agatha	unpopular and butch
Agnes	inert, homely
Alberta	dynamic but not well-liked
Alexandra	formal
Alfreda	a bit masculine, a wallflower
Alice	simple and seemly
Alma	ladylike
Almira	rather dull
Althea	plodding
Alva	masculine
Alvina	slow
Amanda	cultured
Amelia	colorless
Amy	active
Anastasia	pampered
Andrea	industrious
Angela	pleasant-looking, somewhat willful
Anita	exceedingly sexy
Ann	ladylike and honest, but not pretty
Anne	beautiful but untrustworthy, sociable
Annette	spirited

Antoinette	regally beautiful, seductive
April	spritely
Arlene	comely, brisk
Astrid	luscious
Audrey	authoritative, strong

B

Barbara	forceful, successful, fat but sexy
Bea	demure
Beatrice	not very popular, but feminine
Becky	cute
Belinda	very girlish
Belle	unpopular
Bernadette	saintly
Bernice	sedate
Bertha	obese
Bess	motherly
Beth	animated and very ladylike
Betsy	friendly and fun
Betty	super-feminine
Beulah	homely, masculine, plodding
Beverly	a bombshell—sexy and lively
Billie	butch, vigorous
Blanche	a trifle lazy
Blythe	blithe
Bobbie	masculine and forceful
Bonnie	girlish and busy
Brenda	aggressive and womanly
Bridget	
(or Brigitte)	as in Bardot, a sex kitten
Brunhilde	blonde and burly

C

Camilla	very ladylike
Candice	pampered
Candy	extremely sexy
Cara	cute
Carla	above average in looks and energy
Carlotta	dark, enigmatic
Carmel	assiduous
Carmen	seductive, Latin
Carole	popular, good-looking, vivacious

Caroline	a mover
Cassandra	doleful
Cassie	tomboyish, athletic
Celeste	aloof
Charity	delicate
Charlotte	girlish, sweet
Clara	dull but very feminine
Clarissa	lethargic
Claudia	diligent
Colleen	girlish and spritely
Connie	lively, well-liked, pretty
Constance	attractive, smart, sophisticated
Cora	mature
Cynthia	aggressively sexy

D

Daisy	like Gatsby's girl—indolent and coquettish
Daphne	spritely
Darlene	seductive
Dawn	beautiful, sexy, ethereal
Deanna	exciting
Deborah	confident, dynamic, extra feminine
Deirdre	zealous
Della	sexy
Denise	popular, feminine and active
Diana	very ladylike and well-liked
Diane	extremely likable, successful, attractive
Dolly	blonde and bumptious
Dolores	diligent, sexy
Dora	dull but physically active
Dorothy	a pampered lady
Dotty	bouncy

E

Edith	sexy
Edwina	lackluster
Effie	vapid
Eileen	lovely
Elaine	quite sexy, admired and active
Eleanor	average in every category
Elise	delicate, but not sought-after
Eliza	vivacious

Elizabeth	seductive
Ella	womanly
Ellen	cheery
Ellie	talkative
Elsa	unpopular
Elvira	drab, slow
Emily	a sideline-sitter
Emma	pretty but silly
Enid	lazy
Erma	sexy, but listless
Ernestine	inert, unloved, masculine
Estelle	a bit slow
Esther	not very exciting
Ethel	ho-hum
Eugenia	slow, not well-liked
Eunice	feminine but unpopular, determined
Eva	girlish
Evangeline	somewhat indolent
Eve	exceedingly feminine
Evelyn	formidable

F

Faith	dainty
Fanny	frisky, if not popular
Fay	fey
Fifi	passionate
Florence	masculine
Frances	appealing
Freda	something of a wallflower, colorless

G

Gabrielle	scintillating
Gail	a social creature
Gay (or Gaye)	gay, athletic
Genevieve	a bit indolent, but girlish
Georgianna	humdrum
Geraldine	not very well liked
Gertrude	dull
Gillian	temperamental but likable
Gina	a winner in all categories
Ginger	cute
Ginny	snappy
Gladys	not very popular or exciting

Glenna	a touch passive
Gloria	dynamic and seductive
Grace	ladylike
Gretchen	frilly
Gwendolyn	not well-liked

H

Hannah	not hard-hearted, but dull and unloved
Harriet	lethargic
Hazel	warm
Heather	girlish
Heidi	cute
Helen	attractive
Henrietta	a wallflower
Hester	unfeminine and unloved
Hilda	lifeless and not terribly likable
Hildegarde	lazy
Honey	sickeningly sweet
Hope	extremely ladylike, sedentary

I

Ida	inert
Ilsa	lackluster
Imogene	not very well-liked, but otherwise average
Inez	passive, unpopular
Ingrid	very feminine, not overactive
Irene	a bit pampered, attractive
Iris	dainty, vulnerable
Isabel	dull
Ivy	drab

J

Jacqueline	a bombshell of femininity, very popular
Jane	certainly not plain
Janet	a winner in all categories
Janice	unrelenting
Jean	ladylike, attractive
Jeanette	very feminine, well-liked
Jennifer	youthful, yet old-fashioned
Jenny	active, not as frilly as Jennifer, but above average
Jerry	butch, athletic, easygoing

Jesse	forceful, masculine
Jessica	ambitious and beautiful
Jewell	sluggish
Jill	likable, active
Jo	a cut above average all around
Joan	womanly and well-liked
Joanne	very sexy, a leader
Jocelyn	not terribly popular or active, but feminine
Joy	girlish, well-liked, spirited
Joyce	eager, serious
Judith	very ladylike
Judy	bouncy, all-American
Julia	decorous
Juliet	slightly pampered
Justine	indifferent

K

Karen	sharp, extremely feminine
Kate	unstoppable
Katharine	determined, strong-willed, comely
Kathie	very likable
Kathleen	always much sought-after
Kay	feminine, spring-like
Kim	very, very popular
Kitty	exceptionally sexy

L

Lana	alluring
Laura	like the song—sexy, mysterious
Laurel	frilly
Laverne	cunning, hard
Leah	far from overactive, but attractive
Lee	a tomboy
Lena	silly and sexy
Leona	not very assertive
Lesley	has lots of friends
Leta	not overly sought-after
Leticia	almost inert, but somewhat seductive
Libby	something of a wallflower
Lil	old-fashioned
Lillian	sultry
Lilly	naive

Linda	utterly feminine, extremely popular and energetic
Lisa	very frail, well-liked
Liza	spirited
Lois	not dynamic, but feminine
Loren	a mover, independent
Loretta	sexy
Lorna	dull but especially attractive
Lorraine	very appealing
Lou	butch
Louise	pretty
Lucia	fiery, alluring
Lucinda	girlish
Lucy	fun
Luella	not very likable
Lydia	very feminine

M

Mabel	unpopular and aggressive
Madeline	sultry
Madge	brisk
Maggie	not terribly well-liked, but active
Maisie	friendless
Mandy	unstirred
Marcia	wily, popular
Margaret	a bit dowdy
Marge	one of the gals
Margot	somewhat lazy and uninvolved
Marian	ladylike, pure
Marie	slim and attractive, intelligent
Marion	womanly, wise
Marjorie	very sexy
Marleen	bold
Marta	assertive
Martha	unexciting
Mary	wholesome, womanly, active
Mathilda	homely, wistful, unloved
Maureen	sultry but surly
Mavis	dull
Maxine	more energetic than most
May	frilly

Meg	dowdy but diligent
Melanie	very delicate, attractive
Melissa	passive but graceful
Melody	sweet
Meredith	neuter
Merle	indifferent
Mildred	gray
Millicent	very pampered
Milly	unconcerned
Minnie	giddy
Miranda	unpopular
Miriam	sneaky
Molly	wholesome, happy, well-liked
Mona	not very dynamic
Monica	passionate
Myra	spiritless
Myrna	sluggish
Myrtle	drab

N

Nancy	spiteful
Nanette	very girlish, lovable
Naomi	not very popular, nor aggressive
Natalie	dynamite—tops in all categories
Nell	unliked but sweet
Nellie	very dull
Nettie	brisk, underappreciated
Nicole	average on all counts
Nina	a comely thing, but tame
Noel	sociable
Nola	sexy
Nona	somewhat drab
Nora	a no-nonsense woman
Norma	lonely

O

Odelia	colorless and often alone
Ola	unexciting
Olga	fat and unloved
Olive	disliked, inert
Opal	shunned

P

Page	good-looking, determined and very bright
Paige	not overly popular
Pamela	hard, ambitious and domineering
Pansy	a pansy
Patience	a homebody
Patricia	plain
Patsy	attractive, relentless
Patty	a winner—dynamic, feminine, very popular
Paula	determined
Paulette	frilly
Pauline	pampered and very, very feminine
Pearl	not very bright
Peggy	spirited, cute
Penelope	extremely girlish, not overly popular
Penny	pert
Phoebe	unloved
Phyllis	vulnerably feminine
Pia	uninvolved, detached
Polly	cute, one of the girls
Priscilla	prissy
Prudence	inert, properly feminine

R

Rachel	serious, sincere
Rae	not very feminine
Ramona	romantic
Reba	unloved
Rebecca	sweet
Regina	aristocratic
Rennie	sexy
Rhoda	a bit of a *schlemiel,* but attractive
Rita	pretty, seductive
Robbie	a tomboy
Roberta	competent, level-headed
Robin	pert
Rollene	an introvert
Ronny	too mannish
Rosa	sexy
Rosalie	determined, comely
Rosamond	baffling

Rose	wholesome, loving and feminine
Rosie	very girlish and somewhat spirited
Rowena	drab
Roxanne	diligent
Ruby	colorless
Ruth	an earth mother

S

Sabrina	sultry
Sadie	a wallflower
Salena	untrustworthy
Sally	blonde and sassy
Sandra	exceptionally feminine and popular
Sarah	sensual and selfish
Selma	a wallflower
Sheila	flirty
Sherry	vibrant
Shirley	attractive and highly sociable
Sonia	mysterious
Sophia	à la Loren—a bombshell
Sophie	hard-working
Stacey	brisk but sexless
Stephanie	attractive and life-loving
Sue	lovely and never alone
Susan	dynamic, well-liked, exceedingly attractive
Susanne (or Suzanne)	lively, sexy, popular
Suzie	zealous and young
Sybil	intelligent
Sylvia	lively, very feminine

T

Tammy	mischievous, pert and redheaded
Tania (or Tanya)	exotic
Teddy	masculine, industrious
Tess	unhappy
Thelma	rather lethargic
Theo	neuter

Theodora	indolent
Theresa	determined, very feminine
Thomasina	ladylike, pampered
Tilly	silly
Toby	tomboyish
Toni	energetic
Tracey	everybody's friend, spritely
Trixie	cute
Trudy	one of the girls

U

Ursula	very dynamic, tremendously popular and appealing

V

Val	resolute
Valerie	extremely feminine, popular
Velma	one who is avoided
Vera	predatory
Verna	unexciting
Vicky	very sexy, exceedingly well-liked and frisky
Victoria	pampered, cultured
Viola	overlooked
Violet	fragile
Vivian	brisk, elegant

W

Wanda	voluptuous
Wendy	spritely
Wilda	lazy
Willa	a wallflower
Wilma	stodgy
Winifred	unpopular
Winnie	flighty

Y

Yolanda	not terribly well-liked
Yvette	a bombshell in every area
Yvonne	stunning

Z

Zelda	aggressive

Boys List

A

Aaron	masculine, though not very active
Abe	very manly and industrious
Abraham	strong
Adam	diligent
Adolph	very unpopular
Adrian	average
Al	a winner
Alan	very sexy, loaded with friends
Albert	not terribly well-liked, lazy
Alden	hardworking
Aldo	slothful
Aldous	quiet
Alex	diligent, virile
Alfred	neuter
Allan (or Allen)	serious, sincere, sensitive
Alvin	very tame
Andre	sophisticated
Andrew	sincere but immature
Andy	a bit of a laggard, but popular
Anthony	tall, wiry, elegant
Antoine	sissified
Anton	very attractive
Archibald	effeminate, sedentary
Arlie	neuter, passive
Armand	not aggressive
Arnold	masculine if unexciting
Art	lively, manly, likable
Arthur	a bit lazy

B

Baird	listless, but masculine
Barney	a wallflower
Barrett	stuffy
Barry	exceptionally masculine, dynamic
Bart	very macho
Barth	dull
Bartholomew	sexless
Barton	very masculine

Basil	sinister
Baxter	indifferent
Ben	very manly, zealous, popular
Benedict	unpopular
Benjamin	dishonest
Bennett	very masculine but lethargic
Benson	slothful
Bernard	exceptionally manly
Bernie	a nice guy
Bertram	very dull
Bill	super-macho, sexy, successful
Billy	very active and well-liked, but less manly than Bill
Blair	exciting
Bob	exceptionally masculine and dynamic
Bobby	a winner in all categories
Booth	unpopular
Boyd	manly, but rather passive
Bradford	diligent, likable, popular
Brandon	masculine
Brant	aggressive
Brett	a winner
Brian	a superstar—macho, dynamic
Bruce	a loner
Bruno	brutish
Burke	above average all around
Burton	exciting

C

Caleb	unassertive
Calvin	a touch inert
Cameron	sexy, relentless
Carl	extremely masculine
Carroll	sissified, pampered
Casper	a milquetoast
Cass	very manly
Cecil	passive, with few friends
Cedric	sedentary, not widely admired
Chandler	quite sexy
Charles	masculine, popular, but not overly active
Charley	very well-liked, spirited

Charlton	solid
Chauncey	lazy
Chester	disliked, though manly
Chet	persevering, manly
Chris	extremely popular and very dynamic
Christian	soft
Christopher	diligent, intelligent
Chuck	very masculine, but quiet
Clarence	neuter, but industrious
Clark	very forceful and manly
Claud	a clod
Cliff	bold, sexy
Clifford	gentlemanly
Clifton	intelligent, attractive, but a bit passive
Clyde	cloddish
Colin	lazy but virile
Conrad	a tiger
Cort	industrious
Courtney	dainty
Craig	a winner—exceedingly masculine, active
Curt	exceptionally popular, exceedingly manly, very active
Curtis	masculine, dynamic—but less so than Curt
Cyril	sneaky
Cyrus	an unsympathetic sort

D

Dale	reasonably sedulous
Damon	assertive
Dana	very active but unexciting, neuter
Dane	manly
Daniel	very virile
Danny	a nice guy, if not overly industrious
Darcy	passive, not masculine
Darrell	brisk
Dave	a superstar—a he-man, an achiever
David	not quite as terrific as Dave, but still an undeniable winner
Davis	above average in all areas
Davy	lazy, neuter
Dean	a winner

Delbert	a loser—effeminate, inert
Denny	very popular, industrious
Derk	indolent, but exceedingly masculine
Derrick	a winner
Dexter	somewhat sexless, cerebral
Dick	exceptionally manly, well-liked
Dillon	a cut above the pack
Dimitri	strong
Dion	feminine
Dominic	above average in all categories
Don	a charmer
Donald	smooth
Dorian	
(or Dorien)	lean, elegant, quite intelligent
Doug	strong, likable
Douglas	a winner—supermasculine and a dynamo
Drew	not terribly active, but manly and admired
Duane	masculine but lazy
Dudley	a dud
Duncan	not very dynamic
Durward	insipid
Dwight	not exactly the life of the party, but strong and industrious

E

Eaton	slothful but manly
Ed	very masculine, popular, dynamic
Eddie	lively
Edgar	not very exciting, nor popular
Edmund	average
Edward	thoughtful
Edwin	not much of a mover
Eldon	unconcerned
Eli	hard-driving but friendless
Elias	manly but passive
Ellery	a bit effeminate, rather lazy
Elliot	manly, industrious
Ellis	lackluster
Elmer	a loser—unloved, slothful, not bright
Elroy	a real loser—sissified, sedentary
Emil	active, unliked
Emmett	a laggard

Emory	friendless, plodding, neuter
Ephraim	boring but sincere, a loner
Eric	a big winner—very strong
Ernest	passive and unpopular
Ernie	more active than Ernest, and more manly
Erwin	a bit uninvolved
Eugene	not ambitious
Evan	a slacker
Everett	a bore
Ezra	dull

F

Farly	not well-liked
Farrell	indifferent
Felix	neuter, unpopular
Fenton	sedentary and friendless
Ferd	a big loser
Fletcher	lethargic
Floyd	not popular
Forrest	unstirred
Foster	manlier than most, but uninspired
Francis	passive, neuter
Frank	forceful, likable
Franklin	masculine, active
Fred	unflappable
Freddy	flip
Frederick	pushy

G

Gale	sissified, spritely
Gardiner	assertive, moderately hard-working
Garrick	very masculine
Garth	forceful, industrious
Gary	very, very popular, masculine and diligent
Gay	limp-wristed
Gaylord	neuter, slothful
George	aggressive
Gerald	active, masculine
Gil	a regular guy
Gilbert	lonely
Glen	exceedingly dynamic
Gordon	hardworking but unsuccessful

Graham	masculine
Grant	dynamic, extremely manly
Gregory	intelligent, cultured
Griff	tough
Griffith	passive and unpopular
Gunther	lazy and exceedingly unpopular
Gus	firm

H

Hal	industrious
Halsey	reserved
Hank	virile, active
Hans	macho, likable, not passive
Harlan	cautious
Harley	vapid
Harold	coarse
Harry	very manly, but in need of friends
Harvey	a bit of a klutz
Henry	solid
Herbert	less than diligent, not very masculine
Herman	sedentary
Hiram	colorless
Hollis	dull
Homer	very passive
Horace	stodgy and unloved
Howard	lackluster
Hubert	inert
Hugh	mediocre
Hugo	manly, but not extremely well-liked
Humphrey	terribly unpopular, sedentary

I

Ian	passive, but quite masculine
Ira	neuter, passive, a loser
Irvin	a *schlemiel*—extremely passive
Irving	intellectual, neuter
Irwin	somewhat lethargic
Isaac	stern
Isidore	sissified, self-effacing and lazy
Ivan	not particularly lovable
Izzy	dizzy—a loser

J

Jack	diligent, very sexy
Jacob	a bit dull, but manly
Jake	implacable
James	a big winner in all categories
Jamie	somewhat neuter, but a charmer
Jan	feminine but active
Jason	hugely popular
Jay	masculine, brisk
Jeff	a winner—manly, dynamic, popular
Jeffrey	exceptionally personable, sexy, lively
Jerome	masculine
Jesse	sexless and unpopular, but diligent
Jim	virile, industrious, very popular
Jimmy	a likely success
Joe	a truck driver
Joey	dynamic, virile, charming
John	trustworthy, surprisingly passive but very manly
Johnny	a winner across the board
Jon	honest
Jonah	unpopular
Joseph	intelligent, earnest but dull
Josh	unswerving
Justin	vigorous

K

Keith	hard, self-reliant, ambitious
Ken	energetic
Kendall	nonviolent
Kenneth	a big winner
Kenny	manly, popular, spirited
Kent	macho, zealous, a big winner
Kenyon	a trifle unexciting
Kermit	very unpopular
Kerr	firm
Kerry	a cut above average but sexually ambiguous
Kevin	very popular, virile
Kim	a bit feminine, but very popular and quite vivacious
Kirby	unloved
Kirk	a crowd-pleaser—super-macho, dynamic

L

Lambert	a Little Lord Fauntleroy
Lance	slim
Lane	spirited
Larry	strong, dependable
Lawrence	masculine
Lee	a spectator at life
Lem	a loser
Lennie	a regular guy
Leo	not overly zestful
Leonard	lethargic, unpopular
Lewis	serious
Lincoln	respected
Lloyd	diligent, very masculine
Lorenzo	hard-working but unpopular
Lou	a yawn
Lowell	manly but not very active
Luke	strong
Luther	passive but masculine
Lyle	sedentary

M

Mac	macho, but not too friendly
Madison	a charming gentleman
Malcolm	lethargic
Manuel	a lonesome soul
Mark	
(or Marc)	spoiled
Marshall	strong
Martin	well thought of
Marvin	very unpopular, dull
Mason	a cut above average
Matt	a huge winner—macho, dynamic
Matthew	supportive
Maurice	dull
Maury	so-so
Max	brusque
Maximilian	very manly
Maynard	lazy, a loser
Melvin	wilted
Merle	extremely unassertive
Michael	very, very popular, extremely manly

	but surprisingly not too dynamic
Micky	boyish
Mike	as masculine and popular as Michael, more active
Miles	solid
Milt	lethargic, manly
Milton	sedentary
Mitch	well-liked, strong, zealous
Mitchell	slightly better than average
Monroe	passive
Monte	energetic, slick
Montgomery	a winner
Morgan	not overactive, but masculine enough
Morley	boring
Mort	dull
Moses	not very popular, passive but manly
Murray	uninspired
Myron	pathetic

N

Nat	diligent, dependable
Nate	a he-man
Nathan	vital
Nathaniel	formal
Neal	extremely masculine, industrious—a winner
Ned	manly but lazy
Nelson	energetic
Neville	sexless, unpopular
Nicholas	very strong
Nick	a big winner in all categories
Niles	lifeless
Noble	very manly, but not popular
Noel	sensitive, but an outsider
Nolan	unexciting
Norbert	a loser
Norm	one of the guys
Norman	dull
Norton	sedentary, unpopular, neuter

O

Ogden	inert
Olaf	unloved

Oliver	terribly lazy
Ollie	a real loser—sissified, lethargic
Orson	laggardly
Oscar	not very industrious nor terribly popular
Otis	a loner
Otto	independent, masculine
Owen	manly but unloved
Ozzie	not the best-liked guy in town

P

Paddy	a sissy, a loser
Paine	not very dynamic
Palmer	passive
Park	above average
Patrick	zealous
Paul	cheery, honest and proud
Pearce	manly
Perly	prissy
Perry	average
Peter	admired, animated
Phil	a success
Phillip	as big a winner as Phil
Phineas	lazy, unloved, unmanly
Pierce	unpopular
Porter	strong-willed
Powell	exceedingly masculine and industrious
Prentice	not abounding in friendships
Prescott	masculine
Preston	solid

R

Ralph	an average sort
Ramsey	not terribly well-liked
Randall	mature
Randolph	authoritative
Randy	very sexy
Ray	lethargic, neuter
Raymond	strong
Reed	brisk
Reg	manly
Reginald	lazy
Reuben	inert

Rex	sexy
Reynolds	unpopular, lethargic
Richard	very good-looking
Rick	a winner all around
Ricky	active
Rob	a huge winner
Robert	diffident
Robin	sissified
Rod	solid, reliable
Rodney	diligent
Roger	red and plodding
Roland	unpopular, lethargic
Rollo	a mama's boy
Ron	a big winner all around
Ronald	exceptionally industrious, well thought of
Ronny	popular but not very energetic
Rory	very masculine, pretty active
Roscoe	not widely liked
Ross	more masculine than most
Roy	gutsy
Rudolph	inactive and unpopular
Rudy	masculine
Rufus	sedentary, very unpopular
Russ	very strong but not overly active
Russell	manly

S

Sal	assiduous
Salvador	passive
Sam	a hard worker
Samson	not surprisingly, incredibly strong
Samuel	tough
Sanders	diligent
Sandy	lighthearted
Sargeant	very masculine
Saul	quite strong
Scotty	well-liked
Sean	above average all around
Sebastian	unpopular
Seymour	a loser, sluggish
Shane	a winner

Shaw	industrious but neuter
Shawn	neuter
Shelby	asexual
Sheldon	below average
Shelly	feminine
Shepherd	lethargic
Sherman	below average, but only slightly
Sherwin	not very exciting
Sherwood	passive
Si	unexciting
Sid	manly, but not popular
Sidney	insipid
Silas	passive
Simon	introverted and mean
Sinclair	a bit lazy
Sol	easygoing
Solomon	uh-huh—wise, but passive
Sonny	athletic
Spence	active, sexy
Spencer	an all-around good guy
Stan	very masculine
Stanford	dignified
Stanley	rather dull
Stephen (or Steven)	a winner in all areas
Sterling	stern
Steve	popular, industrious
Stewart	exceptionally masculine, diligent
Stu	strong
Sumner	active
Sutton	unpopular
Sylvester	a big loser

T

Tad	immature
Tate	unrelenting
Taylor	quite masculine
Ted	vigorous, much liked
Teddy	above average, likable
Terrence	not overactive
Thad	very masculine

Thatcher	a passive personality
Thayer	lackluster
Theo	not very active
Theodore	passive, but masculine enough
Thomas	large, soft and cuddly
Thornton	a bit dull
Thorpe	inactive but masculine
Tobias	unpopular
Tom	very manly, diligent
Tony	sociable
Travis	diligent
Tyler	reliable
Tyrone	dynamic

V

Valentine	a sissy
Vaughan	slothful
Vern	a good guy
Vick	very sexy
Victor	quite masculine, active
Vince	tough
Vincent	energetic, masculine
Virgil	neuter and unpopular

W

Wade	very masculine
Wallace	lazy
Walt	a regular guy
Walter	competent, not very athletic
Ward	a winner
Warren	active, manly
Wayne	extremely dynamic
Wendell	unconcerned
Wes	stolid
Wesley	masculine but passive
Whitney	vivacious
Will	average
Willy	not as popular as Will
William	kind but not aggressive
Winston	not overly active
Winthrop	very unpopular, downright lazy
Woodrow	tedious

| Wyatt | quite masculine |
| Wylie | not terribly popular |

Y

Yale	average
Yates	something of an egghead, a loner
York	uninvolved

Z

| Zachary | strong of character |
| Zeke | rough-hewn |

A Glossary of 2,500 Names and Their Etymology

Alberta may have come from the Teutonic words for "noble and brilliant" and Basil may be traced to the Greek for "kingly," but these are certainly not the qualities we usually associate with these names. Both conjure up essentially negative images, in spite of the fact that their original meanings were glowing. To appreciate fully how much the real meanings of names have changed in our society, it is necessary to compare the reality (pages 147–172) with the etymology. What follows is a glossary giving the origins and meanings of 2,500 names.

Glossary of Girls' Names

A

ABIGAIL "a source of joy" (Hebrew); Dim.—Abby, Ab, Gail, Gale, Gayle

ADA "joyous" or "prosperous" (Teutonic); Dim.—Addy, Addie

ADABELLE "joyous and fair" (Teutonic + Hebrew); Var.—Adabel

ADAH "ornament" (Hebrew)

ADDIE, ADDY See Ada, Adelaide

ADELAIDE "noble and kind" (Teutonic); Dim.—Addy, Addie, Adeline, Della, Del, Alice, Heidi

ADELINE see Adelaide

ADINE "delicate" (Hebrew); Dim.—Adina

ADORA "adored" (Teutonic); Dim.—Dora

ADRIENNE "from the Adriatic Sea" (Latin); Dim.—Adriana, Adria, Adrianne

AGATHA "good" (Greek); Dim.—Aggie, Aggy, Ag

AGNES "pure" (Greek); Var. and dim.—Inez, Nessie

AILEEN see Helen

AIMEE "beloved" (French)

ALANNA   "comely" or "fair" (Celtic) ; Dim.—Lana, Lane

ALARICE   "ruler of all" (Teutonic) ; Fem. of Alaric

ALBERTA   "noble and brilliant" (Teutonic) ; Fem. of Albert; Var. and dim.—Elberta, Berta, Bertha

ALDA   "rich" (Teutonic)

ALEXANDRA   "helper of mankind" (Greek) ; Fem. of Alexander; Var. and dim.—Alexandrine, Alexis, Alex, Sandra, Sondra

ALEXIS   *see* Alexandra

ALFREDA   "supernaturally wise" or "elf lady" (Teutonic) ; Fem. of Alfred; Dim.—Ally, Freda

ALICE   "truth" (Greek) , or perhaps Teutonic for "noble and of good cheer," or variation of Adelaide, q.v.

ALINE   *see* Helen

ALLEGRA   "cheerful" (Latin)

ALLY   *see* Alfreda

ALMA   "nourishing, cherishing" (Latin) , or Arabic for "learned"

ALMIRA   "princess, or the exalted" (Arabic) ; Fem. of Elmer

ALOYSE   "famous in war" (Teutonic)

ALTHEA   "wholesome, healing" (Greek) ; Dim.—Athee, Thea

ALVA   "white or fair" (Latin)

ALVINA   "beloved" (Teutonic) ; Fem. of Alvin; Dim.—Vinnie

AMANDA   "worthy of love" (Latin) ; Dim.—Mandy, Manda

AMARANTHA   "immortal" (Greek)

AMBER   "jewel" (Arabic)

AMELIA   "industrious" or "persuasive" (Teutonic); Fem. of Emil; Dim.—Millie

AMENA   "honest" (Celtic)

AMY   "beloved" (Latin)

ANASTASIA   "one who shall rise again" (Greek) ; Dim.—Ana, Stacy, Stacey

ANATOLA   "of the East" (Greek) ; Fem. of Anatole

ANDREA   "womanly" (Greek) ; Fem. of Andrew

ANGELA   "angelic" (Greek/Italian) ; Dim.—Angie

ANITA   Spanish diminutive of Ann, q.v.; Dim.—Nita

ANN   "full of grace, mercy or prayer" (Hebrew) ; Var. and dim.— Anne, Anna, Annie, Annette, Edna, Hannah, Nancy, Nanette, Nina, Anita

ANTHEA   "flower-like" (Greek) ; Dim.—Thea

ANTONIA   "beyond excellence" (Latin) ; Fem. of Anthony; Dim.— Netta, Nettie, Toni

APRIL   "to open" (Latin) , meaning the opening of spring

ARABELLA "fair altar" (Latin) ; Dim.—Bell, Bella, Belle
ARDIS "fervent" (Latin)
ARDITH "rich gift" (Teutonic)
ARIADNE "holy one" (Greek)
ARLENE "a pledge" (Celtic)
ASTRA "starlike" (Greek)
ATHENA "wise" (Greek)
AUDREY "strong, noble" (Teutonic)
AUGUSTA "majestic" (Latin) ; Fem. of August; Dim.—Gussie
AURELIA "golden" (Latin) ; Dim.—Ora, Oralie, Aura
AVIS "a bird" (Latin)

B

BABS *see* Barbara
BARBARA "stranger" (Greek) ; Dim.—Babs, Babby, Barbie
BEATA "divine, blessed" (Latin)
BEATRICE "she who makes happy" (Latin) ; Var. and dim.—Beatrix, Bea, Trix, Trixy
BECKY *see* Rebecca
BELINDA "wise" or "serpent" (Italian) ; Dim.—Bel, Linda, Lindy
BELL, BELLE *see* Arabella, Isabel, Mabel, Mirabel
BELLA "beautiful" (Latin) , or diminutive of Arabella, q.v.
BENA "wise" (Hebrew)
BENEDICTA "blessed" (Latin) ; Fem. of Benedict
BERNICE "bringer of victory" (Greek) ; Var.—Berenice
BERTA *see* Alberta
BERTHA "shining, glorious" (Teutonic) , or variation of Alberta, q.v.; Var.—Berthe, Berta
BERYL "precious jewel" (Hebrew or Greek)
BESS, BESSIE *see* Elizabeth
BETH *see* Elizabeth
BETSEY, BETSY *see* Elizabeth
BETTE, BETTINA, BETTY *see* Elizabeth
BEULAH "she who will be married" (Hebrew)
BEVERLY "ambitious" (Anglo-Saxon)
BILLIE "wise protector" (Teutonic) ; Fem. of William
BINA *see* Sabina
BIRDIE "birdlike" (Modern English)
BLANCHE "white" (French)
BLYTHE "blithe" (Anglo-Saxon)
BOBBI, BOBBIE *see* Roberta

BONNIE   "pretty" (Middle English) ; Dim.—Boni, Bonni, Bonny, Bunny
BRENDA   "firebrand" (Teutonic) ; Fem. of Brandt; Dim.—Bren
BRENNA   "maiden with raven hair" (Celtic)
BRIDGET   "strong" (Celtic) ; Var. and dim.—Brigitte, Brieta, Brita, Brie
BRIE, BRIETA   see Bridget
BRINA   see Zabrina
BRITA   see Bridget
BRUNHILDE   "heroine on the battlefield" (Teutonic)
BUNNY   see Bonnie

C

CALIDA   "the ardent" (Latin)
CALVINA   "bald" (Latin) ; Fem. of Calvin
CAMILLA   "noble and righteous" (Latin) ; Dim.—Camille, Cammie, Cam, Milly.
CANDACE   "pure and glowing" (Greek) ; Dim.—Candie, Candy
CARA   "dear one" (Celtic)
CARLA   "strong" (Italian) ; Fem. of Charles (Carlo) ; Var.—Carlene, Carly, Karla
CARLOTTA   Italian form of Charlotte, q.v.
CARMEL   "God's woodland" (Hebrew) ; Var.—Carmela, Carmelita
CARMEN   "song" (Latin/Spanish) ; Var.—Carmine
CAROL   "joyous song" (French) ; Var. and dim.—Carole, Caryl, Karol, Cary
CAROLINE   "strong" (Teutonic) ; Var. and dim.—Carolina, Carolyn, Carrie, Karolyn, Karolina, Karoline
CARRIE, CARRY   see Charlotte
CARY, CARYL   see Carol
CASSIE   see Cassandra, Katharine
CASSANDRA   "prophetess" (Greek); Dim.—Cass, Cassie
CATALINA   see Katharine
CATHARINE, CATHERINE   see Katharine
CATHLEEN   see Katharine
CATHRYN, CATHY   see Katharine
CECILIA   "blind" (Latin) ; Fem. of Cecil; Dim.—Cissy, Cis, Cecile, Celia, Cille
CELESTE   "heavenly" (Latin) ; Var.—Celestine
CELIA   "heaven" (Latin) or diminutive of Cecilia, q.v.
CHANDRA   "illustrious" (Sanskrit)
CHARITY   "loving" (Latin) ; Dim.—Charry, Cherry, Cher
CHARLOTTE   "strong and womanly" (French) ; Fem. of Charles; Var. and dim.—Carlotta, Carrie, Carry, Lotta, Lotty, Lottie, Lotte

CHARMAINE "little song" (Latin)

CHER *see* Charity

CHERIE "dear one" (French) ; Var. and dim.—Cheryl, Cheri, Sheryl, Sherry

CHERRY *see* Charity

CHERYL *see* Cherie

CHLOE "blooming" (Greek)

CHRISTINE "the anointed" (Greek) ; Var. and dim.—Christina, Chris, Chrissy, Teena, Tina, Kirsten, Kristin, Kristine

CILLE *see* Cecilia

CINDY *see* Cynthia

CIS, CISSY *see* Cecilia

CLAIRE *see* Clara

CLARA "bright and shining" (Latin) ; Var.—Claire, Clare, Clarette, Clarice

CLARABELLE "clear and beautiful" (Latin and French) ; Var.—Claribel

CLARICE *see* Clara, Clarissa

CLARISSA "destined for fame" (Latin) ; Var.—Clarice, Clarisa, Clarise

CLAUDETTE "little lame one" (Latin) ; Fem. of Claude

CLAUDIA "the lame" (Latin) ; Fem. of Claude; Var. and dim.— Claude, Claudine, Claudette

CLEO "famed" (Greek)

CLEOPATRA "her father's fame" (Greek)

CLOTILDE "battle maiden" (Teutonic) ; Var. and dim.—Clothilde, Tilda

COLETTE "victorious" (Latin) ; Fem. dim. of Nicholas; Var.—Collette

COLLEEN "girl" (Irish) ; Var.—Coleen, Colene

CONSTANCE "constant" (Latin) ; Dim.—Connie, Coni, Con

CONSUELO "consolation" (Latin) ; Var. and Dim.—Connie, Con

CORA "maiden" (Greek) ; Var.—Corene, Coretta, Corinne, Corrie, Corry

CORAL "coral" (Greek)

CORENE *see* Cora

CORETTA *see* Cora

CORINNE *see* Cora

CORNELIA "wifely virtue" (Latin) ; Var. and dim.—Cornela, Nell, Nellie

CORRIE, CORRY *see* Cora

CRYSTAL "crystal" (Greek)

CYNTHIA "the moon" (Greek) ; Dim.—Cindy, Cynthie

CYRENA "water nymph" (Greek)

D

DAFFY   *see* Daphne

DAGMAR   "joy of the Danes" (Danish) ; Dim.—Dag

DAISY   "day's eye" (Anglo-Saxon)

DALE   "dweller in the valley" (Anglo-Saxon)

DAPHNE   "laurel tree" (Greek) ; Dim.—Daph, Daphie, Daffy

DARLENE   "tenderly beloved" (Anglo-Saxon) ; Var.—Darleen, Darline

DARYL   "beloved" (Old English)

DAVINA   "beloved" (Hebrew)

DAWN   "dawn" (Anglo-Saxon)

DEANNA   *see* Diana

DEBORAH   "the bee" (Hebrew) ; Var. and dim.—Debra, Debora, Deb, Debbie, Debby

DEE   *see* Deirdre, Dorothy, Perdita

DEIRDRE   "sorrow" (Gaelic) ; Dim.—Dee

DELIA   "from the island of Delos" (Greek)

DELILAH   "the temptress" (Hebrew) ; Dim.—Lila, Lilah

DELLA   *see* Adelaide

DELORA   "from the seashore" (Latin)

DELORES   *see* Dolores

DELPHINE   "calmness" (Greek) ; Dim.—Del

DENISE   "wine goddess" (Greek) ; Fem. of Dennis

DIANA   "virgin moon goddess" (Greek) ; Var. and dim.—Deanna, Dianna, Dianne, Dian, Diann, Diane, Di

DINAH   "judged" (Hebrew) ; Var.—Dina

DIONE   "daughter of heaven and earth" (Greek)

DITA   *see* Perdita

DIXIE   "girl from the South" (American) ; Dim.—Dix

DODI   *see* Doris

DOL, DOLLY   *see* Dolores, Dorothy

DOLORES   "lady of sorrows" (Latin/Spanish) ; Var. and dim.—Delores, Dor, Dolly, Dol

DONNA   "lady" (Italian) ; Var.—Dona

DOR   *see* Dolores

DORA   "a gift" (Greek) ; *see also* Adora, Eudora, Isadora, Pandora, Theodora

DOREEN   Irish form of Dorene, q.v.

DORENE   "golden girl" (French) ; Var. and dim.—Doreen, Dori, Dorie, Dory

DORIE   *see* Dora, Dorene

DORIS   "of the sea" (Greek) or diminutive of Theodora, q.v.; Dim.—Dodi

DOROTHY "God's gift" (Greek); Fem. of Theodore; Var. and dim.—
Dorothea, Dee, Dol, Dolly, Dore, Dot

DRUSILLA "dewy-eyed" (Greek) ; Dim.—Dru, Drus, Drussie

DULCIA "sweet and delightful" (Latin) ; Var.—Dulcine, Dulci

E

EADIE, EADITH *see* Edith

EDA "happy and rich" (Anglo-Saxon) , or diminutive of Edith, q.v.

EDE *see* Edith

EDEN "delightful" (Hebrew)

EDITH "rich gift" (Teutonic); Var.—Eadith, Eda, Edythe, Eadie, Ede,
Edy

EDLYN "noble" (Anglo-Saxon) ; Dim.—Lynn

EDOMONDA "prosperous protector" (Anglo-Saxon) ; Fem. of Edmond;
Var.—Edmunda

EDNA "rebirth or pleasure" (Hebrew) or variation of Ann, q.v.; Dim.
—Edny, Ed

EDWINA "valuable friend" (Anglo-Saxon) ; Fem. of Edwin; Dim.—
Eddie, Ed, Winnie

EDY, EDYTHE *see* Edith

EFFIE "fair and famous" (Greek) ; Var.—Effy

EILEEN Irish/Gaelic form of Helen, q.v.

ELAINE Old French form of Helen, q.v.; Var.—Alaine, Alayne, Elana,
Laine, Lani

ELBERTA *see* Alberta

ELDREDA "noble and wise" (Teutonic) ; Fem. of Albert

ELEANOR Old Provençal form of Helen, q.v.

ELENA Italian form Helen, q.v.

ELENORE, ELINOR *see* Helen

ELISA *see* Elizabeth

ELISE "consecrated to God" (Hebrew) ; variation of Elizabeth

ELIZA *see* Elizabeth

ELIZABETH "consecrated to God" (Hebrew); Var. and dim.—Elise,
Elisa, Elisabeth, Eliza, Elsa, Elsbeth, Elsie, Bess, Bessie, Beth, Betsy,
Bette, Bettina, Betty, Libby, Lisa, Lise, Liza, Lizzie, Lizzy, Ilsa

ELLA "elfin" (Anglo-Saxon) , or form of Helen, q.v.

ELLEN *see* Helen

ELMA "amiable" (Greek)

ELNORA, ELNORE *see* Helen

ELOISE "battle-famed" (Teutonic) , or variation of Louise, q.v.

ELSA *see* Elizabeth

ELSBETH *see* Elizabeth

ELSIE   *see* Elizabeth

ELVIRA   "elf-like" (Spanish)

EMILY   "industrious" (Teutonic) ; Fem. of Emil; Var. and dim.—
Emilie, Em, Emmy, Millie

EMMA   "the healer" (Teutonic) ; Dim.—Em, Emie, Emmie, Emmy

ENID   "pure soul" (Celtic)

ERICA   "royal" (Teutonic) ; Fem. of Eric; Var.—Erika

ERMA   *see* Irma

ERNESTINE   "earnest" (Teutonic) ; Fem. of Ernest; Dim.—Teena, Tina

ESTELLE   Old Provençal form of Esther, q.v., or Stella, q.v.

ESTHER   "a star" (Hebrew)

ETHEL   "noble" (Teutonic)

ETTA   *see* Henrietta

EUDORA   "delightful gift" (Greek) ; Dim.—Dora

EUGENIA   "well-born" (Greek) ; Fem. of Eugene; Dim.—Gena, Gene,
Genie, Gina

EUNICE   "happily victorious" (Greek) ; Dim.—Eunie

EVA   Greek and Latin form of Eve, q.v.

EVANGELINE   "bearer of good news" (Greek)

EVE   "life" (Hebrew) ; Var. and dim.—Eva, Evelyn, Evita, Evonne,
Evie, Evelyn

EVELYN   *see* Eve

EVIE, EVITA   *see* Eve

EVONNE   *see* Eve

F

FAITH   "faithful" (Latin) ; Var.—Fay, Faye

FANNY   "free" (Teutonic) ; Var. and dim.—Fannie, Fan

FAY, FAYE   *see* Faith

FELICIA   "happy" (Latin) ; Fem. of Felix; Var.—Felice, Felise

FERN   "a fern" (Anglo-Saxon) , from Sanskrit "a wing or feather"

FLAVIA   "blonde" (Latin)

FLEUR   *see* Florence

FLO, FLORA   *see* Florence

FLORENCE   "to bloom" (Latin) ; Dim.—Fleur, Flora, Floris, Flo,
Flossie

FLORIS   *see* Florence

FRANCES   "free" (Teutonic) ; Fem. of Francis; Var. and dim.—France,
Francesca, Francine.

FREDA   "peace" (Teutonic) ; *see also* Alfreda, Wilfreda, Winifred; Var.
and dim.—Freida, Freddie

FREDERICA   "rich peace" (Teutonic); Fem. of Frederick

FREIDA   *see* Freda
FRITZIE   "peaceful ruler" (Teutonic) ; Fem. of Fritz

G

GABRIELLE   "woman of God" or "God is my strength" (Hebrew) ; Dim.—Gabey, Gaby, Gabby, Gab
GAIL, GALE   *see* Abigail
GAY   "gay" (French-Teutonic) ; Var.—Gae, Gaye
GAYLE   *see* Abigail
GENA   *see* Eugenia, Regina
GENE   *see* Eugenia
GENEVIEVE   "pure" (Celtic)
GENIE   *see* Eugenia
GEORGETTE   "husbandman" (Greek) ; Fem. of George
GEORGIANNA   "earth-lover" (Greek) ; also Fem. of George & Ann; Var.
   —Georgia, Georgiana, Georgina, Georgine, Georgi, Georgie
GERALDINE   "spear-ruler" (Teutonic) ; Fem. of Gerald; Dim.—Gerri, Jerry
GERDA   "the protected" (Teutonic) ; Dim.—Gerdi
GERMAINE   "German" (Latin) ; Dim.—Gerry, Jerry
GERTRUDE   "spear maiden" (Teutonic) ; Dim.—Gerta, Gerti, Gertie, Trudy, Trude
GILDA   "servant of God" (Celtic) Dim.—Gilli
GINA   *see* Eugena, Regina
GINGER, GINNY   *see* Virginia
GISELLE   "promise" (Teutonic)
GLADYS   "delicate" (Latin) ; Dim.—Glad, Gladdie
GLENNA   "from the glen" (Gaelic) ; Dim.—Glen, Glennie
GLORIA   "glorious" (Latin) ; Dim.—Glo, Glorie, Glory
GLORIANA   "glorious grace" (Latin) ; Dim.—Glo, Glorie, Glory
GRACE   "graceful" (Latin) ; Var. and dim.—Grayce, Gracie
GREDEL   *see* Margaret
GREER   "watchwoman" (Greek)
GRETA, GRETCHEN   *see* Margaret
GRISELDA   "heroine" (Teutonic) ; Dim.—Zelda
GUINEVERE   "white or fair lady" (Celtic) ; Var. and dim.—Jennifer, Jennie, Gwen, Gwennie
GUSSIE   *see* Augusta
GWENDOLEN   "white-browed" (Celtic) ; Dim.—Gwenn, Gwyn, Wendy

H

HANNAH   *see* Ann
HAPPY   "happy" (modern American)

HARRIET   *see* Henrietta; Dim.—Hattie
HAZEL   "commander" (Anglo-Saxon)
HEATHER   "flower" (Anglo-Saxon)
HEDDA   "war" (Teutonic) ; Dim.—Hedy, Heddy
HEIDI   *see* Adelaide
HELEN   "light" (Greek) ; Var. and dim.—Helena, Helene, Aileen,
    Aline, Eileen, Elaine (q.v.) , Eleanor, Eleanora, Elena, Elene, Elenore,
    Elinor, Elinora, Ella, Ellen, Ellie, Elnore, Ilene, Lenora, Lenore,
    Leonora, Leonore, Lora, Lorine, Lennie, Nell, Nellie, Nora
HELGA   "holy" (Scandinavian)
HELOISE   French variation of Louise, q.v.
HENRIETTA   "mistress of the home" (Teutonic) ; Fem. of Henry; Var.
    and dim.—Harriet, Etta, Henni, Hennie, Hetti, Hetty
HERMIONE   "of the earth" (Greek) ; Fem. of Herman
HESPER   "evening star" (Greek)
HESTER   "star" (Persian) ; Dim.—Hetti, Hetty
HETTI, HETTY   *see* Henrietta, Hester
HILDA   "battle" (Teutonic) ; Dim.—Hildie, Hildy
HILDEGARD   "battle-maiden" (Teutonic)
HOLLY   "good fortune" (Anglo-Saxon)
HONORA   "honor" (Latin) ; Dim.—Nora, Norah
HOPE   "hope" (English)
HORTENSE   "gardener" (Latin) ; Var.—Hortensa

I

IANTHE   "violet flower" (Greek)
IDA   "happy" (Teutonic)
IDELIA   "noble" (Teutonic)
ILENE   *see* Helen
ILKA   "industrious" (Celtic-Teutonic-Latin)
ILSA   *see* Elizabeth
IMOGENE   "likeness" (Latin) ; Var.—Imogen
INA   *see* Katharine
INEZ   Spanish form of Agnes, q.v.
INGA   *see* Ingrid
INGRID   "daughter" (Old Norse) ; Var.—Inga
IONA   "purple jewel" (Greek)
IRENE   "peace" (Greek) ; Var. and dim.—Irena, Rena, Rene, Reni,
    Renny
IRIS   "rainbow" (Greek)
IRMA   "strong" (Teutonic) ; Var. and dim.—Erma, Irmine

IRMINE   *see* Irma
ISABEL   "oath to God" (Hebrew) ; Var. and dim.—Isabella, Isbel, Bel, Bell, Belle
ISADORA   "gift of Isis" (Greek) ; Dim.—Dora, Dory, Issy, Izzy
ISBEL   *see* Isabel
ISOLD   "fair" (Celtic)
IVANA   *see* Jane
IVY   "ivy" (Greek)
IZZY   *see* Isadora

J

JACINTA   "comely" (Greek)
JACQUELINE   "the supplanter" (Hebrew) ; Fem. of Jacob; Dim.— Jackie
JAN   *see* Jane
JANE   "God's gracious gift" (Hebrew) ; Fem. of John; Var. and dim. —Janet, Janice, Jayne, Jean, Jeanette, Joan, Joana, Joanna, Joanne, Johanna, Juanita, Jan, Janey, Jeanie, Joanie, Juana, Ivana
JANET, JANICE   *see* Jane
JASMINE   "flower" (Persian)
JAYNE   *see* Jane
JEAN, JEANETTE   *see* Jane
JENNIE   *see* Guinevere, Virginia
JENNIFER   *see* Guinevere
JERRY   *see* Geraldine, Germaine
JESSICA   "God's grace" (Hebrew) ; Dim.—Jesse, Jessie, Jess
JEWEL   "precious stone" (Latin)
JILL   *see* Julia
JINN, JINNY   *see* Virginia
JOAN, JOANA   *see* Jane
JOANNA, JOANNE   *see* Jane
JOCELYN   "merry" (Latin)
JODIE, JODY   *see* Judith
JOHANNA   *see* Jane
JOSEPHINE   "she shall add" (Hebrew/French) ; Fem. of Joseph
JOY   "joy" (Latin)
JOYCE   "joyful" (Latin)
JUANA, JUANITA   Spanish forms of Jane, q.v.
JUDITH   "praised" (Hebrew) ; Dim.—Judy, Jodie, Jody
JULIA   "youthful" (Greek); Fem. of Julius; Var. and dim.—Juliana, Julie, Juliet, Jill, Juliette
JULIET   *see* Julia

JUNE "youthful" (Latin) ; Dim.—Junie

JUSTINE "just" (Latin) ; Fem. of Justin; Var. and dim.—Justina, Tina

K

KARA *see* Katharine

KAREN, KARENA *see* Katharine

KARIN *see* Katharine

KARLA *see* Carla

KAROL *see* Carol

KAROLINA *see* Caroline

KAROLINE, KAROLYN *see* Caroline

KARYN *see* Katharine

KATE *see* Katharine

KATHARINE "pure" (Greek) ; Var. and dim.—Katherine, Catalina, Cathleen, Catharine, Catherine, Cathy, Karen, Karena, Karin, Karyn, Katharina, Kathryn, Kathleen, Katrina, Ina, Cassie, Kara, Kate, Kathy, Katie, Kit, Kitty, Trina

KATHLEEN, KATHY *see* Katharine

KATIE *see* Katharine

KATRINA *see* Katharine

KAY "exultant" (Greek)

KENDRA "the knowing" (Anglo-Saxon)

KIM "glorious leader" (Anglo-Saxon?)

KIRSTEN *see* Christine

KIT, KITTY *see* Katharine

KOTEN "young maiden" (Greek)

KRISTIN, KRISTINA *see* Christina

L

LANA, LANE *see* Alanna

LARA "well-known" (Latin)

LARAINE *see* Larraine

LARISSA "cheerful" (Latin)

LAURA "the air" or "the laurel" (Latin) ; Fem. of Lawrence; Var. and dim.—Laurel, Lauren, Lora, Loralie, Loren, Loretta, Lorette, Lorinda, Lorna, Lorne, Loree, Lori, Lorie, Lorrie

LAUREL, LAUREN *see* Laura

LAVERNE "springlike" (French) ; Var. and dim.—Lavern, Verna, Verne, Vern

LAVINIA "woman of Rome" (Latin) ; Dim.—Vina, Vinia, Lee

LEA "lioness" (Latin) ; Fem. of Leo

LEAH "the weary" (Hebrew); Var.—Leigh

LEE *see* Lavinia, Leila, Leona

LEIGH *see* Leah

LEILA "black as night" (Arabic) ; Dim.—Lee

LELA, LELAH, LELIA *see* Lillian

LENA "light" (Greek) ; a diminutive of Helena

LENNIE *see* Helen, Leona

LENORA, LENORE *see* Helen

LEONA "the lioness" (Latin) ; Fem. of Leo; Dim.—Lee, Lennie, Leoni

LEONORA, LEONORE *see* Helen

LESLEY "from the gray fort" (Celtic) ; Fem. of Leslie; Dim.—Les

LETA *see* Letitia

LETITIA "joy" (Latin) ; Dim.—Leta, Letty, Tish, Tisha

LIBBY *see* Elizabeth

LILA, LILAH *see* Delilah, Lillian

LILLIAN "a lily" (Latin) Var. and dim.—Lela, Lelah, Lelia, Lila, Lilah, Lilian, Lil, Lilla, Lilli, Lilly, Lily

LINDA "beautiful" (Spanish) or diminutive of Belinda, q.v.; Var. and dim.—Lynda, Lindy, Lindie, Lyndy, Lynd

LINDIE, LINDY *see* Belinda, Linda

LISA, LISE *see* Elizabeth *and* Melissa

LIZA *see* Elizabeth

LIZZIE, LIZZY *see* Elizabeth

LIVI, LIVIA, LIVVY *see* Olivia

LOIS "war maiden" (Greek) ; Fem. of Louis

LOLA "strong" (Spanish) ; Dim. of Carlota, the Spanish Fem. of Charles; Dim.—Lolita

LORA *see* Helen, Laura

LORALIE *see* Laura

LOREE *see* Laura

LORELEI "a siren" (Teutonic) ; Dim.—Lori

LOREN *see* Laura

LORETTA, LORETTE *see* Laura

LORI, LORIE *see* Laura, Lorelei

LORINDA *see* Laura

LORINE *see* Helen

LORNA, LORNE *see* Laura

LORRAINE "famous in war" (Old High German) ; Var.—Laraine, Lorain

LORRIE *see* Laura

LOTTA, LOTTE *see* Charlotte

LOTTIE, LOTTY *see* Charlotte

LOUELLA *see* Luella

LOUISE "battle maiden" (Teutonic) ; Fem. of Louis; Var. and dim.—
Heloise, Louisa, Eloise, Lou, Uisie, Weezy

LUCIA "bright" (Latin); Fem. of Lucius

LUCILLE French form of Lucy, q.v.

LUCINDA *see* Lucy

LUCY "light" (Latin) ; Fem. of Lucius; Var. and dim.—Lucia, Lucille,
Lucinda, Lucie, Lu, Lulu

LUELLA "appeaser" (Latin) Var.—Louella

LYDIA "from the province of Lydia," or "cultured" (Greek)

LYND, LYNDA, LYNDY *see* Linda

LYNN "cascade" (Anglo-Saxon) or diminutive of Edlyn, q.v., or of
Marilyn—*see* Mary; Var.—Lyn, Lynne

M

MABEL "lovable" (Latin) ; Var. and dim.—Maybelle, Belle, Mae

MADELINE "tower of strength" (Hebrew) ; Var. and dim.—Madelene,
Magdalen, Marleen, Marlene, Marline, Maddie, Magda, Mae

MADGE *See* Margaret

MAE *see* Mabel, Madeline, Mary, May

MAG *see* Margaret

MAGDA, MAGDALEN *see* Madeline

MAGGIE *see* Margaret

MAIDA "maiden" (Teutonic) ; Dim.—Maidy

MAIRE *see* Mary

MAISIE *see* Margaret

MAMIE *see* Mary

MANDA, MANDY *see* Amanda

MANETTE, MANON *see* Mary

MANUELA "God with us" (Hebrew/Spanish) ; Fem. of Manuel

MARA *see* Mary

MARCELLA *see* Marcia

MARCIA "hammer" (Latin) ; Fem. of Mark; Var. and dim.—Marcella,
Marsha, Marcie, Marcy

MARELLA *see* Mary

MARGARET "a pearl" (Greek) ; Var. and dim.—Madge, Margarete,
Margareta, Margarita, Margery, Margo, Margot, Marjorie, Gredel,
Greta, Gretchen, Mag, Maggie, Maisie, Marge, Margie, Meg, Peg,
Peggy

MARGERY *see* Margaret

MARGARITE *see* Margaret

MARGO, MARGOT *see* Margaret

MARJORIE *see* Margaret

MAREA, MARIAN *see* Mary

MARICE *see* Mary

MARIE, MARIEL *see* Mary

MARIETTA, MARIETTE *see* Mary

MARILLA, MARILYN *see* Mary

MARINA "sea maiden" (Latin) : Dim.—Mary, Rina, Rinie

MARLA *see* Mary

MARLEEN, MARLENE, MARLINE *see* Madeline

MARSHA *see* Marcia

MARTHA "mistress" or "lady" (Aramean) ; Dim.—Marta, Mattie, Matty, Martie, Marti

MARY "bitter" (Hebrew) ; Var. and dim.—Mara, Maria, Marya, Marie, Marian, Mariel, Marla, Marella, Marilla, Marilyn, Marietta, Mariette, Marice, Miriam, Manon, Manette, Maureen, Moyam, Moira, Maire, May, Mae, Minnie, Mollie, Molly, Polly, Mitzi, Mimi, Mamie, Moll, Pol

MARYA *see* Mary

MATHILDA "brave in battle" (Teutonic) ; Var. and dim.—Maud, Maude, Matti, Matty, Tilda, Tilly

MAUD, MAUDE *see* Mathilda

MAUREEN *see* Mary

MAVIS "song-thrush" (Celtic)

MAXINE "greatest" (Latin) ; Fem. of Maximilian

MAY "maiden" (Middle English) or variation of Mary, q.v.; Var.—Mae

MAYBELLE *see* Mabel

MEG *see* Margaret

MEGAN "able or strong" (Anglo-Saxon)

MEHETABEL "God's favored" (Hebrew) ; Var.—Mehitabel, Metabel

MELANIE "clad in black" (Greek) ; Var. and dim.—Mel, Mellie, Melly

MELBA *see* Melvina

MELISSA "honey bee" (Greek) ; Dim.—Mel, Lisa

MELODY "song" (Greek)

MELVINA "chief elf lady" (Celtic) ; Fem. of Melvin; Dim.—Melba, Melva

MENA *see* Philomena

MERCEDES "the rewarding" (Spanish) ; Dim.—Mercy, Merci

MERCI, MERCY *see* Mercedes

MEREDITH "protector of the sea" (Celtic)

MERLE "the blackbird" (French) ; Var.—Merla, Meryl

MERRITT "of merit" (Anglo-Saxon)

MERT *see* Myrtle

MERYL *see* Merle

METABEL   *see* Mehetabel

MIGNON   "dainty" (French)

MILDRED   "mild" or "gentle" (Anglo-Saxon) ; Dim.—Millie

MILLICENT   "strength" (Teutonic) ; Dim.—Milli, Millie, Milly

MILLY   *see* Amelia, Camilla, Emily, Mildred, Millicent

MIMI   *see* Mary

MINERVA   "wise" (Latin) ; Dim.—Min, Minnie

MINNA   "loving memory" (Teutonic) ; Dim.—Min, Minni, Minnie

MINNIE   *see* Mary, Minerva, Minna

MIRABEL   "very beautiful" (Spanish) ; Var. and dim.—Mirabelle, Mir, Bell, Belle

MIRANDA   "admirable" (Latin) ; Dim.—Randy

MIRIAM, MITZI   *see* Mary

MOIRA   *see* Mary

MOLLIE, MOLLY   *see* Mary

MONA   "peaceful, and alone" (Latin) or diminutive of Ramona, q.v.

MONICA   "adviser" (Latin) ; Var.—Monique

MOYAM   *see* Mary

MURIEL   "myrrh" (Arabic)

MYRA   "wonderful" (Latin)

MYRNA   "tender and gentle" (Gaelic)

MYRTLE   "crown of victory" (Greek) ; Var. and dim.—Myrta, Mert

N

NADA   "hope" (Slavic) ; Var.—Nadia, Nadine

NADIA   *see* Nada

NADINE   French form of Nada, q.v.

NANCY, NANETTE   *see* Ann

NAOMI   "sweet or pleasant" (Hebrew) ; Dim.—Nomi

NARA   "joyous" (Gaelic)

NARDA   "the anointed" (Persian)

NATALIE   "child of Christmas" (Latin) ; Var. and dim.—Natala, Natalia, Natasha, Nathalie, Nat, Nattie, Netta, Nettie

NATASHA   *see* Natalie

NEALA   "chief" (Celtic) ; Fem. of Neal

NELL, NELLIE   *see* Cornelia, Helen

NERINE   "sea nymph" (Greek)

NERISSA   "of the sea" (Greek) ; Var.—Nerita

NERITA   *see* Nerissa

NESSIE   *see* Agnes

NETTA, NETTIE   *see* Antonia, Natalie

NICOLE "victory of the people" (Greek); Fem. of Nicholas; Var and dim.—Nicola, Nicolette, Niki, Nikki

NINA *see* Ann

NITA *see* Anita

NOEL "Christmas child" (Latin); Fem. of Noel; Var.—Noella

NOLA "famous" (Celtic); Fem. of Nolan

NOLETA "unwilling" (Latin)

NOMI *see* Naomi

NONA "the ninth" (Latin); Dim.—Nonnie

NORA *see* Helen, Honora

NORMA "the model or pattern" (Latin)

NYDIA "a refuge" (Latin)

O

OCTAVIA "the eighth" (Latin); Fem. of Octavius

ODELIA "wealthy" (Teutonic)

ODELE "a melody" (Greek); Var.—Odell

ODETTE "home-lover" (French)

OLA "daughter" (Teutonic)

OLGA Russian form of Helga, q.v.

OLIVIA "the olive of peace" (Latin); Fem. of Oliver; Var. and dim. —Olive, Livia, Livi, Livvi, Ollie, Ollie

OONA *see* Una

OPAL "jewel" (Sanskrit)

OPHELIA "immortal and wise" (Greek); Dim.—Phelia

ORA, ORALIE *see* Aurelia

ORIEL "golden" (Latin); Var.—Oriole

ORLENA "golden" (Latin); Var.—Orlene, Orlina

OTTILIE "battle maiden" (Teutonic); Dim.—Ottie

P

PAIGE "child" (Anglo-Saxon); Var.—Page

PAMELA "loving" (English); Dim.—Pam

PANDORA "gifted" (Greek); Dim.—Dorie, Dora

PANSY "flower" (Greek)

PATIENCE "the patient" (Latin)

PATRICIA "noble" (Latin); Fem. of Patrick; Dim.—Pat, Patsy, Patti, Patty

PAULA "little" (Latin); Fem. of Paul; Var. and dim.—Paulette, Paulina, Pauline, Pauli, Paulie

PAULETTE *see* Paula

PAULINA, PAULINE *see* Paula
PEARL "a pearl" (Latin); Var. and dim.—Perle, Perl, Perlie
PEG, PEGGY *see* Margaret
PEGEEN "pearl" (Celtic)
PENELOPE "the weaver" (Greek) ; Dim.—Pen, Penny
PEONY "flower-like" (Greek)
PERDITA "the lost one" (Latin) ; Dim.—Dita, Dee
PERL, PERLE *see* Pearl
PETRINA "resolute" (Greek) ; Fem. of Peter; Dim.—Peti, Petie
PHELIA *see* Ophelia
PHILANA "lover of mankind" (Greek)
PHILIPPA "lover of horses" (Greek) ; Fem. of Philip; Dim.—Pippa
PHILLIS *see* Phyllis
PHILOMENA "friend," or "nightingale" (Greek) ; Dim.—Mena
PHOEBE "wise, shining one" (Greek)
PHYLLIS "a green bough" (Greek) ; Var. and dim.—Phillis, Phylis,
   Phyl, Phil
PIA "devout" (Italian)
PIPPA Italian form of Philippa, q.v.
POL, POLLY *see* Mary
POMONA "fruitful" (Latin)
POPPY "flower-like" (Latin)
PORTIA "of the Roman clan of swineherds" (Latin)
PRIMA "the first" (Latin)
PRIMROSE "the first rose" (Latin) ; Dim.—Rose, Rosie
PRISCILLA "the ancient" (Latin) ; Dim.—Pris, Prissie, Prissy, Sil
PRUDENCE "the prudent" (Latin) ; Dim.—Pru, Prudi, Prudy
PRUNELLA "plum-colored" (Latin)
PSYCHE "the spirit" (Greek)

Q

QUEENIE "the queen" (Teutonic) ; Var.—Queena, Queeny
QUENBY "womanly" (Teutonic/Scandinavian)
QUINTA "the fifth" (Latin) ; Fem. of Quentin; Var.—Quintina

R

RACHEL "lamblike" (Hebrew) ; Var. and dim.—Rochelle, Rae, Ray,
   Shelley
RAINA "queenlike" (Latin)
RAMONA "protectress" (Teutonic) ; Dim.—Mona, Rama, Rae
RANA "royal" (Sanskrit) ; Var.—Rani

RANDY *see* Miranda

RANI *see* Rana

RAPHAELA "blessed healer" (Hebrew) ; Fem. of Raphael

RAY "doe" (Scandinavian) or diminutive of Rachel, q.v.

REBA *see* Rebecca

REBECCA "the ensnarer" (Hebrew) ; Var. and dim.—Rebekah, Becky, Reba, Riba, Riva

REGINA "queenly" (Latin) ; Var. and dim.—Regan, Regine, Gena, Gina, Reggie, Reg

RENA *see* Irene

RENATA "born again" (Latin)

RENE *see* Irene

RENEE "reborn" (French)

RENI, RENNY *see* Irene

RHEA "mother" (Greek)

RHODA "rose" (Greek) ; Dim.—Rodie, Roe

RIBA *see* Rebecca

RITA "pearl" (Greek) , or a diminutive of Margarita—*see* Margaret

RIVA *see* Rebecca

ROANNE "gracious" (Latin) ; Var.—Roanna

ROBERTA "of shining fame" (Teutonic) ; Fem. of Robert; Var. and dim.—Ruperta, Bobbi, Bobbie, Robin, Robbie

ROBBIE, ROBIN *see* Roberta

ROCHELLE *see* Rachel

RODERICA "famous ruler or princess" (Teutonic) ; Fem. of Roderick

RODIE, ROE *see* Rhoda

ROLANDA "famous" (Teutonic) ; Fem. of Roland; Dim.—Rola, Roe

ROMOLA "woman of Rome" (Latin)

RON, RONNIE, RONNY *see* Ronalda, Veronica

RONALDA "mighty and powerful" (Teutonic) ; Fem. of Ronald; Dim. —Ronnie, Ron

ROSA "rose" (Latin)

ROSABEL "beautiful rose" (Latin) ; Var.—Rosabelle, Rosabella

ROSALIE *see* Rose

ROSALIND "fair rose" (Spanish) ; Var. and dim.—Rosalinde, Roselyn, Roslyn, Rosalyn, Ros, Roz

ROSAMOND, ROSAMUND *see* Rose

ROSE "rose" (Latin) or diminutive of Primrose, q.v.; Var. and dim. —Rosa, Rosalee, Rosalia, Rosalie, Rosamond, Rosamund, Rosena, Rosetta, Roselle, Rosie

ROSELLE *see* Rose

ROSEMARIE *see* Rosemary
ROSEMARY "Mary's rose" (Hebrew) or "dew of the sea" (Latin);
  Dim.—Rosie, Rose
ROSENA *see* Rose
ROSETTA "little rose" (Italian), a diminutive of Rose
ROSLYN *see* Rosalind
ROWENA "white mane" (Celtic); Dim.—Ro
ROXANE "dawn" (Persian); Dim.—Rox, Roxie, Roxy, Roxanne
RUBY "red" (Latin)
RUE "herb" (Greek)
RUPERTA *see* Roberta
RUTH "beauty" or "a friend" (Hebrew); Dim.—Ruthie

S

SABINA "Sabine" (Latin); Dim.—Bina
SACHA "helping" (Greek), also Fem. of the Russian form Alexander
SADIE, SADY *see* Sarah
SAL, SALLIE, SALLY *see* Sarah
SALOME "peaceful"' (Hebrew)
SAMARA "of Samaria" (Hebrew); Dim.—Sam, Sammy
SANDRA *see* Alexandra
SARAH "princess" (Hebrew); Var. and dim.—Sadie, Sady, Sadye, Sara,
  Sarena, Saretta, Sari, Shari, Sal, Sally, Sallie
SERENA, SARETTA *see* Sarah
SARI *see* Sarah
SELENA "the moon" (Greek)
SERAPHINE "ardent" (Hebrew)
SERENA "serene" (Latin)
SHARI *see* Sarah
SHARON "plain" (Hebrew); Var.—Sharron
SHEILA "musical" (Celtic)
SHELLY *see* Rachel
SHERRY see Cherie, Shirley
SHERYL *see* Cheri
SHIRLEY "from the white meadow" (Old English); Var.—Shirlee,
  Sherry, Sheri, Shirl, Shirlie
SIBYL *see* Sybil
SIL *see* Priscilla
SILVIA *see* Sylvia
SIMONE "heard" (Hebrew); Fem. of Simon; Var.—Simona
SONDRA *see* Alexandra
SONIA *see* Sophia

SOPHIA "wisdom" (Greek) ; Dim.—Sophie, Soph, Sonia

STACEY, STACY *see* Anastasia

STARR "star" (Anglo-Saxon)

STELLA "star" (Latin) ; Var. and dim.—Estelle, Stell

STEPHANIE "a crown or garland" (Greek) ; Fem. of Stephen; Dim.—Stevi

SUSAN "lily" (Hebrew) ; Var. and dim.—Susanna, Susanne, Susann, Suzanna, Susie, Suzy, Sue

SYBIL "prophetic" (Greek) ; Var.—Sibyl

SYDNEY "ensnarer" (Hebrew) ; Fem. of Sidney; Dim.—Syd

SYLVIA "forest maiden" (Latin) ; Fem. of Silvanus; Var. and dim.—Silvia, Syl, Sy

T

TABITHA "gazelle" (Aramaic) ; Dim.—Tabby

TALITHA "damsel" (Aramaic)

TALLULAH "terrible" (American Indian: Chickasaw)

TAMARA "palm" (Hebrew) ; Dim.—Tammy, Tamma

TANIA "fairy queen" (Russian)

TEDDI *see* Theodora

TEENA *see* Christine, Ernestine

TERESA "harvester" (Greek) ; Var. and dim.—Terese, Theresa, Therese, Tracy

THALIA "blooming" (Greek)

THEA "divine" (Greek) ; *see also* Althea, Anthea, Theodora; Var.—Theda

THEDA *see* Thea

THEODORA "God's divine gift" (Greek) ; Fem. of Theodore; Var. and dim.—Theodosia, Teddi, Thea, Theo, Dora, Doris

THEODOSIA *see* Theodora

THERA "wild" (Greek)

THERESE *see* Teresa

THETIS "sea nymph" (Greek)

THOMASINA "the twin" (Hebrew) ; Fem. of Thomas; Var.—Thomasine

THORA "thunderclap" (Teutonic)

TILDA "battle maiden" (Teutonic), or diminutive of Clotilde, q.v., or Mathilda, q.v.; Dim.—Tildy, Tilly

TIMOTHEA "honoring God" (Greek) ; Fem. of Timothy

TINA *see* Christine, Ernestine, Justine

TISH, TISHA *see* Letitia

TOBEY "God is good" (Hebrew) ; Fem. of Tobias; Var. and dim.—Tobi, Toby

Toni   *see* Antonia
Tracy   *see* Teresa
Trina   *see* Katharine
Trix, Trixie   *see* Beatrice
Trude, Trudy   *see* Gertrude

U

Udele   "rich" (Anglo-Saxon)
Uisie   *see* Louise
Ula   "sea jewel" (Celtic)
Ulrika   "ruler of all" (Teutonic) ; Fem. of Ulric
Una   "one" (Latin) ; Var.—Oona
Undine   "of the waters" (Latin)
Ursa   "she-bear" (Latin) ; Var. and dim.—Ursel, Ursula
Ursula   "little she-bear" (Latin) ; Var.—Ursel

V

Val   *see* Valda, Valentina, Valerie, Valora
Valda   "battle heroine" (Teutonic) ; Dim.—Val
Valeda   *see* Velda
Valentina   "the brave and strong" (Teutonic) ; Fem. of Valentine;
    Dim.—Val, Valli
Valerie   "strong" (Teutonic) ; Dim.—Val
Valora   "the valorous" (Latin) ; Dim.—Val
Vanessa   "butterfly" (Greek) ; Dim.—Vanni, Van
Vania   "God's gracious gift" (Russian) ; Fem. of Ivan
Veda   "wise" (Sanskrit)
Vedis   "spirit of the forest" (Teutonic)
Velda   "of great wisdom" (Teutonic) ; Var.—Valeda
Velma   *see* Wilhelmina
Vera   "the true" (Latin)
Verda   "springlike" (Latin)
Vern, Verna, Verne   *see* Laverne
Veronica   "true image" (Latin) ; Dim.—Ronnie, Ronny
Vesta   "goddess of hearth and home" (Latin)
Victoria   "the victorious" (Latin) ; Dim.—Vicky
Vina, Vinia   *see* Lavinia
Vinnie   *see* Alvina
Violet   "shy" (Latin) ; Var. and dim.—Violetta, Violette, Viola, Vi
Virginia   "pure" (Latin) ; Dim.—Ginger, Jinny, Ginny, Jennie, Jinn
Vita   "vital" (Latin) ; Dim.—Vi

VIVIAN "animated" (Latin); Var. and dim.–Vivien, Vivienne, Viv, Vivi, Vivie

VONNIE *see* Yvonne

W

WANDA "the wanderer" (Teutonic)

WEEZY *see* Louise

WENDY *see* Gwendolen

WENONA "first-born daughter" (American Indian); Var.–Wenonah

WILDA "the wild one" (Anglo-Saxon); Dim.–Willy, Will

WILFREDA "peacemaker" (Teutonic); Fem. of Wilfred; Dim.–Freda, Will

WILHELMINA "protectress" (Teutonic); Fem. of William; Var. and dim.–Welma, Wilma, Velma

WILLA "desired" (Anglo-Saxon); Fem. of William

WINIFRED "friend of peace" (Teutonic); Dim.–Winny, Freda

WINNIE, WINNY *see* Edwina

WYNNE "fair" (Celtic)

X

XANTHE "golden-haired" (Greek)

XENIA "hospitable" (Greek)

XYLIA "of the wood" (Greek)

Y

YOLANDA "shy" (Latin); Var.–Yolande

YVETTE *see* Yvonne

YVONNE "the archer" (French); Var. and dim.–Yvette, Vonnie

Z

ZABRINA "noble" (Anglo-Saxon); Dim.–Brina

ZAMORA "of Zamora" (Spanish)

ZANDRA "friend of mankind" (Greek)

ZEBADA "gift of God" (Hebrew)

ZELDA *see* Griselda

ZENA "hospitable" (Greek)

ZOE "life" (Greek)

ZORAH "dawn" (Latin); Var.–Zora

ZULEIKA "fair" (Arabic)

Glossary of Boys' Names

A

AARON   "mountain high" or "the enlightened" (Hebrew)
ABBIE   *see* Abelard, Abner
ABBOTT   "father" (Hebrew)
ABEL   "breath" (Hebrew)
ABELARD   "resolute" (Teutonic) ; Dim.—Abbie
ABNER   "father of light" (Hebrew) ; Dim.—Abbie
ABRAHAM   "exalted father of many" (Hebrew) ; Var. and dim.—Abram, Avram, Abie, Abe
ABRAM   *see* Abraham
ADAIR   "from the ford, near the oak trees" (Celtic)
ADALBERT   *see* Albert
ADAM   "man of red earth" (Hebrew)
ADDISON   "descendant of Adam" (Hebrew)
ADIN   "delicate, sensual" (Hebrew)
ADOLPH   "noble wolf" (Teutonic) ; Var.—Adolf, Adolphe, Adolphus
ADRIAN   "from Adria on the sea" (Latin) ; Var.—Adrien
AKSEL   *see* Axel
ALAN   "harmony" (Celtic); Var.—Allen, Alain, Allan, Al
ALARIC   "ruler of all" (Teutonic) ; Var. and dim.—Alarick, Ulri, Ricky, Rick
ALASTAIR   *see* Alexander
ALBAN   "white" (Latin) ; Var.—Alben, Alva
ALBER   "noble bear" (Teutonic) ; Dim.—Al
ALBERT   "noble, bright" (Teutonic) ; Var. and dim.—Adalbert, Delbert, Elbert, Ethelbert, Bert, Bertie, Al
ALDEN   "old friend" (Old English) ; Var. and dim.—Aldin, Alwin, Al
ALDIS   *see* Aldous
ALDO   "rich" (Teutonic) ; Dim.—Al
ALDOUS   "from the old house" (Anglo-Saxon) ; Var.—Aldis, Aldus
ALEC   see Alexander
ALEXANDER   "helper of mankind" (Greek) ; Var. and dim.—Al, Alastair, Alec, Alex, Alexis, Alick, Sanders, Saunders, Sandy
ALEXIS   *see* Alexander
ALWIN   *see* Alden
ALFONSO   *see* Alphonse
ALFRED   "wise man" (Anglo-Saxon) ; Dim.—Al, Alf, Alfie, Alfy
ALGER   "noble spearman" (Anglo-Saxon) ; Var.—Algar
ALGERNON   "whiskered" (French) ; Dim.—Algie, Al

ALLAN *see* Alan
ALLEN *see* Alan
ALONZO *see* Alphonse
ALPHONSE "ready for battle" (Teutonic); Var. and dim.—Alfonso, Alonzo, Lon, Lonny
ALSTON "from the old village" (Anglo-Saxon); Dim.—Al
ALTON "from the old village" (Anglo-Saxon); Dim.—Al
ALVA *see* Alban
ALVIN "everyone's friend" (Teutonic); Var.—Alvan, Alwin, Elvin
ALWIN *see* Alvin
AMADIS "love of God" (Latin)
AMBERT "shining, bright" (Teutonic); Dim.—Bert, Bertie
AMBROSE "immortal" (Greek)
ANATOLE "from the East" (Greek); Var.—Anatol
ANDERS *see* Andrew
ANDRE *see* Andrew
ANDREAS *See* Andrew
ANDREW "manly" (Greek); Var. and dim.—Anders, Andreas, Andre, Andy, Drew
ANGELO "messenger" (Greek); Dim.—Angie
ANGUS "outstanding and strong" (Celtic); Dim.—Gus, Gussie
ANSEL "divine helmet" (Teutonic); Var.—Anselm
ANSELM *see* Ansel
ANSON "son of Ann" (Anglo-Saxon)
ANTHONY "beyond praise, priceless" (Latin); Var. and dim.—Anton, Antony, Antonio, Antoine, Tony
ARCHIBALD "sacred and bold prince" (Teutonic); Dim.—Archie, Arch
ARDEN "eager" (Latin)
ARGUS "all-seeing" (Greek); Dim.—Gus
ARLIE "from the hare meadow" (Anglo-Saxon); a form of Harley
ARMAND French variation of Herman, q.v.; Var.—Armond
ARNOLD "mighty as an eagle" (Teutonic); Dim.—Arnie
ARTHUR "rock-like" (Celtic); Var. and dim.—Arturo, Art, Artie
ARVEL "wept over" (Welsh)
ARVIN "friend of the people" (Teutonic); Dim.—Arv, Arvie
ASA "healer" (Hebrew)
ASHLEY "dweller in the ash-tree meadow" (Anglo-Saxon)
AUBIN "white" (Latin); Var.—Aubyn
AUBREY "ruler of the elves" (Teutonic); Dim.—Bree
AUGUST "the exalted" (Latin); Var. and dim.—Augustine, Augus, Augustus, Augie, Gus, Gussie, Austin

AUSTIN   *see* August

AVERILL   "like a wild boar," or "of the month of April" (Anglo-Saxon) ;
Var.—Averil

AVERY   "ruler of the elves" (Anglo-Saxon) ; Dim.—Av

AVRAM   *see* Abraham

AXEL   "father of peace" (Hebrew) ; Var.—Aksel

AYLWIN   "awesome friend" (Teutonic)

B

BAIRD   "bard or minstrel" (Celtic) ; Var.—Bard

BALDWIN   "bold and princely friend" (Teutonic)

BANCROFT   "from the bean field" (Anglo-Saxon)

BARCLAY   "from the meadow of birches" (Anglo-Saxon) ; Var.—Berk

BARNABY   "son of prophecy" (Hebrew) ; Var. and dim.—Barnabas,
Barney

BARNARD   *see* Bernard

BARRET   "mighty as a bear" (Teutonic)

BARRY   "dweller at the barrier" (Old French)

BARTHOLOMEW   "plowman" (Hebrew); Dim.—Barth, Bart, Bat

BARTON   "farmer" (Anglo-Saxon) ; Dim.—Bart

BARUCH   "blessed" (Hebrew) ; Dim.—Barry

BASIL   "kingly" (Greek)

BAXTER   "baker" (Teutonic/English)

BENEDICT   "blessed" (Latin) ; Var. and dim.—Benedic, Bennett, Beny,
Ben, Dixon

BENJAMIN   "son of the right hand" (Hebrew) ; Dim.—Benjie, Ben,
Bennie, Benny

BENNETT   *see* Benedict

BENTON   "of the moors" (Anglo-Saxon) ; Dim.—Ben, Benny

BERKELEY   "from the meadow of birches" (Anglo-Saxon) ; Var.—
Barclay

BERNARD   "bearlike warrior" (Teutonic) ; Var. and dim.—Barnard,
Barnet, Bernhard, Barney, Barn, Bernie, Bern

BERT   "bright" (Teutonic), also a diminutive form of Albert, Ambert,
Bertram, Burton, Egbert, Elbert, Herbert, Lambert, etc.

BERTRAM   "glorious raven" (Teutonic) ; Var. and dim.—Bertrand,
Bertie, Bert

BERTRAND   *see* Bertram

BERWICK   "from the barley grange" (Anglo-Saxon)

BEVERLY   "from the beaver meadow" (Anglo-Saxon) ; Dim.—Bev,
Bevvy

BILL, BILLY   *see* William

BLAIR "of the plain" (Celtic)

BOB, BOBBY *see* Robert

BOOTH "from the market" (Teutonic)

BORIS "warrior" (Slavic)

BOWEN "son of Owen" (Celtic)

BOYCE "of the woodlands" (Teutonic)

BOYD "blond" (Celtic)

BRADEN "from the broad valley" (Anglo-Saxon) ; Dim.—Brad

BRADFORD "from the broad ford" (Anglo-Saxon) ; Dim.—Brad

BRADLEY "from the broad meadow" (Anglo-Saxon) ; Dim.—Brad

BRANDON "from the beacon hill" (Celtic) ; Var.—Brendon, Brendan

BRANT "fiery" (Teutonic)

BREE *see* Aubrey

BRENDAN, BRENDON *see* Brandon

BRENT "from the steep hill" (Anglo-Saxon)

BRETT "a Breton" (French)

BRIAN "powerful" (Celtic) ; Var.—Bryan, Bryant

BRICE "alert" (Celtic)

BRODERICK "son of Roderick" (Welsh)

BROOKS "dweller by the stream" (Anglo-Saxon)

BRUCE "from the brushwood thicket" (French)

BRUNO "dark" (Teutonic)

BRYAN, BRYANT *see* Brian

BURGESS "citizen" (Teutonic)

BURKE "from the stronghold" (Teutonic)

BURTON "famous" (Anglo-Saxon) ; Dim.—Bert, Burt

BYRON "from the cottage" (Teutonic)

C

CAESAR "long-haired" (Latin)

CALEB "faithful" (Hebrew)

CALVIN "bald" (Latin) ; Dim.—Cal

CAMERON "twisted nose" (Celtic) ; Dim.—Cam

CAREY "from the fortress" (Celtic) ; Var.—Cary

CARL *see* Charles

CARLO, CARLOS *see* Charles

CARLTON "from Carl's farm" (Anglo-Saxon) ; Var.—Carleton

CAROL, CARROLL *see* Charles

CARY *see* Carey

CASIMIR "peace" (Slavic) ; Dim.—Cassy, Cass

CASPAR "treasure" (Persian) ; Var. and dim.—Casper, Jasper, Cass, Cassy

CASSIUS "vain" (Latin) ; Dim.—Cass, Cassy

CECE *see* Cecil

CECIL "blind" (Latin) ; Dim.—Cece

CEDRIC "chieftain" (Celtic)

CHALEY, CHALIE *see* Charles

CHALMER "lord of the manor" (Teutonic) ; Var.—Chalmers

CHANDLER "candle-maker" (French)

CHANNING "member of the Bishop's council" (French)

CHARLES "man" (Teutonic) ; Var. and dim.—Carl, Carol, Carroll, Karl, Karol, Charley, Charlie, Chas, Carlo, Carlos, Chuck, Chuckie

CHARLTON "from Charles' farm" (Anglo-Saxon) ; Var.—Charleton, Carlton, Carleton

CHAS *see* Charles

CHAUNCEY "chancellor" (Latin)

CHESTER "dweller in the fortified camp" (Anglo-Saxon) ; Dim.—Ches

CHRISTIAN "Christian" (Latin) ; Var. and dim.—Kristian, Kristin, Chris, Kit

CHRISTOPHER "Christ-bearer" (Greek) ; Dim.—Chris, Kit, Christie, Kris

CHUCK, CHUCKIE *see* Charles

CLARENCE "illustrious" (Latin) ; Dim.—Clare

CLARK "wise" (Latin)

CLAUDE "lame" (Latin) ; Dim.—Claudy

CLAUSE *see* Nicholas

CLAY *see* Clayton

CLAYBORNE *see* Clayton

CLAYTON "mortal" (Teutonic) ; Var. and dim.—Clayborne, Clay

CLEMENCE *see* Clement

CLEMENT "merciful" (Latin) ; Var. and dim.—Clemence, Clem

CLEVE *see* Clive

CLIFFORD "from the ford at the cliff" (Anglo-Saxon) ; Dim.—Cliff

CLIFTON "from the farm near the cliff" (Anglo-Saxon) ; Dim.—Cliff

CLINTON "from the headland farm" (Anglo-Saxon) ; Dim.—Clint

CLIVE "cliff" (Anglo-Saxon) ; Var.—Cleve

CLYDE "heard from afar" (Celtic)

COLEMAN "dove" (Celtic) ; Var. and dim.—Colman, Cole, Col

COLIN "victorious and strong" (Celtic) ; also a form of Nicholas, q.v.

COLMAN *see* Coleman

CON "wise" (Celtic) ; Var.—Conal, Conant, Connel, Conn

CONRAD "worthy counsel" (Teutonic) ; Var. and dim.—Konrad, Connie

CONROY "wise" (Celtic)

CONSTANTINE "steadfast" (Latin) ; Dim.—Constant, Conn, Connie

CONWAY "hound of the plain" (Celtic)

CORBIN "the raven" (Latin) ; Dim.—Corby
CORDELL "rope" (French)
COREY "of the ravine" (Celtic)
CORNELIUS "war horn" (Latin)
COURTENAY "from the court" (Anglo-French) ; Var.—Courtland, Courtney
COURTLAND *see* Courtenay
COURTNEY *see* Courtenay
CRAIG "crag-dweller" (Celtic)
CRAWFORD "from the crow ford" (Anglo-Saxon)
CROSBY "of the crossroads" (Teutonic)
CULBERT "brilliant" (Teutonic) ; Var.—Cuthbert, Colbert
CULVER "dove" (Anglo-Saxon)
CURTIS "courteous" (French) ; Dim.—Court, Kurt
CYRIL "lordly" (Greek)
CYRUS "sun" (Persian) ; Dim.—Cy

D

DAIN *see* Dana
DALE "of the dale" (Teutonic) ; Var.—Dalton
DALLAS "of the waterfall" (Celtic)
DALTON *see* Dale
DAMION *see* Damon
DAMON "tame" (Greek) ; Var.—Damion
DANA "Dane" (Scandinavian) ; Var.—Dane, Dain
DANE *see* Dana
DANIEL "God is the judge" (Hebrew) ; Dim.—Danny, Dan
DARCY "dark" (Celtic) or "dweller in the stronghold" (French)
DARRYL "beloved" (Anglo-Saxon) ; Var.—Darrell, Darrel, Daryl
DAVID "beloved one" (Hebrew) ; Dim.—Dave, Davie, Davy
DEAN "from the valley" (Anglo-Saxon)
DELBERT *see* Albert
DELMAR "of the sea" (Old French-Latin)
DEMETRIUS "earth-lover" (Greek) ; Var.—Dimitri, Dmitri
DEMPSTER "judge" (Anglo-Saxon)
DENNIS "wine-lover" (Greek) ; Var.—Denis, Dennison, Denny
DENNISON *see* Dennis
DEREK Middle Dutch form of Theodoric, q.v.; Var.—Derrick, Derk, Dirk
DESMOND "protector" (Anglo-Saxon)
DEVIN "poet" (Celtic)
DEXTER "right-handed, on the right hand, fortunate" (Latin)

DICK, DICKY   *see* Richard
DILLON   "faithful and true" (Celtic)
DIMITRI   *see* Demetrius
DION   "wine-lover" (Greek) ; Variation of Dennis
DIRK   *see* Derek
DMITRI   *see* Demetrius
DOANE   "from the dunes" (Celtic)
DOMINIC   "the Lord's" (Latin) ; Var. and dim.—Dominick, Dom, Nicky, Nick
DON   "dark" (Celtic) , or a diminutive form of Donald, q.v.
DONA   *see* Donald
DONALD   "ruler of the world" (Celtic); Dim.—Don, Donny, Donal
DORAN   "stranger" (Celtic)
DORIAN   "a Doricman" (Greek) ; Var. and dim.—Dorien, Dory
DORIEN   *see* Dorian
DORY   *see* Dorian, Isidore
DOUGLAS   "dweller by the black stream" (Celtic) ; Dim.—Doug
DOYLE   "black stranger" (Celtic)
DREW   "honest and capable" (Teutonic) , or diminutive of Andrew, q.v.
DRISCOLL   "the interpreter" (Celtic)
DRUCE   "Druid" (Celtic)
DUANE   "singing" (Celtic)
DUDLEY   "from the town of Dudley" (Anglo-Saxon) ; Dim.—Lee, Dudd
DUKE   "leader" (Latin)
DUNCAN   "dark warrior" (Celtic) ; Dim.—Dunc
DUNSTAN   "dweller from the brown quarry" (Anglo-Saxon)
DURAND   "enduring" (Latin)
DURWARD   "gatekeeper" (Anglo-Saxon)
DURWIN   "good friend" (Anglo-Saxon)
DUSTIN   "valiant" (Teutonic)
DWIGHT   "white" (Teutonic)

E

EARL   "chief, nobleman, warrior" (Anglo-Saxon) ; Var.—Earle, Errol
EBEN   "rock" (Hebrew)
EBENEZER   "rock of help" (Hebrew)
EBERHART   *see* Everett
EDAN   "flame" (Celtic)
EDGAR   "fortunate spear" (Anglo-Saxon) ; Dim.—Ed, Eddie
EDISON   *see* Edson
EDMOND   *see* Edmund
EDMUND   "wealthy protector" (Anglo-Saxon) ; Dim.—Ed, Eddie, Ned

EDSEL "from the halls of the rich" (Anglo-Saxon)

EDSON "son of Ed" (Anglo-Saxon) ; Var.—Edison

EDWARD "prosperous guardian" (Anglo-Saxon) ; Dim.—Ed, Eddie, Ned, Ted, Teddy

EDWIN "valuable friend" (Anglo-Saxon) ; Dim.—Ed, Eddie

EGAN "ardent" (Celtic) ; Var.—Egon

EGBERT "shining sword" (Anglo-Saxon) ; Dim.—Bertie, Bert

EGON *see* Egan

ELBERT "brilliant" (Teutonic), or a variation of Albert, q.v.; Dim.— Bert

ELDON "the elder" (Teutonic)

ELDRED *see* Eldridge

ELDRIDGE "adviser" (Anglo-Saxon); Var.—Eldred, Eldwin

ELDWIN *see* Eldridge

ELI "the highest" (Hebrew) ; Var.—Ely

ELIAS "Jehovah is God" (Hebrew) ; Var.—Elihu, Elijah, Eliot, Elliot, Elliott, Ellis

ELIHU *see* Elias

ELIJAH *see* Elias

ELLERY "dweller by the adlers" (Teutonic)

ELLIOT "Jehovah is God" (French), a French form of the Hebrew Elias; Var.—Eliot, Elliott

ELLIS *see* Elias

ELMER "of awe-inspiring fame" (Teutonic)

ELROY "royal" (Teutonic)

ELTON "from the old farmstead" (Anglo-Saxon)

ELVIN *see* Elwin

ELWIN "friend of elves" (Anglo-Saxon) or variation of Alvin, q.v.; Var.—Elvin, Elwyn

ELY *see* Eli

EMANUEL "God is with us" (Hebrew) ; Var.—Emmanuel, Manuel

EMERSON "son of Emery" (Anglo-Saxon)

EMERY *see* Emory

EMIL "hard-working" (Teutonic) ; Var.—Emile, Emlyn

EMLYN *see* Emil

EMMET "diligent ant" (Anglo-Saxon) ; Var.—Emet, Emmett

EMORY "ambitious" (Teutonic); Var.—Emery

ENOCH "devoted" (Hebrew)

ENOS "mortal man" (Hebrew)

ENRICO *see* Henry

EPHRAIM "fruitful" (Hebrew) ; Var.—Ephrem

EPHREM *see* Ephraim

ERASTUS "beloved" (Greek)

ERIC "kingly" (Teutonic) ; Var. and dim.—Erich, Erick, Erik, Rick

ERNEST "earnest" (Teutonic) ; Dim.—Ernie

ERROL *see* Earl

ERSKINE "from the town of Erskine in Scotland" (Anglo-Saxon/Celtic)

ERVIN *see* Irving

ERWIN "lover of the sea" (Anglo-Saxon) ; Var.—Irwin

ESMOND "gracious protector" (Anglo-Saxon)

ETHAN "strong" (Hebrew)

ETHELBERT *see* Albert

EUGENE "noble" (Greek) ; Dim.—Gene

EUSTACE "fruitful" (Greek) ; Var.—Eustis

EVAN Welsh variation of John, q.v.

EVERARD *see* Everett

EVERETT "strong as a wild boar" (Teutonic) ; Var. and dim.—Everard, Eberhart, Everet, Ev

EZEKIEL "strength of God" (Hebrew) ; Dim.—Zeke

EZRA "helper" (Hebrew) ; Dim.—Ez

F

FABIAN "farmer" (Latin)

FAIRFAX "blond" (Anglo-Saxon)

FARLEY "from the pasture where the bulls graze" (Anglo-Saxon) ; Var.—Farleigh, Fairley

FARRELL "the brave one" (Celtic) ; Var.—Farrel

FELIX "fortunate" (Latin)

FENTON "from the marshes" (Anglo-Saxon)

FERDINAND "adventurous" (Teutonic) ; Var. and dim.—Fernand, Fernan, Ferde, Hernando

FERGUS "manly and strong" (Celtic) ; Dim.—Fergie

FERNAN, FERNAND *see* Ferdinand

FERRIS "rock" (Celtic)

FITZGERALD "son of Gerald" (Teutonic)

FLETCHER "arrowsmith" (Teutonic)

FLORIAN "flowering" (Latin)

FLOYD "gray" (Celtic)

FORREST "of the forest" (Teutonic)

FOSTER "forester" (Anglo-Saxon)

FOWLER "fowl-keeper" (Anglo-Saxon)

FRANCHOT *see* Francis

FRANCIS "free" (Teutonic) ; Var. and dim.—Franz, Franchot, Frank, Frankie

FRANK   "a freeman" (Teutonic) ; Var. and dim.—Franklin, Franklyn, Frankie

FRANZ   *see* Francis

FRED   *see* Frederick, Wilfred

FREDERICK   "peaceful ruler" (Teutonic) ; Var. and dim.—Freddie, Fred, Fritz

FREEMAN   "a free man" (Anglo-Saxon)

FRITZ   *see* Frederick

FULTON   "of the farm" (Anglo-Saxon)

G

GABRIEL   "God is strong" (Hebrew) ; Dim.—Gabe, Gabby

GAIL   "lively" (Celtic) ; Var.—Gale

GALE   *see* Gail

GALEN   "physician" (Greek)

GALVIN   "sparrow" (Celtic) ; Dim.—Vinny, Vin

GAMALIEL   "the Lord is my judge" (Hebrew)

GARDINER   "gardener" (Teutonic) ; Var.—Gardener, Gardner

GARNER   "protector" (Teutonic)

GARNET   "garnet" (Latin)

GARRETH   *see* Garrett

GARRETT   "mighty spear" (Anglo-Saxon) ; Var. and dim.—Garett, Garreth, Garth, Gerard, Jaret, Gary, Gerry, Garry

GARRICK   "spear king" (Teutonic) ; Dim.—Rick, Ricky, Gary, Garry, Gerry

GARRY   *see* Garrett, Garrick

GARTH   *see* Garrett

GARVIN   "friend in battle" (Teutonic) ; Dim.—Gary, Gar, Gerry

GARY   *see* Garrett, Garrick, Garvin

GASPAR   *see* Jasper

GAYLORD   "happy lord" (Anglo-Saxon)

GENE   *see* Eugene

GEOFFREY   Old French form of Godfrey, q.v.; Var. and dim.—Jeffrey, Jeffers, Geof, Geoff, Jeff

GEORGE   "farmer" (Greek) ; Var. and dim.—Georges, Jorge, Georgie

GERALD   "mighty warrior with a spear" (Teutonic) ; Var. and dim.—Gerrald, Jerrold, Gerry, Jerry, Jer, Gerry

GERARD   *see* Garrett

GERRY   *see* Garrett, Garrick, Garvin, Gerald

GERSHOM   "the exiled" (Hebrew)

GIDEON   "hewer" (Hebrew)

GIFFORD   "gift" (Teutonic) ; Dim.—Giff

GILBERT "shining pledge" (Teutonic) ; Var. and dim.–Gilpin, Wilbert, Wilbur, Gil

GILES "shield carrier" (Latin) ; Var. and dim.–Gilles, Gilly

GILMORE "Mary's servant" (Celtic) ; Dim.–Gilly, Gil

GILPIN *see* Gilbert

GILROY "the King's servant" (Celtic) ; Dim.–Gil, Roy

GIOVANNI Italian form of John, q.v.

GLENN "from the glen" (Celtic) ; Var.–Glen, Glynn

GODFREY "God's peace" (Teutonic)

GOODWIN "good friend" (Teutonic)

GORDON "from the three-cornered hill" (Anglo-Saxon) ; Dim.–Gordie

GRAEME *see* Graham

GRAHAM "from the gray house" (Teutonic) ; Var.–Graeme

GRANT "great" (Latin)

GREGORY "watchman" (Greek) ; Dim.–Greg

GRESHAM "from the grassland" (Anglo-Saxon)

GRIFFITH "redheaded" (Celtic) ; Var. and dim.–Rufus, Rufe, Griff

GROVER "dweller in the grove" (Anglo-Saxon)

GUNTHER "noble and brave warrior" (Teutonic)

GUS, GUSSIE *see* Angus, August, Gustave

GUSTAVE "noble staff of the Goths" (Teutonic) ; Var. and dim.–Gustavus, Gustaf, Gus, Gussie

GUY "guide" (French) ; Var.–Wyatt

H

HAL *see* Harold, Henry

HALDEN "half-Dane" (Teutonic)

HALE "robust" (Teutonic)

HALSEY "from Hal's island" (Anglo-Saxon)

HAMILTON "from the mountain" (French)

HANK *see* Henry

HANS diminutive of the German Johannes, a form of John, q.v.

HANSEL another form of John, q.v.

HARLAN "from the land of the battles" (Teutonic)

HARLEY "from the stag's meadow" (Anglo-Saxon) ; Var.–Arlie, Harleigh, Har

HAROLD "army dominion" (Anglo-Saxon) ; Dim.–Hal, Harry

HARRY *see* Harold, Henry

HARVEY "bitter" (French) ; Dim.–Harve

HAYDEN "from the hedged down" (Teutonic)

HEATH "from the wasteland" (Anglo-Saxon)

HECTOR "steadfast" (Greek)

HEINRICH *see* Henry

HENDRICK *see* Henry

HENNY *see* Henry

HENRI *see* Henry

HENRY "ruler of the home" (Teutonic); Var. and dim.—Heinrich, Hendrick, Henri, Enrico, Harry, Hal, Hank, Henny

HERBERT "bright warrior" (Teutonic); Dim.—Herbie, Herb, Bert, Bertie

HERMAN "warrior" (Teutonic); Var. and dim.—Armand, Armond, Hermon, Herm, Hermie

HERNANDO *see* Ferdinand

HEYWOOD "from the green forest" (Teutonic)

HEZEKIAH "God is my strength" (Hebrew); Dim.—Zeke

HILARY "merry" (Latin); Var.—Hillary

HILLIARD "guardian during war" (Teutonic)

HIRAM "exalted" (Hebrew)

HOBART "bright of mind" (Teutonic); Var. and dim.—Hubbard, Hobbie, Hubie

HOLDEN "gracious" (Teutonic)

HOLLIS "dweller by the holly trees" (Anglo-Saxon); Dim.—Holl

HOMER "a pledge" (Greek)

HORACE "time keeper" (Latin); Var.—Horatio

HORATIO *see* Horace

HOSEA "salvation" (Hebrew)

HOWARD "chief protector" (Teutonic); Dim.—Howie

HOYT *see* Hubert

HUBBARD *see* Hobart, Hubart

HUBERT "bright of mind" (Teutonic); Var. and dim.—Hubbard, Hoyt, Hubie

HUBIE *see* Hobart, Hubert

HUGH "intelligent" (Teutonic); Var.—Hugo, Huey, Hughes

HUGO *see* Hugh

HUMBERT "shining home" (Teutonic)

HUMPHREY "supporter of the peace" (Teutonic)

HUNTLEY "from the hunter's meadow" (Anglo-Saxon)

HYMAN "life" (Hebrew); Masc. of Eve; Dim.—Hy, Hymie

I

IAN Scottish form of John, q.v.

ICHABOD "gone is glory" (Hebrew)

IGNATIUS "the ardent" (Latin); Var.—Ignace

IRA "descendant" (Hebrew)

IRVIN *see* Irving

IRVING "the west" (Celtic) ; Var. and dim.—Ervin, Erwin, Irvin, Irwin, Marvin, Mervin, Merwin, Merv, Marv

IRWIN *see* Erwin, Irving

ISAAC "laughing" (Hebrew)

ISADOR *see* Isidore

ISAIAH "the Lord's salvation" (Hebrew)

ISIDORE "gift of Isis" (Greek) ; Var. and dim.—Isadore, Dory, Issy, Izzy

ISRAEL "the Lord's soldier" (Hebrew)

IVAN Russian form of John, q.v.

IVER "archer" (Scandinavian) ; Var.—Ivar, Ivor, Yves

IZZY *see* Isidore

J

JACK *see* Jacob, John

JACOB "the supplanter" (Hebrew); Var. and dim.—Jake, Jack, James, Jacques

JACQUES *see* Jacob

JAKE *see* Jacob

JAMES Old French variation of Jacob, q.v.; Dim.—Jim, Jimmy, Jamie, Jame

JAN *see* John

JARED "the descendant" (Hebrew) ; Dim.—Jerry

JARET *see* Garrett

JARVIS "sharp as the spear" (Teutonic)

JASON "the healer" (Greek) ; Dim.—Jase

JASPER "carrier of the treasure" (Persian), or variation of Caspar, q.v.; Var. and dim.—Caspar, Gaspar, Jasp

JAY "lively" (Anglo-Saxon)

JEAN French form of John, q.v.

JEDEDIAH "beloved of the Lord" (Hebrew) ; Var. and dim.—Jedidiah, Jed

JEFFREY "God's peace" (Teutonic) ; a form of Geoffrey and Godfrey; Dim.—Jeff

JER *see* Gerald, Jeremiah, Jerome

JEREMIAH "exalted of God" (Hebrew) ; Var. and dim.—Jeremy, Jerry, Jer

JEREMY *see* Jeremiah

JEROME "holy" (Greek) ; Dim.—Jerry, Jer

JESSE "rich" (Hebrew)

JETHRO "superlative" (Hebrew)

JIM *see* James

JOACHIM   "God will judge" (Hebrew)

JOCK   *see* John

JOEL   "Jehovah is God" (Hebrew) ; Dim.—Joey, Joe

JOHN   "God's gracious gift" (Hebrew) ; Var. and dim.—Evan, Giovanni, Hans, Ian, Ivan, Jan, Johann, Johanne, Jon, Juan, Sean, Shawn, Shane, Jack, Jock, Johnny, Jackie, Jean, Zane

JONAH   *see* Jonas

JONAS   "dove of peace" (Hebrew) ; Var.—Jonah

JONATHAN   "gift of the Lord" (Hebrew)

JORDAN   "the descender" (Hebrew)

JORGE   *see* George

JOSEPH   "he shall add" (Hebrew) ; Var. and dim.—Josef, Joey, Joe

JOSHUA   "saved by the Lord" (Hebrew) ; Dim.—Josh

JUAN   Spanish form of John, q.v.

JULIUS   "youthful" (Latin) ; Var. and dim.—Jules, Julian, Julie, Julio

JUNIUS   "born in the month of June" (Latin)

JUSTIN   "the just" (Latin)

K

KANE   "fair" (Celtic) ; Var.—Kayne

KARL, KAROL   *see* Charles

KARSTEN   "the Christian" (Greek)

KAYNE   *see* Kane

KEIR   "dark" (Celtic)

KEITH   "dweller in the forest" (Celtic)

KENDALL   "of the valley" (Celtic) ; Dim.—Kenny, Ken

KENDRICK   "royal ruler" (Anglo-Saxon) ; Dim.—Kenny, Ken

KENNETH   "comely" (Celtic) ; Dim.—Kenny, Ken

KENT   "handsome" (Celtic)

KENYON   "blond" (Celtic) ; Dim.—Kenny, Ken

KERBY   *see* Kirby

KERMIT   "son of the god of arms" (Celtic)

KERR   "dark" (Celtic) ; Var.—Kerrin, Kieran

KERRIN   *see* Kerr

KEVIN   "kind or gentle" (Celtic) ; Dim.—Kev

KIERAN   *see* Kerr

KIMBAL   "royally brave" (Anglo-Saxon) ; Dim.—Kim

KINGSLEY   "from the king's meadow" (Anglo-Saxon)

KIRBY   "from the church" (Teutonic) ; Var.—Kerby

KIRK   "of the church" (Scandinavian)

KIT   *see* Christian, Christopher

KONRAD   *see* Conrad

KRIS   *see* Christopher
KRISTIAN, KRISTIN   *see* Christian
KURT   *see* Curtis

L

LAMBERT   "the glory of his land" (Teutonic) ; Dim.—Bert
LANCE   "spear" (Anglo-Saxon) ; Var.—Lancelot
LANDON   "from the long hill" (Anglo-Saxon) ; Var. and dim.—Langston, Langdon, Lanny
LANE   "from the lane" (Anglo-Saxon)
LANG   "tall" (Teutonic)
LANGDON, LANGSTON   *see* Landon
LARRY   *see* Lawrence
LARS   Swedish form of Lawrence, q.v.
LAURENCE   *see* Lawrence
LAWRENCE   "the laurel" (Latin) ; Var. and dim.—Laurence, Lorenz, Lorenzo, Lars, Larry
LAZARUS   "assisted by God" (Hebrew)
LEE   "meadowed" (Anglo-Saxon), or diminutive of Dudley, q.v., or Stanley, q.v.
LEN, LENNY   *see* Leonard
LEO   "lion" (Latin); Var.—Leon
LEON   Spanish form of Leo, q.v.
LEONARD   "strong or brave as a lion" (Teutonic) ; Var. and dim.— Lenny, Len
LEOPOLD   "patriotic" (Teutonic)
LEROY   "royal" (French)
LESLIE   "from the gray fort" (Celtic) ; Dim.—Les
LESTER   "from the camp" (Anglo-Saxon) ; Dim.—Les
LEW, LEWIS   *see* Louis
LINCOLN   "from the river bank" (Celtic) ; Dim.—Linc
LIONEL   "young lion" (Old French)
LISLE   *see* Lyle
LLEWELLYN   "lion-like" (Celtic) ; Dim.—Lew
LLOYD   "gray" (Celtic)
LON, LONNIE   *see* Alphonse, Zebulon
LORENZ, LORENZO   *see* Lawrence
LOUIS   "famous as a warrior" (Teutonic) ; Var. and dim—Lew, Lewis, Lou, Louie
LOWELL   "beloved" (Anglo-Saxon)
LUCIUS   "light" (Latin) ; Var. and dim.—Lucian, Lucas, Luke
LUKE   *see* Lucius

LUTHER "famous fighter" (Teutonic)
LYLE "from the island" (French) ; Var.—Lisle

M

MAC "the son of" (Celtic)
MADISON "son of a mighty battle maiden" (Teutonic)
MAGNUS "great" (Latin)
MALCOLM "servant of the dove" (Celtic)
MALLORY "without good fortune" (Latin)
MALVIN *see* Melvin
MANUEL *see* Emanuel
MARCEL *see* Mark
MARCUS, MARCY *see* Mark
MARK "hammer" (Latin) ; Var. and dim.—Marcus, Marcel, Marcy
MARLEN, MARLIN *see* Merlin
MARMADUKE "leader on the seas" (Celtic)
MARSHALL "marshal" (French)
MARTIN "warlike" (Latin) ; Dim.—Marty
MARVIN *see* Irving
MASON "a mason" (Teutonic)
MATHIAS *see* Matthew
MATTHEW "gift from the Lord" (Hebrew) ; Var. and dim.—Mathias, Matty, Matt
MAURICE "moorish" (Latin) ; Var. and dim.—Morris, Mury, Morry
MAXIMILIAN "the greatest" (Latin) ; Dim.—Maxie, Max
MAYNARD "mighty and valorous" (Anglo-Saxon)
MELVILLE "a place" (French) ; Dim.—Mel
MELVIN "chief" (Celtic) ; Var. and dim.—Malvin, Mel
MEREDITH "protector from the sea" (Welsh)
MERLE "the blackbird" (French)
MERLIN "the falcon" (Anglo-Saxon) ; Var. and dim—Marlen, Marlin, Merl
MERRILL "famous" (Teutonic)
MERTON "dweller at the seaside farm" (Anglo-Saxon)
MERV, MERVIN *see* Irving
MERWIN *see* Irving
MEYER "farmer" (Teutonic)
MICAH "like unto the Lord" (Hebrew)
MICHAEL "Godlike" (Hebrew) ; Var. and dim.—Mitchell, Mike, Mikey
MILES "millstone" (Greek) ; Var.—Milo
MILLER "a miller" (Latin)
MILTON "from the mill farm" (Anglo-Saxon)

MITCHELL *see* Michael

MONROE "from the swamp" (Celtic)

MONTGOMERY "mountain hunter" (French) ; Dim.—Monty

MORGAN "dweller by the sea" (Welsh)

MORLEY "from the meadow on the moor" (Anglo-Saxon)

MORRIS *see* Maurice

MORTIMER "from the still water" (French) ; Dim.—Morty, Mort

MORTON "dweller in the village on the moor" (Anglo-Saxon) ; Dim.—Morty

MOSES "child" (Ancient Egyptian), or "drawn from the water" (Greek) ; Dim.—Moe, Mose

MURRAY "sailor" (Celtic)

MYRON "good-smelling" (Greek)

N

NAHUM "the comforter" (Hebrew)

NAHAN "given, gift" (Hebrew) ; Dim.—Nat, Nate

NATHANIEL "gift of the Lord" (Hebrew) ; Dim.—Nate, Nat

NEAL "chief" (Celtic) ; Var.—Neil

NED *see* Edmund, Edward, Norton

NEIL *see* Neal

NELSON "Nell's son" (Celtic)

NERO "black" (Italian)

NEVILLE "from the new town" (Latin)

NEVIN "nephew" (Anglo-Saxon)

NEWELL *see* Noel

NEWTON "from the new estate" (Anglo-Saxon)

NICHOLAS "the people's victory" (Greek) ; Var. and dim.—Nichol, Niles, Claus, Colin, Nicky, Nick

NICK, NICKY *see* Dominic, Nicholas, Nicodemus

NICODEMUS "conqueror of the people" (Greek) ; Dim.—Nicky, Nick

NIGEL "dark" (Latin)

NILES *see* Nicholas

NOAH "rest" (Hebrew)

NOEL "Christmas" (French/Latin) ; Var.—Newell

NOLAN "noble" (Latin)

NORBERT "brightness of the sea" (Teutonic)

NORMAN "man from the North" (Teutonic) ; Var. and dim.—Norris, Norm

NORRIS *see* Norman

NORTON "from the northern village" (Anglo-Saxon) ; Dim.—Ned

O

OBADIAH "God's servant" (Hebrew) ; Dim.—Obie
OBIE *see* Obadiah
OCTAVIUS "the eighth" (Latin)
ODELL "rich man" (Teutonic) ; Var.—Odin
ODIN *see* Odell
OGDEN "dweller in the oak valley" (Anglo-Saxon)
OLAF "peace" (Scandinavian) ; Var.—Olen, Olin, Olie
OLEN, OLIN, OLIE *see* Olaf
OLIVER "olive" (Latin) ; Var. and dim.—Olivier, Ollie
OREN "white-skinned" (Celtic) ; Var.—Oran, Orin
ORSON "the bear" (Latin)
OSBORN "divine bear" (Teutonic)
OSCAR "divine warrior" (Anglo-Saxon) ; Dim.—Oz, Ozzie
OSWALD "divinely powerful" (Anglo-Saxon) ; Dim.—Oz, Ozzie
OTIS "sharp of hearing" (Greek)
OTTO "wealthy" (Teutonic)
OWEN "well-born" (Greek) or "young warrior" (Celtic)
OZZIE *see* Oscar, Oswald

P

PADDY *see* Patrick
PAGE "page" (French)
PAINE "countryman" (Latin)
PALMER "palm-bearing pilgrim" (Latin)
PARKE "of the park" (Anglo-Saxon) ; Var.—Park
PARNELL *see* Peter
PATRICK "patrician" (Latin) ; Dim.—Patty, Pat, Paddy
PAUL "little" (Latin)
PEDRO *see* Peter
PEMBROKE "from the headland" (Welsh)
PERCIVAL "the destroyer" (Greek) ; Dim.—Percy
PERNELL *see* Peter
PERRY "the pear tree" (Anglo-Saxon)
PETER "a rock" (Greek) ; Var. and dim.—Parnell, Pedro, Pierce, Pernell, Pierre, Petie, Pete
PHELAN "wolf" (Celtic)
PHILIP "lover of horses" (Greek) ; Dim.—Phil
PHINEAS "oracle" (Hebrew)
PIERCE *see* Peter
PIERRE *see* Peter

PORTER "gatekeeper" (Latin)
POWELL "son of Powel, the alert one" (Celtic) ; Dim.–Powie
PRENTICE "the apprentice" (Latin)
PRESCOTT "from the dwelling of the priest" (Anglo-Saxon)
PRESTON "from the domain of the church" (Anglo-Saxon)
PUTNAM "dweller near the pond" (Anglo-Saxon)

Q

QUENTIN "fifth" (Latin) ; Dim.–Quent
QUINCY "from the fifth son's house" (Latin) ; Dim.–Quince
QUINN "the wise one" (Celtic)

R

RAMON *see* Raymond
RAMSEY "from Ram's island" (Teutonic)
RANDALL *see* Randolph
RANDOLPH "protected by wolves" (Anglo-Saxon) ; Var. and dim.–
    Randall, Rolfe, Rolph, Randy
RAPHAEL "God's healer" (Hebrew) ; Dim.–Rafe
RAYMOND "mighty protector" (Teutonic) ; Var. and dim.–Ramon,
    Raymund, Ray
REDMOND "adviser" (Teutonic)
REGAN "royal" (Celtic)
REGINALD "mighty ruler" (Teutonic) ; Var. and dim.–Reggie, Ron-
    ald, Ron, Ronnie
REUBEN "Behold, a son!" (Hebrew) ; Dim.–Rube
REX "king" (Latin)
RICHARD "wealthy and powerful" (Teutonic) ; Dim.–Rich, Ricky,
    Rick, Dicky, Dick
RICHMOND "mighty protector" (Teutonic)
RICK, RICKY *see* Alaric, Eric, Richard, Ulric
ROBERT "of shining fame" (Teutonic) ; Var. and dim.–Robin, Rupert,
    Robby, Rob, Bobby, Bob
ROBIN *see* Robert
RODERICK "famous ruler" (Teutonic) ; Dim.–Rod, Roddy, Rory
RODNEY "famous" (Teutonic) ; Dim.–Rod, Roddy
ROGER "renowned spear warrior" (Teutonic) ; Dim.–Rog
ROLAND "fame of the land" (Teutonic) ; Var. and dim.–Rowland,
    Rollin, Rollo, Rolland
ROLFE, ROLPH *see* Randolph, Rudolph
ROLLAND *see* Roland
ROLLIN *see* Roland, Rudolph

ROLLO   *see* Roland

RONALD   Old Norse form of Reginald, q.v.; Dim.—Ron, Ronnie

RORY   "ruddy" (Celtic) , or diminutive of Roderick, q.v.

ROSCOE   "from the deer forest" (Teutonic)

ROSS   "horse" (Teutonic)

ROSWELL   "mighty steed" (Teutonic)

ROWLAND   *see* Roland

ROY   "redheaded" (Celtic) or diminutive of Gilroy, q.v.

ROYCE   "son of Roy, the kingly" (French)

RUDOLPH   "famed wolf" (Teutonic) ; Var. and dim.—Rollin, Rudolf, Rolfe, Rolph, Rudy

RUFUS   "redheaded" (Latin) ; Dim.—Rufe

RUPERT   *see* Robert

RUSSELL   "fox-like" (Anglo-Saxon) ; Dim.—Russ

S

SAMSON   "shining like the sun" (Hebrew) ; Dim.—Sammy, Sam

SAMUEL   "asked of God" (Hebrew) ; Dim.—Sammy, Sam

SANDERS   "son of Alexander" (Greek) or a dimunitive of Alexander, q.v.; Dim.—Sandy

SANDY   *see* Alexander, Sanders

SAUNDERS   *see* Alexander

SARGENT   "sergeant" (Latin); Var. and dim.—Sargeant, Sarge

SAUL   "desired" (Hebrew)

SCHUYLER   "scholar" (Dutch)

SCOTT   "Scottish" (Latin) ; Dim.—Scotty

SEAN   Irish form of John, q.v.

SEBASTIAN   "revered" (Greek)

SELBY   "from the manor farm" (Teutonic) ; Var.—Shelby

SELWYN   "friend at the court" (Anglo-Saxon)

SEWARD   "protector of the seacoast" (Anglo-Saxon)

SEYMOUR   "of the sea moor" (Anglo-Saxon)

SHANE   *see* John

SHAW   "from the grove" (Anglo-Saxon)

SHAWN   *see* John

SHELBY   *see* Selby

SHELDON   "from the hill on the ledge" (Anglo-Saxon) ; Var. and dim. —Shelton, Shelly, Shell

SHELLEY   "from the ledge" (Anglo-Saxon)

SHELTON   *see* Sheldon

SHEPARD   "shepherd" (Anglo-Saxon) ; Var. and dim.—Sheppard, Shep

SHERMAN   "wool-shearer" (Anglo-Saxon) ; Dim.—Shermy, Sherm

SHERWIN "swift runner" (Anglo-Saxon) ; Dim.—Sher

SHERWOOD "from the bright forest" (Anglo-Saxon)

SIDNEY "a follower of St. Denys" (French) ; Var. and dim.—Sid, Sydney, Syd

SIEGFRIED "glorious peace" (Teutonic)

SIGMUND "victorious guardian" (Teutonic) ; Dim.—Sig, Siggy

SILAS *see* Sylvester

SIMON "heard" (Hebrew)

SINCLAIR "illustrious and bright" (Latin)

SLOAN "warrior" (Celtic)

SOL "the sun" (Latin) ; also a diminutive form of Solomon, q.v.

SOLOMON "peaceful" (Hebrew) ; Dim.—Sol

SPENCER "dispenser" (French) ; Dim.—Spence

STAFFORD "from the landing ford" (Anglo-Saxon)

STANFORD "from the paved ford" (Anglo-Saxon) ; Dim.—Stan

STANLEY "glory of the camp" (Slavic) ; Dim.—Stan, Lee

STEPHEN "crown" (Greek) ; Var. and dim.—Steven, Stephan, Stefan, Steve, Stevie

STERLING "sterling" (Teutonic)

STEVEN *see* Stephen

STEWART "a steward" (Anglo-Saxon) ; Var. and dim.—Stuart, Stew, Stu

STILLMAN "peaceable man" (Anglo-Saxon)

STUART *see* Stewart

SUMNER "a summoner" (French)

SUTTON "from the village in the south" (Anglo-Saxon)

SYLVESTER "man from the forest" (Latin) ; Var. and dim.—Silas, Si, Syl, Sy

T

TAD *see* Theodore

TATE "happy" (Teutonic)

TAVIS "son of David" (Celtic)

TAYLOR "the tailor" (Latin)

TED *see* Edward, Theodore, Theodoric

TERENCE "tender" (Latin) ; Var. and dim.—Terrence, Terry

THADDEUS "praise to God" (Hebrew) ; Dim.—Thad

THATCHER "thatcher" (Anglo-Saxon)

THAYER "of the nation's army" (Teutonic)

THEODORE "gift of God" (Greek) ; Dim.—Tad, Ted, Teddy, Theo

THEODORIC "ruler of the people" (Teutonic) ; Var. and dim.—Ted, Teddy, Theo, Derek, Derrick, Derk

THOMAS "the twin" (Hebrew) ; Var. and dim.—Tomas, Tommy, Tom
THORNTON "from the thorny trees" (Anglo-Saxon)
THORPE "from the hamlet" (Teutonic)
THURSTON "Thor's jewel" (Scandinavian)
TIMOTHY "honoring God" (Greek) ; Dim.—Tim, Timmy
TITUS "the safe" (Latin)
TOBIAS "God's goodness" (Hebrew) ; Dim.—Toby
TODD "the fox" (Latin) ; Dim.—Toddy
TOM, TOMAS *see* Thomas
TONY *see* Anthony
TOWNSEND "from town's end" (Anglo-Saxon)
TRAVERS "from the crossroads" (Latin) ; Var.—Travis
TRAVIS *see* Travers
TRISTAN "full of sorrow" (Latin)
TRUMAN "true man" (Anglo-Saxon)
TURNER "worker with a lathe" (Latin)
TYLER "title-maker" (Anglo-Saxon) ; Dim.—Ty
TYRONE the meaning of Tyrone is not clear, but it has Celtic origins;
  poss. from the county in Ireland
TYSON "son of the Teuton (German)" (Teutonic) ; Dim.—Ty

U

ULRI *see* Alaric
ULRIC "of the noble land" (Teutonic) ; Var. and dim.—Ulrich, Rick,
  Ricky
ULRICH *see* Ulric
ULYSSES "the wrathful" (Greek)
UPTON "from the hill town" (Anglo-Saxon)
URIAH "God is light" (Hebrew)

V

VAIL "from the valley" (French)
VAL "power" (Teutonic) or diminutive of Valentine, q.v., and
  Valerian, q.v.
VALENTINE "healthy" (Latin)
VALERIAN "strong" (Latin)
VARIAN "fickle" (Latin)
VAUGHAN "small" (Celtic) ; Var.—Vaughn
VERE "true" (Latin)
VERNON "flourishing" (Latin) ; Dim.—Vern
VICTOR "the victor" (Latin) ; Dim.—Vick, Vic

VIN, VINNY *see* Galvin, Vincent
VINCENT "the conquering" (Latin) ; Dim.—Vince, Vin, Vinny
VINSON "son of Vinn" (Anglo-Saxon)
VIRGIL "flourishing" (Latin) ; Dim.—Virg
VITO "vital" (Latin)
VIVIEN "animated" (Latin)
VLADIMIR "ruler of the world" (Slavic)

W

WADE "wanderer" (Anglo-Saxon)
WALCOTT "dweller in the cottage" (Anglo-Saxon)
WALKER "forester" (Anglo-Saxon)
WALLACE "Welshman" (Teutonic)
WALTER "mighty warrior" (Teutonic) ; Dim.—Walt, Wally
WARD "watchman" (Teutonic)
WARNER "guarding warrior" (Teutonic)
WARREN "game warden" (Teutonic)
WARRICK "stronghold" (Anglo-Saxon)
WATSON "warrior's son" (Anglo-Saxon)
WAYLAND "dweller near the highway" (Teutonic)
WAYNE "wagonmaker" (Teutonic)
WEBSTER "weaver" (Anglo-Saxon) ; Dim.—Webb
WENDELL "wanderer" (Teutonic)
WESLEY "from the west meadow" (Anglo-Saxon) ; Dim.—Wes
WHITELAW "from the white hill" (Anglo-Saxon)
WHITNEY "from the white island" (Anglo-Saxon)
WILBERT *see* Gilbert
WILBUR *see* Gilbert
WILFRED "defender of the peace" (Teutonic) ; Var. and dim.—
   Wilfrid, Fred
WILLIAM "determined protector" (Teutonic) ; Var. and dim.—Willis,
   Bill, Billy, Billie, Willy, Will
WILLIS *see* William
WINFIELD "pleasure field" (Anglo-Saxon) ; Dim.—Win, Winny, Winnie
WINSLOW "from the friendly hill" (Teutonic) ; Dim.—Win, Winny,
   Winnie
WINSTON "from the friendly town" (Anglo-Saxon) ; Dim.—Win,
   Winny, Winnie
WINTHROP "from the friendly village" (Teutonic) ; Dim.—Win,
   Winny, Winnie
WOLFE "wolf" (Teutonic)
WOODROW "from the forest hedgerow" (Anglo-Saxon) ; Dim.—Woodie

WRIGHT "workman" (Anglo-Saxon)
WYATT "guide" (French) ; Var.—Guy
WYLIE "beguiling" (Anglo-Saxon)

X

XAVIER "brilliant" (Arabic)
XERXES "king" (Persian)

Y

YALE "yielder" (Teutonic)
YANCY "Englishman" (French)
YARDLEY "from the enclosed yard" (Anglo-Saxon)
YATES "dweller by the gates" (Anglo-Saxon)
YORICK *see* York
YORK "sacred tree" (Latin) ; Var.—Yorick
YVES "the archer" (Scandinavian) ; Var.—Yvon
YVON *see* Yves

Z

ZACHARIAH "remembered by God" (Hebrew); Var. and dim.—
Zacharias, Zachary, Zack
ZACHARIAS, ZACHARY *see* Zachariah
ZANE *see* John
ZEBADIAH "gift of the Lord" (Hebrew) ; Dim.—Zeb
ZEBULON "dwelling place" (Hebrew) ; Dim.—Lon, Lonny, Zeb
ZEKE *see* Ezekiel, Hezekiah

A State-by-State Guide to the Law of Names

Anyone who may wish to go through the formality of having his or her name legally changed by the courts should first consider what is on the books in the various states. Summaries of those laws pertaining to names follow. All the material is based on J. Bander's *Change of Name and Law of Names* and *Shana Alexander's State-by-State Guide to Women's Legal Rights*.

Alabama

A declaration of intent to change one's name must be filed with the Probate Court, accompanied by the reasons for the change. A married woman is free to use her maiden name.

Alaska

"A person may bring an action for change of name in the Superior Court. No change of name of a person except a woman upon her marriage or divorce shall be made unless the court finds sufficient reasons."

Arizona

An application, setting forth detailed reasons for the change, must be filed in Superior Court of the County of Residence. Minors over 16 years of age may file their own petitions. Final divorce decree may change the wife's name.

Arkansas

An application with reasons for the change must be made to the Chancery and Circuit courts. The Court may restore a maiden name to a divorced wife, but only if no children were born to the marriage.

California

An application or petition is made to the Superior Court of the County of Residence. The petition must show the reasons for the change, and they must be sufficient in the eyes of the judge who is presiding.

Colorado

A petition is filed with the District, Superior or County Court setting forth reasons for the change. Once the Court approves and orders the change, a notice is to be published at least three times in the newspaper within 20 days of the order. A wife may not use her maiden name without restrictions.

Connecticut

A wife must list maiden and married names on voter registration forms. A divorce decree may provide for the change of name of a divorced wife. All applications are made to the Superior Court in the County of Residence.

Delaware

A wife who changes her name by marriage must re-register to vote under her married name. On the granting of a divorce, the maiden name or the name of a former deceased husband may be adopted with court approval. Petitions are made to the Superior Court for name changes.

District of Columbia

A resident must file an application in the District Court of the United States for the District of Columbia, setting forth reasons for the requested change. The Court has discretion to grant or refuse the application. Before the hearings, a notice of filing must be published in the newspaper once a week for three consecutive weeks. A wife may hold on to her maiden name without restrictions.

Florida

Petition is filed in the Chancery Court of residence, showing the new name, and the court shall make the decree. A married woman may use her maiden name without any restrictions.

Georgia

An application is filed with the Superior Court, which may authorize the change. Notice of filing is to be published once a week for four weeks to allow for any objections. A woman may freely use her maiden name after marriage.

Hawaii

"Every married woman shall adopt her husband's name as a family name." The Court may permit a divorced woman to use her maiden name or that of a former spouse. All petitions for a name change must be published in the newspaper.

Idaho

A petition is filed with the District Court where the applicant lives. The notice of the hearing for a name change is published for four consecutive weeks, so that objections may be filed. The Judge has the discretion to grant or refuse the petition.

Illinois

An application or petition is made to the Circuit Court of the County of Residence. The notice of application is published for three consecutive weeks, with the first publication at least six weeks before the application is actually filed. A married woman may not use her maiden name without restrictions.

Indiana

A notice of the filing of an application must be published by three different weekly newspapers, the last of which must be at least 30 days before the hearing for a change of name in the Circuit Court. A married professional woman may vote or be a candidate for office under her maiden name if that is the name she uses in her profession.

Iowa

A petition is filed with the Clerk of the District Court in the County of Residence, and the petition must contain the reasons for the requested change and a statement of all the real estate owned by the applicant. No person may change his name more than once, and married women may not use their maiden names without certain restrictions specified in the statutes.

Kansas

To allow for possible objections, a notice of the name change hearing is published for three consecutive weeks, with the first publication at least 30 days before the hearing itself. The change must appear reasonable in the eyes of the Court. A married woman is not allowed to change her name, though she may revert to a maiden or former name after her divorce.

Kentucky

A married woman may not change her name. A petition is filed with the County Court, which may permit a woman to go back to her maiden name after a divorce.

Louisiana

A petition is filed in the District Court of the parish where the applicant resides. Reasons must be shown. A wife may use her maiden name.

Maine

Petition is submitted to the Judge of Probate in the County of Residence, and notice must be published in the newspapers. The Court may allow a divorced woman to return to using her maiden name in the decree of divorce. When a woman marries, the voter registration is automatically changed to her married name.

Maryland

An application is filed with the Court of Equity in the county where the petitioner resides. Reasons for the change must be outlined. A wife may use her maiden name without restrictions.

Massachusetts

The application is heard in the Probate Court, where sufficient reasons for the change must be given. Public notice of the hearing

226 The Name Game

is required. A woman must re-register to vote when she marries, though she may go back to her former name after a divorce.

Michigan

A petition is filed with the Probate Court, which may grant the change if there is sufficient reason. A wife is not required to re-register as a voter under her married surname, but a husband's petition for a name change is automatically assumed to include his wife and children.

Minnesota

A petition filed with the District Court must describe the real estate in which the petitioner has interest, or liens. Petitioner must prove identity with two witnesses. If a divorce action is brought by a woman, she may use her maiden name. When married, a woman may not use her maiden name without restrictions.

Mississippi

The individual must file a petition with the Chancery Court. Notice is not required, but reasons should be shown for the requested legal change of name. Wife may use maiden name freely.

Missouri

An application is made to the Circuit Court, with notice of change published three times within 20 days after the court order. Although there are restrictions on a married woman's use of her maiden name, she may revert to it once she is divorced.

Montana

Petition is filed in the District Court of the County of Residence, and reasons must be shown for the change. Notice of hearing is published in the newspaper for four successive weeks. Wife may use a separate name without restriction.

Nebraska

Application is filed with the District Court of the County of Residence, and notice must be filed 30 days prior to the hearing. A woman must re-register to vote when she marries.

Nevada

An application is made to the District Court, and a notice of the petition is published once a week for three consecutive weeks. If there are no objections and there is sufficient reason, the Court will order the change. A hearing is held if there are objections. A wife may not use her maiden name without restrictions.

New Hampshire

A petition is filed with the Probate Court, and cause must be shown. A divorce decree may change a wife's name back to the original, but in some cases, the name of a divorced woman "shall not be changed" from her married name.

New Jersey

An application is filed in the County Court or the Superior Court, which may order a divorced wife to resume her maiden name, or to refrain from using her divorced husband's surname. A wife must re-register to vote upon marriage, and a female notary public who marries must sign her hyphenated maiden and surnames.

New Mexico

An application is filed in the District Court. Notice of making application is published once each week for two consecutive weeks. A woman must re-register in order to vote after she marries. She need not indicate marital status when re-registering, but must sign her given, middle and married names.

New York

A petition is filed in the County Court or in the Supreme Court, although a resident of New York City may file a petition in the Supreme Court or any branch of the Civil Court of the City of New York in any county. The application must show the reasons for the requested change, whether or not the petitioner was ever convicted of a crime or declared bankrupt, whether there are any judgments or liens or proceedings pending against him. A birth certificate must be attached. The Court will order the change of a minor's name if the interests of the minor will be substantially promoted. Change of name takes effect not less than 30 days after the order is entered. A married woman may choose to vote under her maiden name, but an 1881 decision that still stands held that, upon marriage, a wife's maiden name is lost and her married name is the legal one.

North Carolina

Petition is made to the Superior Court of the County of Residence and ten days' notice must be given by posting on the courthouse door. Proof of good character, attested to by two citizens, must be filed. A divorced wife may resume her maiden name or the name of a prior deceased husband on application to the Clerk of the Court.

North Dakota

An application is filed with county's District Court. Before he can actually file the petition, however, the individual must publish notice of his intention to file at least 30 days before in a newspaper. The applicant must provide some acceptable reason for the change. Maiden name may be used freely by a wife.

Ohio

Petition is filed in the Court of Common Pleas or in the Probate Court of the County of Residence. Petitioner must list the reasons for the change and notice must be published at least 30 days before the petition is filed with the Court. Upon marriage, a woman's voter registration automatically ends, unless she wants to maintain her maiden name. In that event, she must inform the proper authorities that she intends to do so, and must use her name consistently so that it can be argued that she never changed her surname.

Oklahoma

Application is filed in the District Court by a person who has resided in the state for at least three years and in the county for a minimum of 30 days. The petition must show a birth certificate and reasons for the requested change. If her husband is found guilty in a divorce action, a woman may resume her maiden name following the divorce.

Oregon

A petition is filed in the Probate Court, and must show sufficient cause. Public notice must be given. Birth certificates of children will be changed upon the change of name by a parent. A wife must re-register to vote once she marries.

Pennsylvania

An application is filed in the Court of Common Pleas, and reasons must be set forward. The petitioner must list his residences for the previous five years. Notice must be published in two newspapers on filing. Assuming a different name without application to the Court is unlawful. A woman may, with the approval of the Court, resume her maiden name after her divorce. A wife may also use her maiden name freely during her marriage.

Rhode Island

Application must be made to the Probate Court. A wife may not use her maiden name without some restrictions.

South Carolina

Petition is filed with the Circuit Court, and reasons for the change must be described. A wife may freely use her maiden name.

South Dakota

A petition is filed in the Circuit Court and reasons must be shown. Notice must be published once a week for two successive weeks prior to the court hearing. A wife may not use her maiden name without court sanction.

Tennessee

Application is made to the appropriate Circuit, Probate or County Court, and the reasons must be outlined in the petition. A woman must re-register to vote when she marries.

Texas

Petition is filed in the District Court where the petitioner resides, and shall be granted "so long as the change does not release the petitioner from responsibilities or destroy the rights of third persons." A husband or wife may apply for a name change on the basis of the granting of a divorce decree. While married, a wife may freely use her maiden name.

Utah

Application is filed in the District Court of the County of Residence, laying out reasons for the proposed change. The petitioner must be a resident of the county for at least one year prior to filing the petition. The Court may require that notice be given prior to the hearing in court. A wife is allowed to use her maiden name if she so wishes.

Vermont

A petition stating change of name is signed, sealed and acknowledged before a judge of the Probate Court in the District of Legal Residence. A married person must have the consent of his or her spouse, and he or she must also sign, seal and acknowledge it. When a married man changes his name legally, the names of his wife and minor children change automatically. Notice of filing for a change is to be published weekly in a newspaper for three consecutive weeks. On granting a divorce to a woman, a judge may allow her to resume her maiden name or the name of a former husband. The court may change the names of the minor children of divorced parents if such a change is requested in the divorce action.

Virginia

Petition is filed in the Circuit Court or the Corporation Court, or in the Circuit Court of the City of Richmond. A wife must notify the Registrar of Voters if she chooses to hold on to her maiden name after marriage. A divorce decree may also be cause enough for a woman to resume her maiden name.

Washington

An application is filed in the Superior Court of the County of Residence, setting forth the grounds for the change. A married woman may freely use her maiden name.

West Virginia

A petition is filed with the Circuit Court or, if the judge is on vacation, any other court of record in the county where the petitioner resides. A wife may not use her maiden name without restrictions, though she may be allowed to resume using it if she gets a divorce.

Wisconsin

A petition is filed with the Circuit Court or the County Court, and the birth and marriage records shall show the new name if the Court approves. Change of name is restricted where the petitioner is practicing a profession under license, unless it can be established at a hearing that there is good cause for the change. Teachers are not subject to this restriction. A wife may freely use her maiden name but, after granting a divorce, the Court may allow the wife to go back to her maiden name only if she requires no alimony.

Wyoming

Application is filed with District Court in the County of Residence, stating the grounds for the requested change. There is a two-year residency requirement. Notice must be given prior to the hearing to allow for any objections from creditors, etc. A wife who is a notary public must inform the Secretary of State of Wyoming that she does not intend to use her husband's name. Any other woman may freely use her maiden name.

Sample Change-of-Name Petition

If you wish to legally change your name, you will have to file an application or petition with the proper court in your jurisdiction. (See summaries of state name laws beginning on page 221.) Here is a sample of the type of petition required to get your name changed in the City of New York. It must be accompanied by a copy of the petitioner's birth certificate.

CIVIL COURT OF THE CITY OF NEW YORK
COUNTY OF NEW YORK

. . . . X

In the Matter of the Application of

                                                    INDEX #

. . . .

                                                    PETITION

for leave to change his name to

. . . . X

TO THE HONORABLE JUDGE OF THE CIVIL COURT OF THE CITY OF NEW YORK FOR THE COUNTY OF NEW YORK:

The petition of . . . ., respectfully alleges:

1. Your petitioner is . . . . . . years of age and resides at . . . . in the City, County and State of New York and has so resided for a period of more than five years prior to the making of this application. Your petitioner is unmarried/married and is employed by . . . . as . . . .

2. Your petitioner desires to assume another name other than the one now recorded on his birth certificate and the name he proposes to assume is . . . .

3. The grounds of this application for such change of name are as follows, to wit:

> Example: For many years past, the petitioner has adopted and used the name . . . ., both for social and for many business purposes. Confusion has arisen by reason of petitioner's use and adoption of the name . . . . as opposed to his present legal name, which confusion petitioner wishes to avoid in the future by legally adopting the name . . . .

4. Your petitioner is a citizen of The United States.

5. Your petitioner was born in the City of . . . . on the . . . . day of . . . . . ., 19 . . and was named . . . .

5. A certified transcript of your petitioner's birth certificate is annexed hereto and made a part hereof.

6. Your petitioner, under the name by which he is now known or under any other name has never been convicted of a crime and has never been adjudicated a bankrupt.

7. There are no judgments or liens of record, and no actions nor proceedings pending against your petitioner in any court of this State or of The United States, or any governmental subdivision thereof, or elsewhere, whether the Court be a Court of record or not. There are no bankruptcy or insolvency proceedings, voluntary or involuntary, pending against your petitioner in any court whatsoever or before any officer, person or body or board having jurisdiction thereof and your petitioner has not at any time made an assignment for the benefit of creditors.

8. There are no claims, demands, liabilities or obligations of any kind whatsoever on a written instrument or otherwise, against your petitioner under the name of . . . ., which is the name sought herein to be abandoned and your petitioner has no creditors who may be adversely affected or prejudiced in any way by the proposed change of name.

9. No previous application for this relief has been made.

WHEREFORE, your petitioner prays that an Order of this Court may be entered granting leave to him to assume the name

of . . . . in place of that of . . . . on the date
to be specified thereto not less than thirty (30) days after the
entry of such order and for such other and further relief as may
be proper.

Petitioner

STATE OF NEW YORK   SS.:
COUNTY OF NEW YORK

. . . ., being duly sworn, deposes and says that
deponent is the petitioner in the within proceeding; that deponent has read the foregoing petition and knows the contents
thereof; that same is true to deponent's own knowledge, except
as to matters stated therein stated to be upon information and
belief, and that as to those matters deponent believes it to be
true.
Sworn to before me this
. . day of . . . . . ., 19 . .

Bibliography

Alexander, Shana, *Shana Alexander's State-by-State Guide to Women's Legal Rights,* Wollenstonecraft Inc., Los Angeles, 1975.

Allen, L.; Brown, V.; Dickerson, L., and Pratt, K. C., "The relations of first name preferences to their frequency in the culture." *Journal of Social Psychology,* 1941, 14, 279–293.

Ames, Winthrop, *What Shall We Name the Baby?,* Simon and Schuster, New York, 1941.

Bander, Edward J., *Change of Name and Law of Names* (Legal Almanac Series No. 34), Oceana Publications, Inc., New York, 1973.

Beadle, Muriel, "Game of the Name," *New York Times Magazine,* October 21, 1973, 38+.

Berne, Eric, *What Do You Say After You Say Hello?,* Grove Press, Inc., New York, 1972.

Buchanan, B., and Bruning, J. L., "Connotative Meanings of Names and Nicknames on Three Dimensions," *Journal of Social Psychology,* 1971, 85, 143–144.

Bugliosi, Vincent, *Helter Skelter,* W. W. Norton & Co., New York, 1974.

Eagleson, O. W., "Students' reactions to their given names," *Journal of Social Psychology,* 1946, 23, 187–195.

Eagleson, O. W., and Clifford, A. D., "A comparative study of the names of white and Negro women college students," *Journal of Social Psychology,* 1945, 21, 57–64.

Ellis, A., and Beechley, M., "Emotional disturbance in children with peculiar given names," *Journal of Genetic Psychology,* 1954, 85, 337–339.

Fast, Julius, *Body Language,* M. Evans and Co., New York, 1970.

Frey, Albert R., *Sobriquets and Nicknames,* Ticknor and Company, Boston, 1888, republished by Gale Research Company, Detroit, 1966.

Gill, Brendan, *Here at the New Yorker,* Random House, Inc., New York, 1975.

Hartman, A. Arthur; Nicolay, Robert C., and Hurley, Jesse, "Unique personal names as a social adjustment factor," *Journal of Social Psychology,* 1968, 75, 107–110.

Hassall, William O., *History Through Surnames,* Pergamon Press, London, 1967.

Jahoda, G., "A note on Ashanti names and their relationship to personality," *British Journal of Psychology,* 1954, 45, 192–195.

Kraepelin, E. Psychiatrie. 1 Band: Allgemeine Psychiatrie. Leipzig: Barth, 1909.

Lambert, Eloise, and Pei, Mario, *Our Names, Where They Came From and What They Mean,* Lothrop, Lee and Shepard Co., New York, 1960.

McDavid, J. W., and Harari, H., "Name stereotypes and teachers' expectations," *Journal of Educational Psychology,* 1973, 65:2, 222–225.

McDavid, J. W., and Harari, H., "Social desirability of a name and popularity in school children," paper presented to the American Psychological Association, Chicago, Ill., 1965; *Child Development,* 1966, 37, 453–459.

Mencken, Henry L., *The American Language* and *The American Language, Supplement II,* Alfred A. Knopf, New York, 1948.

Miller, Jonathan, *Freud: The Man, His World, His Influences,* Little, Brown, Boston, 1972.

Murphy, W. F., "A note on the significance of names," *Psychoanalytical Quarterly,* 1957, 26, 91–106.

Newman, Edwin, *Strictly Speaking,* The Bobbs-Merrill Company, New York, 1974.

Savage, B. M., and Wells, F. L., "A note on singularity in given names, *Journal of Social Psychology,* 1940, 27, 271–272.

Shankle, George Earlie, *American Nicknames: Their Origin and Significance,* H. W. Wilson Company, New York, 1955.

Sharp, Harold S., *Pseudonyms and Personal Nicknames,* Vol. I, The Scarecrow Press, Inc. Metuchen, N.J., 1972.

Smith, Elsdon C., *Naming Your Baby,* Chilton, New York, 1970.

Smith, Elsdon C., *New Dictionary of American Family Names,* Harper & Row, New York, 1973.

Strunk, O., "Attitudes toward one's name and one's self," *Journal of Individual Psychology,* 1958, 14, 54–67.

Wells, Evelyn, *What to Name the Baby (A Treasury of Names),* Doubleday, New York, 1946.